ANCIENT
EGYPT
FROM PREHISTORY TO THE ISLAMIC CONQUEST

THE BRITANNICA GUIDE TO ANCIENT CIVILIZATIONS

ANCIENT EGYPT

FROM PREHISTORY TO THE ISLAMIC CONQUEST

EDITED BY KATHLEEN KUIPER, MANAGER, ARTS AND CULTURE

Educational Publishing

IN ASSOCIATION WITH

EDUCATIONAL SERVICES

Published in 2011 by Britannica Educational Publishing
(a trademark of Encyclopædia Britannica, Inc.)
in association with Rosen Educational Services, LLC
29 East 21st Street, New York, NY 10010.

Distributed exclusively by Rosen Educational Services.
For a listing of additional Britannica Educational Publishing titles, call toll free (800) 237-9932.

First Edition

Britannica Educational Publishing
Michael I. Levy: Executive Editor
J.E. Luebering: Senior Manager
Marilyn L. Barton: Senior Coordinator, Production Control
Steven Bosco: Director, Editorial Technologies
Lisa S. Braucher: Senior Producer and Data Editor
Yvette Charboneau: Senior Copy Editor
Kathy Nakamura: Manager, Media Acquisition
Kathleen Kuiper: Manager, Arts and Culture

Rosen Educational Services
Jeanne Nagle: Senior Editor
Nelson Sá: Art Director
Cindy Reiman: Photography Manager
Matthew Cauli: Designer, Cover Design
Introduction by Sean Price

Library of Congress Cataloging-in-Publication Data

Ancient Egypt : from prehistory to the Islamic conquest / edited by Kathleen Kuiper. — 1st ed.
    p. cm. – (The Britannica guide to ancient civilizations)
"In association with Britannica Educational Publishing, Rosen Educational Services."
Includes bibliographical references and index.
ISBN 978-1-61530-148-5 (library binding)
1. Egypt—Civilization—To 332 B.C. 2. Egypt—Social life and customs—To 332 B.C. 3.
Egypt—Civilization—332 B.C.-638 A.D. 4. Egypt--Social life and customs. I. Kuiper,
Kathleen.
DT61.A612 2010
932—dc22

                                                                    2010008661

Manufactured in the United States of America

On the cover: *A golden image of the "boy king" Tutankhamen, provided by his funerary mask.* Romilly Lockyer/The Image Bank/Getty Images

On pages 15, 31, 42, 59, 84, 102, 114, 133, 149, 178: DEA/C. Sappa/De Agostini/Getty Images

CONTENTS

33

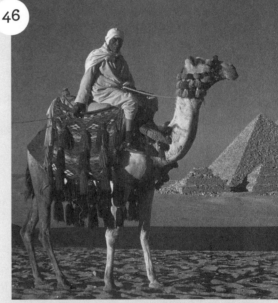

46

47

CHAPTER 5: THE LATE PERIOD AND BEYOND 84

CHAPTER 6: ROMAN AND BYZANTINE EGYPT 102

65

71

90

157

168

174

INTRODUCTION

It can be said that the story of ancient Egypt begins with the Nile River. Settlements along the Nile existed at least 2,000 years before Egypt's first ruling dynasty was founded about 3100 BC. The earliest settlers along the Nile were nomads and pastoralists who grew barley on the fertile floodplain or fished and hunted. The Nile River basin served as the stage for the evolution and decay of an advanced civilization. The river itself enabled the descendants of these seemingly unexceptional people to build a civilization that would tower over the ancient world. This book helps explain how they did it and what it means for us today.

Early Egypt was divided geographically and culturally into Upper Egypt and Lower Egypt. Upper Egypt consisted of the region south of the Nile delta. From these highlands the mighty Nile flowed northward. Lower Egypt was made up of the northern lowlands, where the Nile ended in a fan-shaped delta that emptied into the Mediterranean Sea. Upland people tended to be fierce and rugged, like the terrain that was their home. Lowland northerners were more likely to be prosperous farmers.

Along the banks of the Nile grew the grasslike aquatic plant known as papyrus. The fibres from the stem of this versatile plant were used to make cloth for sails and clothing. Bundled together, papyrus reeds could be fashioned into boats or rope. Without a doubt, the most historically important use of papyrus was as a writing surface. To make this surface, Egyptians crushed the stems of the plant, dampened the layers they created from the strips thus obtained, and finally hammered and dried the result. About 3000 BC papyrus joined clay tablets as preferred writing surfaces. Many documents written on papyrus (the root of the English word *paper*) are still in existence today.

Papyrus documents have provided much of what is known about ancient Egypt, as have inscribed monuments, artwork, and various lists of kings. The most important kings list is Manetho's *Aegyptiaca* (now lost), which offered the basic chronological structure that most historians work from today. Manetho, a priest who lived in the early 3rd century BC, divided Egyptian history, after unification in 3100 BC, into dynasties, 30 of which are recognized.

Ancient Egypt was a land ruled by kings, who were also known as pharaohs. The word *pharaoh* comes from the Egyptian term for "great house," referring to the king's palace. Egyptians believed that their leaders were god-kings who became full-fledged gods after their deaths. The names of some 170 Egyptian kings are known.

The first recorded pharaoh was Menes, who ruled from about 3150 to

King Akhenaton and Queen Nefertiti worship the sun god Aton. Hulton Archive/Getty Images

3125 BC. According to legend, Menes founded the nation's capital at Memphis and united Lower Egypt and Upper Egypt. Yet the archaeological evidence for this early period is sketchy. Excavations have shown that up to two dozen rulers may have carried out the unification. One thing is clear: Egypt's power, stability, and unity in the ancient world made it the first true nation-state.

Perhaps the most recognizable of the ancient Egyptian kings is Tutankhamen, a relatively minor leader in the overarching history of Egyptian rulers. The "Boy King" ascended to the throne in 1333 BC at a very young age and died when he was just 19. He was thrust into the limelight in 1922, when his burial site was discovered by British archaeologist Howard Carter. The funerary chamber was a treasure trove. The kings of ancient Egypt controlled enormous riches, much of which was buried with them. The solid gold inner coffin found in Tutankhamen's tomb would be worth millions of dollars today, for the gold alone. The wealth that accompanied longer-lived kings to their tombs must have been staggering. Unfortunately, this supposition cannot be verified with much certainty because most of the other pharaohs' tombs were looted in ancient times by grave robbers.

Occasionally, women claimed Egypt's throne. The two most important of these women were Hatshepsut (1473–1458 BC) and Cleopatra (51–30 BC). Hatsheput was the daughter of one king, Thutmose I, and the sister and wife of his successor, Thutmose II. For years she ruled jointly with Thutmose III, the young son borne to her husband by another wife, until she proclaimed herself king and adopted full titles and regalia of a (male) pharaoh. Cleopatra came to the throne after her father, then her brother, died. A strong and ambitious ruler, she alternately sought alliances with and waged war against leaders of the Roman Empire. Yet despite her adept leadership, Cleopatra is perhaps best remembered for love affairs she conducted with Julius Caesar and the Roman general Mark Antony.

These women were notable exceptions in regnal matters. Egyptian leaders were overwhelmingly male, and the throne was traditionally passed down to male heirs. By tradition, the eldest son of the pharaoh's chief wife usually had the strongest claim to succeed his father. However, other sons—and other male relatives—could be named pharaoh as well. On occasion, a king might select a successor based on religious oracles.

Religion played an important role in ancient Egypt. The polytheistic Egyptians worshipped a wide array of gods and goddesses. Over the course of 3,000 years, new deities appeared and many old ones faded in importance. Yet Egyptian religion remained remarkably stable over that time and pervaded daily life.

Egypt's pantheon of gods and goddesses can seem strange to modern sensibilities. For instance, Ptah, the creator god, was believed to have made the world from the thoughts in his head. The goddess Nut was believed to swallow Re, the sun god and the creator god, each evening. Each day, he traveled across the sky as the sun and each night he journeyed through the underworld. There he battled against chaos and its allies.

Generally speaking, public religion focused on two objects of devotion: the king and an array of gods. The king held unique status between humanity and the gods. He was believed to commune with the gods, and he constructed huge funerary monuments for his afterlife. The main religious task of the king was to retain the benevolence of the gods. By doing this, he would stave off the disorder and chaos seen in so many kingdoms outside Egypt.

Early kings lived as absolute monarchs surrounded by small groups made up mostly of family. Over time, the kings became the centre of a more complicated government run by a core group of a few hundred wealthy elite. These men, in turn, controlled a few thousand lesser officials. Together, these two groups made up about 5 percent of early populations.

Egyptians believed themselves to be favoured by the gods. They also believed in an afterlife. More important to history, they believed that a body must remain intact to travel through the afterlife. So Egyptians became experts at the art of preserving dead bodies through mummification. Kings especially took elaborate steps to make sure that their bodies were preserved and protected in imposing coffins, sarcophagi, tombs, and pyramids. These instruments of immortality were built to last. Their survival has helped

immeasurably with our understanding of Egypt's civilization.

Writing was a major factor in centralizing the Egyptian state. There were two basic types of writing. Hieroglyphs were used mostly on monuments and for official state occasions. It was the formal writing system. More mundane communications were handled by using hieratic, a cursive form of the language that looks to the casual observer somewhat like modern Arabic.

The individuals who were largely responsible for keeping the machinery of the state running were a highly educated, literate group of scribes, who held a privileged position in society. They were responsible for assessing taxes, keeping legal records, and recording royal achievements. Training to become a scribe started at an early age. Scribes went to schools known as Houses of Life. Often scribes inherited their positions from their fathers, although it was possible for a literate commoner to rise to high office.

Ancient Egypt was also notable for vast building projects. The Egyptians used two main building materials: mud brick and stone. Mud brick was used primarily for building cities. Many of those cities have been washed away over time by the Nile, though Egypt's dry climate has preserved the remains of some. On the other hand, most of the stone tombs and temples were built out of the Nile's reach.

Easily the most recognizable of Egypt's great buildings were the pyramids. Why these structures were built remains something of a mystery, but their monumental scale was guaranteed to impress. The Great Pyramid of Khufu was 481.4 feet (146.7 metres) high. Built in the 2500s BC, it remained the world's tallest building until the late 19th century. Virtually all Egyptian pyramids were constructed early in the history of the Old Kingdom. Scholars speculate that the enormous amounts of money and manpower required for their construction were the chief reason that pyramids fell out of favour. Funerary buildings built thereafter were much smaller and poorer in construction.

Like the pyramids, Egypt's temples justly earned worldwide fame. Perhaps the greatest was the Temple of Luxor, construction of which was begun by Amenhotep III in the 18th dynasty (in the 1300s BC). The Temple of Luxor contained most of the elements found in all of Egypt's great temples. There was an approach avenue lined with sphinxes that led to a great double-towered pylon. Within the pylon was a courtyard leading to a pillar-filled hall. Deep in the temple was a shrine to a deity. Outside the temple was a lake or well to be used for the religious rituals held there. All of this was enclosed within a massive red brick wall. Ramses II (1200s BC)—rightly seen as one of Egypt's greatest builders—is responsible for the two temples at Abu Simbel, featuring four massive statues. They are among the most impressive examples of rock-cut architecture.

The Egyptians' ability to inspire awe has been long-lived. By the time the ancient Greeks first visited Egypt about 500 BC, the pyramids were already thousands of years old. Egypt's grand civilization, however, was in its twilight years. The invasion of Alexander the Great in the 300s BC brought the Ptolemy kings to power as Egypt's final leaders. Then Rome's defeat of Cleopatra in 30 BC brought the Ptolemy dynasty to an end, along with Egypt's independence. Knowledge about Egyptian writing and culture began to fade.

Yet the influence of ancient Egypt was pervasive. Roman emperors built Egyptian gardens in their palaces. Cults based on Egyptian gods and goddesses spread throughout the empire. The goddess Isis, for example, was worshipped from England to Afghanistan. Later, medieval popes constructed obelisks that mimicked those of the pharaohs. Medieval doctors ground up mummies and fed them to patients in the mistaken belief that these well-preserved bodies had supernatural healing powers. Enlightenment philosophers tried to study Egyptian culture with the few sources they had.

The doors of Egyptian history swung wide open again when Napoleon invaded Egypt in 1798. One of his soldiers discovered the Rosetta Stone, which contained a king's decree written in both hieroglyphs and ancient Greek. With this key, French scholar Jean-François Champollion was able to unlock the secrets of hieroglyphs that had eluded scholars for centuries. From this discovery has flowed most of what we know about the ancient Egyptians. Without it, scholars might still be guessing blindly about the meaning of Egypt's temples and tombs.

In the 19th century, Egyptian influence became fashionable in design and the arts. Jewelry, furniture, and an assortment of decorative objects and accent pieces were adorned with designs and images that conjured thoughts of life along the Nile. Egyptian-themed (or at least tinged) operas, plays, and novels were a hit with the general public.

It seemed that the more that was revealed about ancient Egypt, the more the appetite for faux relics and representations grew in America and throughout Europe. The discovery of King Tutankhamen's tomb in the early 20th century sparked yet another round of Egyptomania. Films featuring mummies and compelling characters such as the ever-beguiling Cleopatra flickered across the silver screen, while major cities erected corporate buildings that borrowed heavily from the clean lines of Egyptian design.

Interest in Egypt waned for a time and was then revived in 1978, when the treasures of Tutankhamen's tomb went on traveling display around the world. Another traveling exhibition was begun in 2005. King Tut again made news in 2010 when scientists, using DNA analysis and radiography, revealed that the young pharaoh had most likely died from malaria in combination with degenerative bone disease, thus solving a mystery that had intrigued the masses for decades.

Perhaps interest in Egypt will never truly be a thing of the past. That would be a fate befitting ancient Egypt's status as one of the world's greatest civilizations.

CHAPTER 1

THE STUDY OF ANCIENT EGYPT

Ancient Egyptian civilization developed in northeastern Africa in the 3rd millennium BC. Its many achievements, preserved in its art and monuments, hold a fascination that continues to grow as archaeological finds expose its secrets. The term *ancient Egypt* traditionally refers to northeastern Africa from its prehistory up to the Islamic conquest in the 7th century AD.

ANCIENT EGYPTIAN CIVILIZATION

Ancient Egypt can be thought of as an oasis in the desert of northeastern Africa, dependent on the annual inundation of the Nile River to support its agricultural population. The country's chief wealth came from the fertile floodplain of the Nile valley, where the river flows between bands of limestone hills, and the Nile delta, in which it fans into several branches north of present-day Cairo. Between the floodplain and the hills is a variable band of low desert that supported a certain amount of game. The Nile was Egypt's sole transportation artery.

LIFE IN ANCIENT EGYPT

The First Cataract of the Nile at Aswān, where the riverbed is turned into rapids by a belt of granite, was the country's only well-defined boundary within a populated area. To the south lay the far less hospitable area of Nubia, in which the river flowed through low sandstone hills that in most regions left only a very narrow strip of cultivable land. Nubia was significant for Egypt's periodic southward expansion and for access to products from farther south. West of the Nile was the arid Sahara, broken by a chain of oases some 125 to 185 miles (200 to 300 kilometres) from the river and lacking in all other resources except for a few minerals. The eastern desert, between the Nile and the Red Sea, was more important, for it supported a small nomadic population and desert game, contained numerous mineral deposits, including gold, and was the route to the Red Sea.

To the northeast was the Isthmus of Suez. It offered the principal route for contact with Sinai, from which came turquoise and possibly copper, and with southwestern Asia, Egypt's most important area of cultural interaction, from which were received stimuli for technical development and cultivars for crops. Immigrants and ultimately invaders crossed the isthmus into Egypt, attracted by the country's stability and prosperity. From the late 2nd millennium BC onward, numerous attacks were made by land and sea along the eastern Mediterranean coast.

At first, relatively little cultural contact came by way of the Mediterranean Sea, but from an early date Egypt maintained trading relations with the Lebanese port of Byblos (present-day Jbail). Egypt needed few imports to maintain basic standards of living, but good timber was essential and not available within the country, so it usually was obtained from Lebanon. Minerals such as obsidian and lapis lazuli were imported from as far afield as Anatolia and Afghanistan.

Agriculture centred on the cultivation of cereal crops, chiefly emmer wheat (*Triticum dicoccum*) and barley (*Hordeum vulgare*). The fertility of the land and general predictability of the inundation ensured very high productivity from a single annual crop. This productivity made it possible to store large surpluses against crop failures and also formed the chief basis of Egyptian wealth, which was, until the creation of the large empires of the 1st millennium BC, the greatest of any state in the ancient Middle East.

Basin irrigation was achieved by simple means, and multiple cropping was not feasible until much later times, except perhaps in the lakeside area of Al-Fayyūm. As the river deposited alluvial silt, raising the level of the floodplain, and land was reclaimed from marsh, the area available for cultivation in the Nile valley and delta increased, while pastoralism declined slowly. In addition to grain crops, fruit and vegetables were important, the latter being irrigated year-round in small plots; fish was also vital to the diet. Papyrus, which grew abundantly in marshes, was gathered wild and in later times was cultivated. It may have been used as a food crop, and it certainly was used to make rope, matting, and sandals. Above all, it provided the characteristic Egyptian writing material, which, with cereals, was the country's chief export in Late period Egyptian and then Greco-Roman times.

Cattle may have been domesticated in northeastern Africa. The Egyptians kept many as draft animals and for their various products, showing some of the interest in breeds and individuals that is found to this day in the Sudan and eastern Africa. The donkey, which was the principal transport animal (the camel did not become common until Roman times), was probably domesticated in the region. The native Egyptian breed of sheep became extinct in the 2nd millennium BC and was replaced by an Asiatic breed. Sheep were primarily a source of meat; their wool was rarely used. Goats were more numerous than sheep. Pigs were also raised and eaten. Ducks and geese were kept for food, and many of the vast numbers of wild and migratory birds found in Egypt were hunted and trapped. Desert game, principally various species of antelope and ibex, were hunted by the elite; it was a royal privilege to hunt lions and wild cattle. Pets included dogs, which were also used for hunting, cats (domesticated in Egypt), and monkeys. In addition, the Egyptians had a great interest in, and knowledge of, most species of mammals, birds, reptiles, and fish in their environment.

Most Egyptians were probably descended from settlers who moved to the Nile valley in prehistoric times, with population increase coming through natural fertility. In various periods there were immigrants from Nubia, Libya, and especially the Middle East. They were historically significant and also may have contributed to population growth, but their numbers are unknown. Most people lived in villages and towns in the Nile valley and delta. Dwellings were normally built of mud brick and have long since disappeared beneath the rising water table or beneath modern town sites, thereby obliterating evidence for settlement patterns. In antiquity, as now, the most favoured location of settlements was on slightly raised ground near the riverbank, where transport and water were easily available and flooding was unlikely. Until the 1st millennium BC, Egypt was not urbanized to the same extent as Mesopotamia. Instead, a few centres, notably Memphis and Thebes, attracted population and particularly the elite, while the rest of the people were relatively evenly spread over the land. The size of the population has been estimated as having risen from 1 to 1.5 million in the 3rd millennium BC to perhaps twice that number in the late 2nd millennium and 1st millennium BC. (Much higher levels of population were reached in Greco-Roman times.)

Nearly all of the people were engaged in agriculture and were probably tied to the land. In theory all the land belonged to the king, although in practice those living on it could not easily be removed, and some categories of land could be bought and sold. Land was assigned to high officials to provide them with an income, and most tracts required payment of substantial dues to the state, which had a strong interest in keeping the land in agricultural use. Abandoned land was taken back into state ownership and reassigned for cultivation. The people who lived on and worked the land were not free to leave and were obliged to work it, but they were not slaves. Most paid a proportion of their produce to major officials. Free citizens who worked the land on their own behalf did emerge. Terms applied to them tended originally to refer to poor people, but these agriculturalists were probably not poor.

Slavery was never common, being restricted to captives and foreigners or to people who were forced by poverty or debt to sell themselves into service. Slaves sometimes even married members of their owners' families, so that in the long term those belonging to households tended to be assimilated into free society. In the New Kingdom (from about 1539 to 1075 BC), large numbers of captive slaves were acquired by major state institutions or incorporated into the army. Punitive treatment of foreign slaves or of native fugitives from their obligations included forced labour, exile (in, for example, the oases of the western desert), or compulsory enlistment in dangerous mining expeditions. Even nonpunitive employment such as quarrying in the desert was hazardous. The official record of one expedition shows a mortality rate of more than 10 percent.

Just as the Egyptians optimized agricultural production with simple means, their crafts and techniques, many of which originally came from Asia, were raised to extraordinary levels of perfection. The Egyptians' most striking technical achievement, massive stone building, also exploited the potential of a centralized state to mobilize a huge labour force, which was made available by efficient agricultural practices. Some of the technical and organizational skills involved were remarkable. The construction of the great pyramids of the 4th dynasty (c. 2575–c. 2465 BC) has yet to be fully explained and would be a major challenge to this day. This expenditure of skill contrasts with sparse evidence of an essentially neolithic way of living for the rural population of the time, while the use of flint tools persisted even in urban environments at least until the late 2nd millennium BC. Metal was correspondingly scarce, much of it being used for prestige rather than everyday purposes.

In urban and elite contexts, the Egyptian ideal was the nuclear family, but, on the land and even within the central ruling group, there is evidence for extended families. Egyptians were monogamous, and the choice of partners in marriage, for which no formal ceremony or legal sanction is known, did not follow a set pattern. Consanguineous marriage was not practiced during the Dynastic period, except for the occasional marriage of a brother and sister within the royal family, and that practice may have been open only to kings or heirs to the throne. Divorce was in theory easy, but it was costly. Women had a legal status only marginally inferior to that of men. They could own and dispose of property in their own right, and they could initiate divorce and other legal proceedings. They hardly ever held administrative office but increasingly were involved in religious cults as priestesses or "chantresses." Married women held the title "mistress of the house," the precise significance of which is unknown. Lower down the social scale, they probably worked on the land as well as in the house.

The uneven distribution of wealth, labour, and technology was related to the only partly urban character of society, especially in the 3rd millennium BC. The country's resources were not fed into numerous provincial towns but instead were concentrated to great effect around the capital—itself a dispersed string of settlements rather than a city—and focused on the central figure in society, the king. In the 3rd and early 2nd millennia, the elite ideal, expressed in the decoration of private tombs, was manorial and rural. Not until much later did Egyptians develop a more pronouncedly urban character.

THE KING AND IDEOLOGY: ADMINISTRATION, ART, AND WRITING

In cosmogonical terms, Egyptian society consisted of a descending hierarchy of the gods, the king, the blessed dead, and humanity (by which was understood chiefly the Egyptians). Of these groups, only the king was single, and hence he was individually more prominent than any of the others. A text that summarizes the king's role states that he "is on earth for ever and ever, judging humankind and propitiating the gods, and setting order [ma'at, a central concept] in place of disorder. He gives offerings to the gods and mortuary offerings to the spirits [the blessed dead]." The king was imbued with divine essence, but not in any simple or unqualified sense. His divinity accrued to him from his office and was reaffirmed through rituals, but it was vastly inferior to that of major gods. He was god rather than human by virtue of his potential, which was immeasurably greater than that of any human being. To humanity, he manifested the gods on earth, a conception that was elaborated in a complex web of metaphor and doctrine.

Less directly, he represented humanity to the gods. The text quoted above also gives great prominence to the dead, who were the object of a cult for the living and who could intervene in human affairs; in many periods the chief visible expenditure and focus of display of nonroyal individuals, as of the king, was on provision for the tomb and the next world. Egyptian kings are commonly called pharaohs, following the usage of the Hebrew Bible (Old Testament). The term *pharaoh*, however, is derived from the Egyptian *per 'aa* ("great estate") and dates to the designation of the royal palace as an institution. This term for palace was used increasingly from about 1400 BC as a way of referring to the living king; in earlier times it was rare.

Rules of succession to the kingship are poorly understood. The common conception that the heir to the throne had to marry his predecessor's oldest daughter has been disproved; kingship did not pass through the female line. The choice of queen seems to have been free. Often the queen was a close relative of the king, but she also might be unrelated to him. In the New Kingdom, for which evidence is abundant, each king had a queen with distinctive titles, as well as a number of minor wives.

Sons of the chief queen seem to have been the preferred successors to the throne, but other sons could also become king. In many cases the successor was the eldest (surviving) son, and such a pattern of inheritance agrees with more general Egyptian values, but often he was some other relative or was completely unrelated. New Kingdom texts describe, after the event, how kings were appointed heirs either by their predecessors or by divine oracles, and such may have been the pattern when there was no clear successor. Dissent and conflict are suppressed from public sources. From the Late period (664–332 BC), when sources are more diverse and patterns less rigid, numerous usurpations and interruptions to the succession are known. They probably had many forerunners.

The king's position changed gradually from that of an absolute monarch at the centre of a small ruling group made up mostly of his kin to that of the head of a bureaucratic state—in which his rule was still absolute—based on officeholding and, in theory, on free competition and merit. By the 5th dynasty, fixed institutions had been added to the force of tradition and the regulation of personal contact as brakes on autocracy, but the charismatic and superhuman power of the king remained vital.

The elite of administrative officeholders received their positions and commissions from the king, whose general role as judge over humanity they put into effect. They commemorated their own justice and concern for others, especially their inferiors, and recorded their own exploits and ideal conduct of life in inscriptions for others to see. Thus, the position of the elite was affirmed by reference to the king, to their prestige among their peers, and to their conduct toward their subordinates, justifying to some extent the fact that they—and still more the king—appropriated much of the country's production.

These attitudes and their potential dissemination through society counterbalanced inequality, but how far they were accepted cannot be known. The core group of wealthy officeholders numbered at most a few hundred, and the administrative class of minor officials and scribes, most of whom could not afford to leave memorials or inscriptions, perhaps 5,000. With their dependents, these two groups formed perhaps 5 percent of the early population. Monuments and inscriptions commemorated no more than one in a thousand people.

According to royal ideology, the king appointed the elite on the basis of merit, and in ancient conditions of high mortality the elite had to be open to recruits from outside. There was, however, also an ideal that a son should succeed his father. In periods of weak central control this principle predominated, and in the Late period the whole society became more rigid and stratified.

Writing was a major instrument in the centralization of the Egyptian state and its self-presentation. The two basic types of writing—hieroglyphs, which were used for monuments and display, and the cursive form known as hieratic—were invented at much the same time in late predynastic Egypt (c. 3000 BC). Writing was chiefly used for administration, and until about 2650 BC no continuous texts are preserved; the only extant literary texts written before the early Middle Kingdom (c. 1950 BC) seem to have been lists of important traditional information and possibly medical treatises. The use and potential of writing were restricted both by the rate of literacy, which was probably well below 1 percent, and by expectations of what writing might do.

Hieroglyphic writing was publicly identified with Egypt. Perhaps because of this association with a single powerful state, its language, and its culture, Egyptian writing was seldom adapted to write other languages; in this it contrasts with the cuneiform script of the relatively uncentralized, multilingual Mesopotamia. Nonetheless, Egyptian hieroglyphs probably served in the middle of the 2nd millennium BC as the model from which the alphabet, ultimately the most widespread of all writing systems, evolved.

The dominant visible legacy of ancient Egypt is in works of architecture and representational art. Until the Middle

Ancient Egyptian hieroglyphic numeral system

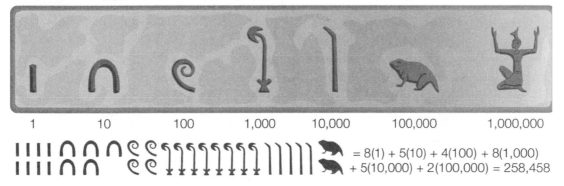

Egyptian hieroglyphic numerals. Encyclopædia Britannica, Inc.

Kingdom, most of these were mortuary, namely royal tomb complexes, including pyramids and mortuary temples, and private tombs. There were also temples dedicated to the cult of the gods throughout the country, but most of these were modest structures. From the beginning of the New Kingdom, temples of the gods became the principal monuments. Royal palaces and private houses, which are very little known, were less important.

Temples and tombs were ideally executed in stone with relief decoration on their walls and were filled with stone and wooden statuary, inscribed and decorated stelae (freestanding small stone monuments), and, in their inner areas, composite works of art in precious materials. The design of the monuments and their decoration dates in essence to the beginning of the historical period and presents an ideal, sanctified cosmos. Little in it is related to the everyday world, and, except in palaces, works of art may have been rare outside temples and tombs. Decoration may record real historical events, rituals, or the official titles and careers of individuals, but its prime significance is the more general assertion of values, and the information presented must be evaluated for its plausibility and compared with other evidence. Some of the events depicted in relief on royal monuments were certainly iconic rather than historically factual.

The highly distinctive Egyptian method of rendering nature and artistic style was also a creation of early times

and can be seen in most works of Egyptian art. In content, these are hierarchically ordered so that the most important figures, the gods and the king, are shown together, while before the New Kingdom gods seldom occur in the same context as humanity. The decoration of a nonroyal tomb characteristically shows the tomb's owner with his subordinates, who administer his land and present him with its produce. The tomb owner is also typically depicted hunting in the marshes, a favourite pastime of the elite that may additionally symbolize passage into the next world. The king and the gods are absent in nonroyal tombs, and, until the New Kingdom, overtly religious matter is restricted to rare scenes of mortuary rituals and journeys and to textual formulas. Temple reliefs, in which king and gods occur freely, show the king defeating his enemies, hunting, and especially offering to the gods, who in turn confer benefits upon him. Human beings are present at most as minor figures supporting the king. On both royal and nonroyal monuments, an ideal world is represented in which all are beautiful and everything goes well; only minor figures may have physical imperfections.

This artistic presentation of values originated at the same time as writing but before the latter could record continuous texts or complex statements. Some of the earliest continuous texts of the 4th and 5th dynasties show an awareness of an ideal past that the present could only aspire to emulate. A few "biographies" of officials allude to strife, but more-nuanced discussion occurs first in literary texts of the Middle Kingdom. The texts consist of stories, dialogues, lamentations, and especially instructions on how to live a good life, and they supply a rich commentary on the more one-dimensional rhetoric of public inscriptions. Literary works were written in all the main later phases of the Egyptian language—Middle Egyptian; the "classical" form of the Middle and New kingdoms that continued in copies and inscriptions into Roman times; Late Egyptian, from the 19th dynasty to about 700 BC; and the demotic script from the 4th century BC to the 3rd century AD—but many of the finest and most complex are among the earliest.

Literary works also included treatises on mathematics, astronomy, medicine, and magic, as well as various religious texts and canonical lists that classified the categories of creation (probably the earliest genre, dating back to the beginning of the Old Kingdom, c. 2575 BC, or even a little earlier). Among these texts, little is truly systematic, a notable exception being a medical treatise on wounds. The absence of systematic inquiry contrasts with Egyptian practical expertise in such fields as surveying, which was used both for orienting and planning buildings to remarkably fine tolerances and for the regular division of fields after the annual inundation of the Nile. The Egyptians also had surveyed and established the dimensions of their entire country by the beginning of the Middle Kingdom. These precise tasks required both knowledge of astronomy and highly ingenious techniques, but they apparently were achieved with little theoretical analysis.

Whereas in the earliest periods Egypt seems to have been administered almost as the personal estate of the king, by the central Old Kingdom it had been divided into about 35 nomes, or provinces, each with its own officials. Administration was concentrated at the capital, where most of the central elite lived and died. In the nonmonetary Egyptian economy, its essential functions were the collection, storage, and redistribution of produce; the drafting and organization of manpower for specialized labour, probably including irrigation and flood protection works, and major state projects; and the supervision of legal matters. Administration and law were not fully distinct, and both depended ultimately on the king. The settlement of disputes was in part an administrative task, for which the chief guiding criterion was precedent, while contractual relations were regulated by the use of standard formulas. State and temple both partook in redistribution and held massive reserves of grain; temples were economic as well as religious institutions. In periods of decentralization similar functions were exercised by local grandees. Markets had only a minor role, and craftsmen were employees who normally traded only what they produced in their free time.

The wealthiest officials escaped this pattern to some extent by receiving their income in the form of land and maintaining large establishments that included their own specialized workers.

The essential medium of administration was writing, reinforced by personal authority over the nonliterate 99 percent of the population. Texts exhorting the young to be scribes emphasize that the scribe commanded while the rest did the work. Most officials (almost all of whom were men) held several offices and accumulated more as they progressed up a complex ranked hierarchy, at the top of which was the vizier, the chief administrator and judge. The vizier reported to the king, who in theory retained certain powers, such as authority to invoke the death penalty, absolutely.

Before the Middle Kingdom, the civil and the military were not sharply distinguished. Military forces consisted of local militias under their own officials and included foreigners, and nonmilitary expeditions to extract minerals from the desert or to transport heavy loads through the country were organized in similar fashion. Until the New Kingdom there was no separate priesthood. Holders of civil office also had priestly titles, and priests had civil titles. Often priesthoods were sinecures: their chief significance was the income they brought. The same was true of the minor civil titles accumulated by high officials. At a lower level, minor priesthoods were held on a rotating basis by "laymen" who served every fourth month in temples. State and temple were so closely interconnected that there was no real tension between them before the late New Kingdom.

SOURCES, CALENDARS, AND CHRONOLOGY

For all but the last century of Egyptian prehistory, whose neolithic and later phases are normally termed "predynastic," evidence is exclusively archaeological. Later native sources have only mythical allusions to such remote times. The Dynastic period of native Egyptian rulers is generally divided into 30 dynasties, following the *Aegyptiaca* of the Greco-Egyptian writer Manetho of Sebennytos (early 3rd century BC), excerpts of which are preserved in the works of later writers. Manetho apparently organized his dynasties by the capital cities from which they ruled, but several of his divisions also reflect political or dynastic changes—that is, changes of the party holding power. He gave the lengths of reign of kings or of entire dynasties and grouped the dynasties into several periods, but, because of textual corruption and a tendency toward inflation, Manetho's figures cannot be used to reconstruct chronology without supporting evidence and analysis.

Manetho's prime sources were earlier Egyptian king lists, the organization of which he imitated. The most significant preserved example of a king list is the Turin Papyrus (Turin Canon), a fragmentary document in the Egyptian Museum in Turin, Italy, which originally listed all kings of the 1st through the 17th dynasty, preceded by a mythical dynasty of gods and one of the "spirits, followers of Horus." Like Manetho's later work, the Turin document gave reign lengths for individual kings, as well as totals for some dynasties and longer multidynastic periods.

In early periods the kings' years of reign were not consecutively numbered but were named for salient events, and lists were made of the names. More-extensive details were added to the lists for the 4th and 5th dynasties, when dates

The Palermo Stone, first side. Courtesy of the Regional Museum of Archaeology, Palermo

were assigned according to biennial cattle censuses numbered through each king's reign. Fragments of such lists are preserved on the Palermo Stone, an inscribed piece of basalt (at the Regional Museum of Archaeology in Palermo, Italy), and related pieces in the Cairo Museum and University College London. These are probably all parts of a single copy of an original document of the 5th dynasty.

The Egyptians did not date by eras longer than the reign of a single king, so a historical framework must be created from totals of reign lengths, which are then related to astronomical data that may allow whole periods to be fixed precisely. This is done through references to astronomical events and correlations with the three calendars in use in Egyptian antiquity. All dating was by a civil calendar, derived from the lunar calendar, which was introduced in the first half of the 3rd millennium BC. The civil year had 365 days and started in principle when Sirius, or the Dog Star—also known in Greek as Sothis (Ancient Egyptian: Sopdet)—became visible above the horizon after a period of absence, which at that time occurred some weeks before the Nile began to rise for the inundation. Every 4 years the civil year advanced one day in relation to the solar year (with 365 ¼, and after a cycle of about 1,460 years it would again agree with the solar calendar. Religious ceremonies were organized according to two lunar calendars that had months of 29 or 30 days, with extra, intercalary months every three years or so.

Five mentions of the rising of Sirius (generally known as Sothic dates) are preserved in texts from the 3rd to the 1st millennium, but by themselves these references cannot yield an absolute chronology. Such a chronology can be computed from larger numbers of lunar dates and cross-checked from solutions for the observations of Sirius. Various chronologies are in use, however, differing by up to 40 years for the 2nd millennium BC and by more than a century for the beginning of the 1st dynasty. The chronologies offered in most publications up to 1985 have been thrown into some doubt for the Middle and New kingdoms by a restudy of the evidence for the Sothic and especially the lunar dates. For the 1st millennium, dates in the Third Intermediate period are approximate; a supposed fixed year of 945 BC, based on links with the Hebrew Bible, turns out to be variable by a number of years. Late period dates (664–332 BC) are almost completely fixed. Before the 12th dynasty, plausible dates for the 11th can be computed backward, but for earlier times dates are approximate. A total of 955 years for the 1st through the 8th dynasty in the Turin Canon has been used to assign a date of about 3100 BC for the beginning of the 1st dynasty, but this requires excessive average reign lengths, and an estimate of 2925 BC is preferable. Radiocarbon and other scientific dating of samples from Egyptian sites have not improved on, or convincingly contested, computed dates. More-recent work on radiocarbon dates from Egypt does,

however, yield results encouragingly close to dates computed in the manner described above.

King lists and astronomy give only a chronological framework. A vast range of archaeological and inscriptional sources for Egyptian history survive, but none of them were produced with the interpretation of history in mind. No consistent political history of ancient Egypt can be written. The evidence is very unevenly distributed. There are gaps of many decades; and in the 3rd millennium BC no continuous royal text recording historical events was inscribed. Private biographical inscriptions of all periods from the 5th dynasty (c. 2465–c. 2325 BC) to the Roman conquest (30 BC) record individual involvement in events but are seldom concerned with their general significance. Royal inscriptions from the 12th dynasty (1938–1756 BC) to Ptolemaic times aim to present a king's actions according to an overall conception of "history," in which he is the re-creator of the order of the world and the guarantor of its continued stability or its expansion. The goal of his action is to serve not humanity but the gods, while nonroyal individuals may relate their own successes to the king in the first instance and sometimes to the gods.

Only in the decentralized intermediate periods did the nonroyal recount internal strife. Kings did not mention dissent in their texts unless it came at the beginning of a reign or a phase of action and was quickly and triumphantly overcome in a reaffirmation of order. Such a schema often dominates the factual content of texts, and it creates a strong bias toward recording foreign affairs, because in official ideology there is no internal dissent after the initial turmoil is over. "History" is as much a ritual as a process of events. As a ritual, its protagonists are royal and divine. Only in the Late period did these conventions weaken significantly. Even then, they were retained in full for temple reliefs, where they kept their vitality into Roman times.

Despite this idealization, the Egyptians were well aware of history, as is clear from their king lists. They divided the past into periods comparable to those used by Egyptologists and evaluated the rulers not only as the founders of epochs but also in terms of their salient exploits or, especially in folklore, their bad qualities. The Demotic Chronicle, a text of the Ptolemaic period, purports to foretell the bad end that would befall numerous Late period kings as divine retribution for their wicked actions.

EGYPTOLOGY: THE RECOVERY AND STUDY OF ANCIENT EGYPT

After the Arab conquest (AD 641), only the Christian Egyptians, the Copts, kept alive the ancient language, written in Greek characters. In Europe the Coptic texts taken from Egypt during the Renaissance awakened interest in the Egyptian language. Up to this time, views of Egypt were dominated by the classical tradition that it was the land of ancient wisdom.

This wisdom was thought to inhere in the hieroglyphic script, which was believed to impart profound symbolic ideas, not—as it in fact does—the sounds and words of texts. Between the 15th and 18th centuries, Egypt had a minor but significant position in general views of antiquity, and its monuments gradually became better known through the work of scholars in Europe and travelers in the country itself; the finest publications of the latter were by Richard Pococke, Frederik Ludwig Norden, and Carsten Niebuhr, all of whose works in the 18th century helped to stimulate an Egyptian revival in European art and architecture. Coptic, the Christian successor of the ancient Egyptian language, was studied from the 17th century, notably by Athanasius Kircher, for its potential to provide the key to Egyptian.

Napoleon I's expedition to and short-lived conquest of Egypt in 1798 was the culmination of 18th-century interest in the East. The expedition was accompanied by a team of scholars who recorded the ancient and contemporary country, issuing in 1809–28 the *Description de l'Égypte*, the most comprehensive study to be made before the decipherment of the hieroglyphic script. The renowned Rosetta Stone, which bears a decree of Ptolemy V Epiphanes in hieroglyphs, demotic script, and Greek alphabetic characters, was discovered during the expedition. It was ceded to the British after the French capitulation in Egypt and became the property of the British Museum in London. This document greatly assisted the decipherment, accomplished by Jean-François Champollion in 1822.

The Egyptian language revealed by the decipherment and decades of subsequent study is a member of the Afro-Asiatic language family. Egyptian is closest to the family's Semitic branch but is distinctive in many respects. During several millennia it changed greatly. The script does not write vowels, and because Greek forms for royal names were known from Manetho long before the Egyptian forms became available, those used to this day are a mixture of Greek and Egyptian.

In the first half of the 19th century, vast numbers of antiquities were exported from Egypt, forming the nucleus of collections in many major museums. These were removed rather than excavated, inflicting, together with the economic development of the country, colossal damage on ancient sites. At the same time, many travelers and scholars visited the country and recorded the monuments. The most important, and remarkably accurate, record was produced by the Prussian expedition led by Karl Richard Lepsius, in 1842–45, which explored sites as far south as the central Sudan.

In the mid-19th century, Egyptology—now defined as the study of pharaonic Egypt, spanning the period c. 4500 BC to AD 641 (the time of the Arab conquest)—developed as a subject in France and in Prussia. The Antiquities Service and a museum of Egyptian antiquities were established in Egypt by the French Egyptologist Auguste Mariette, a great excavator who attempted to preserve sites from destruction, and the Prussian Heinrich Brugsch, who made great progress in the interpretation of texts of many periods and published the first major Egyptian dictionary. In 1880 Flinders (later Sir Flinders) Petrie began more than 40 years of methodical excavation, which created an archaeological framework for all the chief periods of Egyptian culture except for remote prehistory. Petrie was the initiator of much in archaeological method, but he was later surpassed by George Andrew Reisner, who excavated for American institutions from 1899 to 1937. The greatest late 19th-century Egyptologist was Adolf Erman of Berlin, who put the understanding of the Egyptian language on a sound basis and wrote general works that for the first time organized what was known about the earlier periods.

Complete facsimile copies of Egyptian monuments have been published since the 1890s, providing a separate record that becomes more vital as the originals decay. The pioneer of this scientific epigraphy was James Henry Breasted of the Oriental Institute of the University of Chicago, who began his work in 1905 and shortly thereafter was joined by others. He started the Epigraphic Survey in 1924 to make accurate copies of the inscriptions on monuments, which are subject to deterioration from exposure to the elements, and to then publish these records. The

Howard Carter. Encyclopædia Britannica, Inc.

group's current project, which began during the 1990–91 season, is a record of the temple of Amon in Madīnat Habu.

In the first half of the 20th century, some outstanding archaeological discoveries were made. Howard Carter uncovered the tomb of Tutankhamen in 1922, Pierre Montet found the tombs of 21st–22nd-dynasty kings at Tanis in 1939–44, and W.B. Emery and L.P. Kirwan found tombs of the Ballānah culture (the 4th through the 6th century AD) in Nubia in 1931–34. The last of these was part of the second survey of Lower Nubia in 1929–34, which preceded the second raising of the Aswān Dam. This was followed in the late 1950s and '60s by an international campaign to excavate and record sites in Egyptian and Sudanese Nubia before the completion of the Aswān High Dam in 1970. Lower Nubia is now one of the most thoroughly explored archaeological regions of the world. Most of its many temples have been moved, either to higher ground nearby, as happened to Abu Simbel and Philae, or to quite different places, including various foreign museums. The campaign also had the welcome consequence of introducing a wide range of archaeological expertise to Egypt, so that standards of excavation and recording in the country have risen greatly.

Excavation and survey of great importance have continued in many places. For example, at Ṣaqqārah, part of the necropolis of the ancient city of Memphis, new areas of the Sarapeum have been uncovered with rich finds, and a major New Kingdom necropolis is being thoroughly explored. The site of ancient Memphis itself has been systematically surveyed; its position in relation to the ancient course of the Nile has been established; and urban occupation areas have been studied in detail for the first time. More recently, archaeologists in 2009–10 discovered in Alexandria the remains of a temple dedicated to Bastet, a goddess in the shape of a cat.

Egyptology, it should be noted, is primarily an interpretive subject. There have been outstanding contributions—for example in art, for which Heinrich Schäfer established the principles of the rendering of nature, and in language. New light has been cast on texts, the majority of which are written in a simple metre that can serve as the basis of sophisticated literary works. The physical environment, social structure, kingship, and religion are other fields in which great advances have been made, while the reconstruction of the outline of history is constantly being improved in detail.

CHAPTER 2

THE EARLY PERIOD

The peoples of predynastic Egypt were the successors of the Paleolithic inhabitants of northeastern Africa, who had spread over much of its area. During wet phases they had left remains in regions as inhospitable as the Great Sand Sea. The final desiccation of the Sahara was not complete until the end of the 3rd millennium BC. Over thousands of years people must have migrated from there to the Nile valley, the environment of which improved as the region dried out. In this process the decisive change from the nomadic hunter-gatherer way of life of Paleolithic times to settled agriculture has not so far been identified.

Scholars do know that some time after 5000 BC the raising of crops was introduced, probably on a horticultural scale, in small local cultures that seem to have penetrated southward through Egypt into the oases and the Sudan. Several of the basic food plants that were grown are native to the Middle East, so the new techniques probably spread from there. No large-scale migration need have been involved, and the cultures were at first largely self-contained. The preserved evidence for them is unrepresentative because it comes from the low desert, where relatively few people lived. As was the case later, most people probably settled in the valley and delta.

PREDYNASTIC EGYPT

The earliest known Neolithic cultures in Egypt have been found at Marimda Banī Salāma, on the southwestern edge of

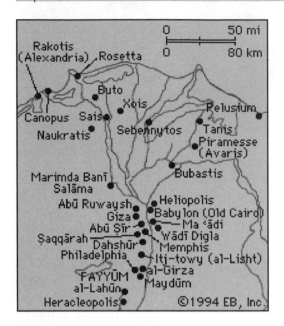

Inset of the Nile delta.

the delta, and farther to the southwest, in Al-Fayyūm. The site at Marimda Banī Salāma, which dates to the 6th–5th millennium BC, gives evidence of settlement and shows that cereals were grown. In Al-Fayyūm, where evidence dates to the 5th millennium BC, the settlements were near the shore of Lake Qārūn, and the settlers engaged in fishing. Marimda is a very large site that was occupied for many centuries. The inhabitants lived in lightly built huts; they may have buried their dead within their houses, but areas where burials have been found may not have been occupied by dwellings at the same time. Pottery was used in both cultures. In addition to these Egyptian Neolithic cultures, others have been identified in the Western Desert, in the

Second Cataract area, and north of Khartoum. Some of these are as early as the Egyptian ones, while others overlapped with the succeeding Egyptian predynastic cultures.

In Upper Egypt, between Asyūṭ and Luxor (Al-Uqṣur), have been found the Tasian culture (named for Dayr Tāsā) and the Badarian culture (named for Al-Badārī); these date from the late 5th millennium BC. Most of the evidence for them comes from cemeteries, where the burials included fine black-topped red pottery, ornaments, some copper objects, and glazed steatite beads. The most characteristic predynastic luxury objects, slate palettes for grinding cosmetics, occur for the first time in this period. The burials show little differentiation of wealth and status and seem to belong to a peasant culture without central political organization.

Probably contemporary with both predynastic and dynastic times are thousands of rock drawings of a wide range of motifs, including boats, found throughout the Eastern Desert, in Lower Nubia, and as far west as Mount 'Uwaynāt, which stands near modern Egypt's borders with Libya and the Sudan in the southwest. The drawings show that nomads were common throughout the desert, probably to the late 3rd millennium BC, but they cannot be dated precisely. They may all have been produced by nomads, or inhabitants of the Nile valley may often have penetrated the desert and made drawings.

Naqādah I, named for the major site of Naqādah but also called Amratian for Al-ʿĀmirah, is a distinct phase that succeeded the Badarian. It has been found as far south as Al-Kawm al-Aḥmar (Hierakonpolis; ancient Egyptian Nekhen), near the sandstone barrier of Mount Silsilah, which was the cultural boundary of Egypt in predynastic times. Naqādah I differs from its Badarian predecessor in its density of settlement and the typology of its material culture but hardly at all in the social organization implied by the archaeological finds. Burials were in shallow pits in which the bodies were placed facing to the west, like those of later Egyptians. Notable types of material found in graves are fine pottery decorated with representational designs in white on red, figurines of men and women, and hard stone mace-heads that are the precursors of important late predynastic objects.

Naqādah II, also known as Gerzean for Girza (Jirza), is the most important predynastic culture. The heartland of its development was the same as that of Naqādah I, but it spread gradually throughout the country. South of Mount Silsilah, sites of the culturally similar Nubian A Group are found as far as the Second Cataract of the Nile and beyond; these have a long span, continuing as late as the Egyptian Early Dynastic period. During Naqādah II, large sites developed at Al-Kawm al-Aḥmar, Naqādah, and Abydos (Abīdūs), showing by their size the concentration of settlement, as

well as exhibiting increasing differentiation in wealth and status. Few sites have been identified between Asyūṭ and Al-Fayyūm, and this region may have been sparsely settled, perhaps supporting a pastoral rather than agricultural population. Near present-day Cairo—at Al-ʿUmāri, Al-Maʿādi, and Wādī Dijlah and stretching as far south as the latitude of Al-Fayyūm—are sites of a separate, contemporary culture. Al-Maʿādi was an extensive settlement that traded with the Middle East and probably acted as an intermediary for transmitting goods

Painted clay vessel with flamingos and ibexes, Gerzean culture, Egypt, c. 3400–c. 3100 BC; in the Roemer-Pelizaeus Museum, Hildesheim, Ger. Holle Bildarchiv, Baden-Baden

to the south. In this period, imports of lapis lazuli provide evidence that trade networks extended as far afield as Afghanistan.

The material culture of Naqādah II included increasing numbers of prestige objects. The characteristic mortuary pottery is made of buff desert clay, principally from around Qinā, and is decorated in red with pictures of uncertain meaning showing boats, animals, and scenes with human figures. Stone vases, many made of hard stones that come from remote areas of the Eastern Desert, are common and of remarkable quality, and cosmetic palettes display elaborate designs, with outlines in the form of animals, birds, or fish. Flint was worked with extraordinary skill to produce large ceremonial knives of a type that continued in use during dynastic times.

Sites of late Naqādah II (sometimes termed Naqādah III) are found throughout Egypt, including the Memphite area and the delta region, and appear to have replaced the local Lower Egyptian cultures. Links with the Middle East intensified, and some distinctively Mesopotamian motifs and objects were briefly in fashion in Egypt. The cultural unification of the country probably accompanied a political unification, but this must have proceeded in stages and cannot be reconstructed in detail. In an intermediate stage, local states may have formed at Al-Kawm al-Aḥmar, Naqādah, and Abydos and in the delta at such sites as Buto (modern Kawm al-Farāʿīn) and Sais (Ṣā al-Ḥajar).

Ultimately, Abydos became preeminent; its late predynastic cemetery of Umm al-Qaʿāb was extended to form the burial place of the kings of the 1st dynasty.

In the latest predynastic period, objects bearing written symbols of royalty were deposited throughout the country, and primitive writing also appeared in marks on pottery. Because the basic symbol for the king, a falcon on a decorated palace facade, hardly varies, these objects are thought to have belonged to a single line of kings or a single state, not to a set of small states. This symbol became the royal Horus name, the first element in a king's titulary, which presented the reigning king as the manifestation of an aspect of the god Horus, the leading god of the country. Over the next few centuries several further definitions of the king's presence were added to this one.

Thus, at this time Egypt seems to have been a state unified under kings who introduced writing and the first bureaucratic administration. These kings, who could have ruled for more than a century, may correspond with a set of names preserved on the Palermo Stone, but no direct identification can be made between them. The latest was probably Narmer, whose name has been found near Memphis, at Abydos, on a ceremonial palette and mace-head from Al-Kawm al-Aḥmar, and at the Palestinian sites of Tall Gat and ʿArad. The relief scenes on the palette show him wearing the two chief crowns of Egypt and defeating northern enemies, but these probably are stereotyped symbols of the king's power and role and not records of specific events of his reign. They demonstrate that the position of the king in society and its presentation in mixed pictorial and written form had been elaborated by the early 3rd millennium BC.

During this time Egyptian artistic style and conventions were formulated, together with writing. The process led to a complete and remarkably rapid transformation of material culture, so that many dynastic Egyptian prestige objects hardly resembled their forerunners.

THE 1ST DYNASTY (C. 2925–C. 2775 BC)

The beginning of the historical period is characterized by the introduction of written records in the form of regnal year names—the records that later were collected in documents such as the Palermo Stone. The first king of Egyptian history, Menes, is therefore a creation of the later record, not the actual unifier of the country; he is known from Egyptian king lists and from classical sources and is credited with irrigation works and with founding the capital, Memphis. On small objects from this time, one of them dated to the important king Narmer but certainly mentioning a different person, there are two possible mentions of a "Men" who may be the king Menes. If these do name Menes, he was probably the same person as Aha, Narmer's probable successor,

Figure perhaps representing Menes on a victory tablet of Egyptian king Narmer, c. 2925–c. 2775 BC. Courtesy of the Egyptian Museum, Cairo; photograph, Hirmer Fotoarchiv, Munich

who was then the founder of the 1st dynasty. Changes in the naming patterns of kings reinforce the assumption that a new dynasty began with his reign.

Aha's tomb at Abydos is altogether more grandiose than previously built tombs, while the first of a series of massive tombs at Ṣaqqārah, next to Memphis, supports the tradition that the city was founded then as a new capital. This shift from Abydos is the culmination of intensified settlement in the crucial area between the Nile River valley and the delta, but Memphis did not yet overcome the traditional pull of its predecessor. The large tombs at Ṣaqqārah appear to belong to high officials, while the kings were buried at Abydos in tombs whose walled complexes have long since disappeared. Their mortuary cults may have been conducted in designated areas nearer the cultivation.

In the late Predynastic period and the first half of the 1st dynasty, Egypt extended its influence into southern Palestine and probably Sinai and conducted a campaign as far as the Second Cataract. The First Cataract area, with its centre on Elephantine, an island in the Nile opposite the present-day town of Aswān, was permanently incorporated into Egypt, but Lower Nubia was not.

Between late predynastic times and the 4th dynasty—and probably early in the period—the Nubian A Group came to an end. There is some evidence that political centralization was in progress around Qustul, but this did not lead to any further development and may indeed have prompted a preemptive strike by Egypt. For Nubia, the malign proximity of the largest state of the time stifled advancement. During the 1st dynasty, writing spread gradually, but because it was used chiefly for administration, the records, which were kept within the floodplain, have not survived. The artificial writing medium of papyrus was invented by the middle of the 1st dynasty. There was a surge in prosperity, and thousands of tombs of all levels of wealth have been found throughout the country. The richest contained magnificent goods in metal, ivory, and other materials, the most widespread luxury products being extraordinarily fine stone vases. The high point of 1st-dynasty development was the long reign of Den (flourished c. 2850 BC).

During the 1st dynasty three titles were added to the royal Horus name: "Two Ladies," an epithet presenting the king as making manifest an aspect of the protective goddesses of the south (Upper Egypt) and the north (Lower Egypt); "Golden Horus," the precise meaning of which is unknown; and "Dual King," a ranked pairing of the two basic words for king, later associated with Upper and Lower Egypt. These titles were followed by the king's own birth name, which in later centuries was written in a cartouche.

THE 2ND DYNASTY (C. 2775–C. 2650 BC)

From the end of the 1st dynasty, there is evidence of rival claimants to the throne. One line may have become the 2nd dynasty, whose first king's Horus name, Hetepsekhemwy, means "peaceful in respect of the two powers" and may allude to the conclusion of strife between two factions or parts of the country, to the antagonistic gods Horus and Seth, or to both. Hetepsekhemwy and his successor, Reneb, moved their burial places to Ṣaqqārah; the tomb of the third king, Nynetjer, has not been found.

EGYPTIAN LAW

Egyptian law originated with the unification of Upper and Lower Egypt under King Menes (c. 2925 BC) and grew and developed until the Roman occupation of Egypt (30 BC). It is older than that of any other civilization. Even after the Roman occupation, elements of Egyptian law were retained outside the major urban areas.

No formal Egyptian code of law has been preserved, although several pharaohs, such as Bocchoris (c. 722–c. 715 BC), were known as lawgivers. After the 7th century BC, however, when the Demotic language (the popular form of the written language) came into use, many legal transactions required written deeds or contracts instead of the traditional oral agreement; and these extant documents have been studied for what they reveal of the law of ancient Egypt.

The ultimate authority in the settlement of disputes was the pharaoh, whose decrees were supreme. Because of the complex nature of legal administration, the pharaoh delegated powers to provincial governors and other officials. Next to the pharaoh, the most powerful individual was the vizier, who directed all administrative branches of the government. He sat in judgment on court cases and appointed magistrates as part of his legal duties.

In a legal proceeding, the plaintiff was required to bring suit. The tribunal then ordered the defendant to appear in court if a point of law seemed to be involved in the dispute. Scribes employed in the legal system supplied procedural information; the parties were not represented by legal advocates. Both parties spoke for themselves and presented any pertinent documentary evidence. Witnesses sometimes were called, but usually the judge ruled on the grounds of the documents and the testimony of each party. The judgment included recommendations for preserving the written record of the trial—possibly the main reason why many of these documents are extant.

Although masculine primogeniture dominated in some periods of Egyptian history, there are records of property being divided equally among the children, male and female. Even with masculine primogeniture, the other children and the surviving spouse usually received a share of the estate. The usual law of succession could be circumvented by a special enregistered document: a parent, for example, could favour a daughter by guaranteeing her rights over the family property. Legal judgments pertaining to the family and rights of succession clearly demonstrate that women as well as men were granted full rights under the laws of ancient Egypt. Women owned and bequeathed property, filed lawsuits, and bore witness in court proceedings without the authority of their father or husband. The working class also had some legal rights; even slaves were allowed to own property under certain circumstances.

Property transfers and contractual agreements were conducted as if they were the same type of legal transaction. Rental of slaves, for example, was regarded as a sales agreement. Work was often bartered for various commodities. The individual parties were allowed to determine restrictions and guarantees in their transaction concerning possible defects in the property or service as well as defects in the law.

Criminal justice necessitated a hierarchy in the judicial system, depending on the severity of the charge. The most heinous criminals could be judged only by the pharaoh, often with the vizier conducting the investigation and turning to the pharaoh for final judgment. In some cases, the pharaoh appointed a special commission with full authority to pass judgment. Punishment for serious crimes included penal servitude and execution; mutilation and flogging were often used to punish lesser offenders.

Although punishment for criminal offenders could be severe—and, in the modern viewpoint, barbaric—Egyptian law nevertheless was admirable in its support of basic human rights. The pharaoh Bocchoris, for example, promoted individual rights, suppressed imprisonment for debt, and reformed laws relating to the transferral of property. His legal innovations are one example of the far-reaching implications of Egyptian law: the Greek lawgiver Solon (6th century BC) visited Egypt and adapted aspects of the legal system to his own ideas for Athens. Egyptian law continued to influence Greek law during the Hellenistic period, and its effects on Roman imperial law may still be felt today.

The second half of the dynasty was a time of conflict and rival lines of kings, some of whose names are preserved on stone vases from the 3rd-dynasty Step Pyramid at Ṣaqqārah or in king lists. Among these contenders, Peribsen took the title of Seth instead of Horus and was probably opposed by Horus Khasekhem, whose name is known only from Kawm al-Aḥmar and who used the programmatic epithet "effective sandal against evil." The last ruler of the dynasty combined the Horus and Seth titles to form the Horus-and-Seth Khasekhemwy, "arising in respect of the two powers," to which was added "the two lords are at peace in him." Khasekhemwy was probably the same person as Khasekhem after the successful defeat of his rivals, principally Peribsen. Both Peribsen and Khasekhemwy had tombs at Abydos, and the latter also built a monumental brick funerary enclosure near the cultivation.

THE 3RD DYNASTY (C. 2650–C. 2575 BC)

There were links of kinship between Khasekhemwy and the 3rd dynasty, but the change between them is marked by a definitive shift of the royal burial place to Memphis. Its first king, Sanakhte, is attested in reliefs from Maghāra in Sinai. His successor, Djoser (Horus name Netjerykhet; reigned 2630–2611 BC), was one of the outstanding kings of Egypt. His Step Pyramid at Ṣaqqārah is both the culmination of an epoch and—as the first large all-stone building, many times larger than anything attempted before—the precursor of later achievements.

The oldest extant monument of hewn stone known to the world, the pyramid consists of six steps and attains a height of 200 feet (61 metres). It is set in a much larger enclosure than that of Khasekhemwy at Abydos and contains reproductions in stone of ritual structures that had previously been built of perishable materials. Architectural details of columns, cornices, and moldings provided many models for later development. The masonry techniques look to brickwork for models and show little concern for the structural potential of stone. The pyramid itself evolved through numerous stages from a flat mastaba (an oblong tomb with a burial chamber dug beneath it, common at earlier nonroyal sites) into a six-stepped, almost square pyramid. There was a second, symbolic tomb with a flat superstructure on the south side of the enclosure, which probably substituted for the traditional royal burial place of Abydos. The king and some of his family were buried deep under the pyramid, where tens of thousands of stone vases were deposited, a number bearing inscriptions of the first two dynasties. Thus, in perpetuating earlier forms in stone and burying this material, Djoser invoked the past in support of his innovations.

The Step Pyramid of King Djoser at Ṣaqqārah, Egypt, c. 2650 BC. Katherine Young/EB Inc.

IMHOTEP

Born in Memphis, Egypt, in the 27th century BC, Imhotep (Greek: Imouthes) was a vizier, a sage, an architect, an astrologer, and the chief minister to Djoser. He was later worshipped as the god of medicine in Egypt and in Greece, where he was identified with the Greek god of medicine, Asclepius.

Although no contemporary account has been found that refers to Imhotep as a practicing physician, ancient documents illustrating Egyptian society and medicine during the Old Kingdom (c. 2575– c. 2130 BC) show that the chief magician of the pharaoh's court also frequently served as the nation's chief physician. Imhotep's reputation as the reigning genius of the time, his position in the court, his training as a scribe, and his becoming known as a medical demigod only 100 years after his death are strong indications that he must have been a physician of considerable skill.

Not until the Persian conquest of Egypt in 525 BC was Imhotep elevated to the position of a full deity, replacing Nefertem in the great triad of Memphis. Imhotep's cult reached its zenith during Greco-Roman times, when his temples in Memphis and on the island of Philae (Arabic: Jazīrat Fīlah) in the Nile River were often crowded with sufferers who prayed and slept there with the conviction that the god would reveal remedies to them in their dreams. The only Egyptian mortal besides the 18th-dynasty sage and minister Amenhotep to attain the honour of total deification, Imhotep is still held in esteem by physicians who, like the eminent 19th-century British practitioner Sir William Osler, consider him "the first figure of a physician to stand out clearly from the mists of antiquity."

Djoser's name was famous in later times, and his monument was studied in the Late period. Imhotep, whose title as a master sculptor is preserved from the Step Pyramid complex, may have been its architect; he lived on into the next reign. His fame also endured, and in the Late period he was deified and became a god of healing. In Manetho's history he is associated with reforms of writing, and this may reflect a genuine tradition, for hieroglyphs were simplified and standardized at that time.

Djoser's successor, Sekhemkhet, planned a still more grandiose step pyramid complex at Ṣaqqārah, and a later king, Khaba, began one at Zawyat al-'Aryan, a few miles south of Giza. The burial place of the last king of the dynasty, Huni, is unknown. It has often been suggested that he built the pyramid of Maydūm, but this probably was the work of his successor, Snefru. Inscribed material naming 3rd-dynasty kings is known from Maghāra to Elephantine but not from the Middle East or Nubia.

The organizational achievements of the 3rd dynasty are reflected in its principal monument, whose message of centralization and concentration of power is reinforced in a negative sense by the archaeological record. Outside the vicinity of Memphis, the Abydos area continued to be important, and four enormous tombs, probably of high officials, were built at the nearby site of Bayt Khallaf; there were small, nonmortuary step pyramids throughout the country, some of which may date to the 4th dynasty.

Otherwise, little evidence comes from the provinces, from which wealth must have flowed to the centre, leaving no rich local elite. By the 3rd dynasty the rigid structure of the later nomes, or provinces, which formed the basis of Old Kingdom administration, had been created, and the imposition of its uniform pattern may have impoverished local centres. Tombs of the elite at Ṣaqqārah, notably those of Hezyre and Khabausokar, contained artistic masterpieces that look forward to the Old Kingdom.

CHAPTER 3

THE OLD AND MIDDLE KINGDOMS

The period discussed in this chapter extends from *c.* 2575 to 1540 BC. It includes the Old Kingdom (encompassing the 4th to 8th dynasties, *c.* 2575–2130 BC), the First Intermediate period (9th to 11th dynasties, *c.* 2130–1938 BC), the Middle Kingdom (12th and 13th dynasties, 1938–1630 BC), and the Second Intermediate period (*c.* 1630–1540 BC).

THE OLD KINGDOM (C. 2575–C. 2130 BC)

The Old Kingdom is usually differentiated from earlier times by the presence of a strong central government. Although the first pyramids had been built by this time—notably Imhotep's Step Pyramid built at Ṣaqqārah for Djoser—it was during the Old Kingdom that the greatest of pyramids were constructed.

THE 4TH DYNASTY (*C.* 2575–*C.* 2465 BC)

In a long perspective, the 4th dynasty was an isolated phenomenon, a period when the potential of centralization was realized to its utmost and a disproportionate amount of the state's resources was used on the kings' mortuary provisions, almost certainly at the expense of general living standards. No significant 4th-dynasty sites have been found away from the Memphite area. Tomb inscriptions show that high officials were granted estates scattered over many nomes, especially in the delta. This pattern of landholding may have avoided the formation of local centres of influence while encouraging intensive exploitation of the land. People who worked on these estates were not free to move, and they paid a high proportion of their earnings in dues and taxes. The building enterprises must have relied on drafting vast numbers of men, probably after the harvest had been gathered in the early summer and during part of the inundation.

The first king of the 4th dynasty, Snefru, probably built the step pyramid of Maydūm and then modified it to form the first true pyramid. Due west of Maydūm was the small step pyramid of Saylah, in Al-Fayyūm, at which Snefru also worked. He built two pyramids at Dahshūr; the southern of the two is known as the Blunted Pyramid because its upper part has a shallower angle of inclination than its lower part. This difference may be due to structural problems or may have been planned from the start, in which case the resulting profile may reproduce a solar symbol of creation. The northern Dahshūr pyramid, the later of the two, has the same angle of inclination as the upper part of the Blunted Pyramid and a base area exceeded only by that of the Great Pyramid at Giza. All three of Snefru's pyramids had mortuary complexes attached to them. Snefru's building achievements were thus at least as great as those of any later king and introduced a century of unparalleled construction.

Snefru's was the first king's name that was regularly written inside the cartouche, an elongated oval that is one of the most characteristic Egyptian symbols. The cartouche itself is older and was shown as a gift bestowed by gods on the king, signifying long duration on the throne. It soon acquired associations with the sun, so that its first use by the builder of the first true pyramid, which is probably also a solar symbol, is not coincidental.

Snefru's successor, Khufu (Cheops), built the Great Pyramid at Giza (Al-Jīzah), to which were added the slightly smaller second pyramid of one of Khufu's sons, Khafre (more correctly Rekhaef, the Chephren of Greek sources), and that of Menkaure (Mycerinus). Khufu's successor, his son Redjedef, began a pyramid at Abū Ruwaysh, and a king of uncertain name began one at Zawyat al-'Aryan. The last known king of the dynasty (there was probably one more), Shepseskaf, built a monumental mastaba at south Ṣaqqārah and was the only Old Kingdom ruler not to begin a pyramid. These works, especially the Great Pyramid, show a great mastery of monumental stoneworking: individual blocks were large or colossal and were extremely accurately fitted to one another. Surveying and planning also were carried out with remarkable precision.

Apart from the colossal conception of the pyramids themselves, the temple complexes attached to them show great mastery of architectural forms. Khufu's temple or approach causeway was decorated with impressive reliefs, fragments of which were incorporated in the 12th-dynasty pyramid of Amenemhet I at

The Blunted, Bent, False, or Rhomboidal Pyramid, so named because of its peculiar double slope, built by King Snefru in the 4th dynasty (c. 2575–c. 2465 BC), Dahshūr, Egypt. © Photos. com/Jupiterimages

Al-Lisht. The best known of all Egyptian sculpture, Khafre's Great Sphinx at Giza and his extraordinary seated statue of Nubian gneiss, date from the middle 4th dynasty.

The Giza pyramids form a group of more or less completed monuments surrounded by many tombs of the royal family and the elite, hierarchically organized and laid out in neat patterns. This arrangement contrasts with that of the reign of Snefru, when important tombs were built at Maydūm and Ṣaqqārah, while the king was probably buried at Dahshūr. Of the Giza tombs, only those of the highest-ranking officials were decorated. Except among the immediate entourage of the kings, the freedom of expression of officials was greatly restricted. Most of the highest officials were members of the large royal family, so that power was concentrated by kinship as well as by other means. This did not prevent factional strife: the complex of Redjedef was deliberately and thoroughly destroyed, probably at the instigation of his successor, Khafre.

The Palermo Stone records a campaign to Lower Nubia in the reign of Snefru that may be associated with graffiti in the area itself. The Egyptians founded a settlement at Buhen, at the north end of the Second Cataract, which endured for 200 years; others may have been founded between there and Elephantine. The purposes of this penetration were probably to establish trade farther south and to create a buffer zone.

No archaeological traces of a settled population in Lower Nubia have been found for the Old Kingdom period. The oppressive presence of Egypt seems to have robbed the inhabitants of their resources, as the provinces were exploited in favour of the king and the elite.

Snefru and the builders of the Giza pyramids represented a classic age to later times. Snefru was the prototype of a good king, whereas Khufu and Khafre had tyrannical reputations, perhaps only because of the size of their monuments. Little direct evidence for political or other attitudes survives from the dynasty, in part because writing was only just beginning to be used for recording continuous texts. Many great works of art were, however, produced for kings and members of the elite, and these set a pattern for later work. Kings of the 4th dynasty identified themselves, at least from the time of Redjedef, as Son of Re (the sun god). Worship of the sun god reached a peak in the 5th dynasty.

THE 5TH DYNASTY
(c. 2465–c. 2325 BC)

The first two kings of the 5th dynasty, Userkaf and Sahure, were sons of Khentkaues, who was a member of the 4th-dynasty royal family. The third king, Neferirkare, may also have been her son. A story from the Middle Kingdom that makes them all sons of a priest of Re may derive from a tradition that they were true worshippers of the sun god

PYRAMIDS OF GIZA AND THE GREAT SPHINX

The three world-famous 4th-dynasty pyramids of Giza (also spelled Gizeh) were erected on a rocky plateau on the west bank of the Nile River near Al-Jīzah (Giza) in northern Egypt. In ancient times they were included among the Seven Wonders of the World.

Nomad on a camel at the pyramids of Giza, near Al-Jīzah, Egypt. © Corbis

The designations of the pyramids—Khufu, Khafre, and Menkaure—correspond to the names of the kings for whom they were built. The northernmost and oldest pyramid of the group, called the Great Pyramid, was built for Khufu (Greek: Cheops), the second king of the 4th dynasty. It is the largest of the three. Constructed near each pyramid was a mortuary temple, which was linked via a sloping causeway to a valley temple on the edge of the Nile floodplain. Also nearby were subsidiary pyramids used for the burials of other members of the royal family.

All three pyramids were plundered both internally and externally in ancient and medieval times. Thus, the grave goods originally deposited in the burial chambers are missing, and the pyramids no longer reach their original heights because they have been almost entirely stripped of their outer casings of smooth white limestone.

The Great Sphinx and the pyramid of Khafre, Giza, Egypt. © Goodshoot/Jupiterimages

To the south of the Great Pyramid, near Khafre's valley temple, lies the Great Sphinx, which is the best known of all Egyptian sculpture. Carved out of limestone and measuring approximately 240 feet (73 metres) long and 66 feet (20 metres) high, the Great Sphinx has human facial features but the body of a recumbent lion. It is the earliest and most famous example of the mythological creature, which was an important image in Egyptian and Greek art and legend. Known to be a portrait statue of Khafre, the sphinx continued as a royal portrait type through most of Egyptian history. (Arabs, however, know the Sphinx of Giza by the name of Abu al-Hawl, or "Father of Terror.")

and implies, probably falsely, that the 4th-dynasty kings were not. Six kings of the 5th dynasty displayed their devotion to the sun god by building personal temples to his cult. These temples, of which the two so far identified are sited similarly to pyramids, probably had a mortuary significance for the king as well as honouring the god. The kings' pyramids should therefore be seen in conjunction with the sun temples, some of which received lavish endowments and were served by many high-ranking officials.

Pyramids have been identified for seven of the nine kings of the dynasty, at Ṣaqqārah (Userkaf and Unas, the last king), Abū Ṣīr (Sahure, Neferirkare, Reneferef, and Neuserre), and south Ṣaqqārah (Djedkare Izezi, the eighth king). The pyramids are smaller and less solidly constructed than those of the 4th dynasty, but the reliefs from their mortuary temples are better preserved and of very fine quality; that of Sahure gives a fair impression of their decorative program. The interiors contained religious scenes relating to provision for Sahure in the next life, while the exteriors presented his "historical" role and relations with the gods. Sea expeditions to Lebanon to acquire timber are depicted, as are aggression against and capture of Libyans. Despite the apparent precision with which captives are named and total figures given, these scenes may not refer to specific events, for the same motifs with the same details were frequently shown over the next 250 years; Sahure's use of them might not have been the earliest.

Foreign connections were far-flung. Goldwork of the period has been found in Anatolia, while stone vases named for Khafre and Pepi I (6th dynasty) have been found at Tall Mardīkh in Syria (Ebla), which was destroyed around 2250 BC. The absence of 5th-dynasty evidence from the site is probably a matter of chance. Expeditions to the turquoise mines of Sinai continued as before. In Nubia, graffiti and inscribed seals from Buhen document Egyptian presence until late in the dynasty, when control was probably abandoned in the face of immigration from the south and the deserts; later generations of the immigrants are known as the Nubian C Group. From the reign of Sahure on, there are records of trade with Punt, a partly legendary land probably in the region of present-day Eritrea, from which the Egyptians obtained incense and myrrh, as well as exotic African products that had been traded from still farther afield. Thus, the reduced level of royal display in Egypt does not imply a less prominent general role for the country.

High officials of the 5th dynasty were no longer members of the royal family, although a few married princesses. Their offices still depended on the king, and in their biographical inscriptions they presented their exploits as relating to him, but they justified other aspects of their social role in terms of a more general morality. They progressed through their careers by acquiring titles in complex ranked sequences that were manipulated by kings throughout the 5th and 6th dynasties. This institutionalization of officialdom has an archaeological parallel in the distribution of elite tombs, which no longer clustered so closely around pyramids. Many are at Giza, but the largest and finest are at Ṣaqqārah and Abū Ṣīr. The repertory of decorated scenes in them continually expanded, but there was no fundamental change in their subject matter. Toward the end of the 5th

Nekhbet, the vulture goddess, hovering over Menkauhor, Egypt, 25th–24th century BC. Alinari/Art Resource, New York

dynasty, some officials with strong local ties began to build their tombs in the Nile valley and the delta, in a development that symbolized the elite's slowly growing independence from royal control.

Something of the working of the central administration is visible in papyri from the mortuary temples of Neferirkare and Reneferef at Abū Ṣīr. These show well-developed methods of accounting and meticulous recordkeeping and document the complicated redistribution of goods and materials between the royal residence, the temples, and officials who held priesthoods. Despite this evidence for detailed organization, the consumption of papyrus was modest and cannot

be compared, for example, with that of Greco-Roman times.

The last three kings of the dynasty, Menkauhor, Djedkare Izezi, and Unas, did not have personal names compounded with "-Re," the name of the sun god (Djedkare is a name assumed on accession); and Izezi and Unas did not build solar temples. Thus, there was a slight shift away from the solar cult. The shift could be linked with the rise of Osiris, the god of the dead, who is first attested from the reign of Neuserre. His origin was, however, probably some centuries earlier. The pyramid of Unas, whose approach causeway was richly decorated with historical and religious scenes, is inscribed inside with spells intended to aid the deceased in the hereafter; varying selections of the spells occur in all later Old Kingdom pyramids. (As a collection, they are known as the Pyramid Texts.) Many of the spells were old when they were inscribed; their presence documents the increasing use of writing rather than a change in beliefs. The Pyramid Texts show the importance of Osiris, at least for the king's passage into the next world: it was an undertaking that aroused anxiety and had to be assisted by elaborate rituals and spells.

THE 6TH DYNASTY (C. 2325–C. 2150 BC)

No marked change can be discerned between the reigns of Unas and Teti, the first king of the 6th dynasty. Around Teti's pyramid in the northern portion of

Ṣaqqārah was built a cemetery of large tombs, including those of several viziers. Together with tombs near the pyramid of Unas, this is the latest group of private monuments of the Old Kingdom in the Memphite area.

Information on 6th-dynasty political and external affairs is more abundant because inscriptions of high officials were longer. Whether the circumstances they describe were also typical of less loquacious ages is unknown, but the very existence of such inscriptions is evidence of a tendency to greater independence among officials. One, Weni, who lived from the reign of Teti through those of Pepi I and Merenre, was a special judge in the trial of a conspiracy in the royal household, mounted several campaigns against a region east of Egypt or in southern Palestine, and organized two quarrying expeditions. In the absence of a standing army, the Egyptian force was levied from the provinces by officials from local administrative centres and other settlements. There were also contingents from several southern countries and a tribe of the Eastern Desert.

Three biographies of officials from Elephantine record trading expeditions to the south in the reigns of Pepi I and Pepi II. The location of the regions named in them is debated and may have been as far afield as the Butāna, south of the Fifth Cataract. Some of the trade routes ran through the Western Desert, where the Egyptians established an administrative post at Balāṭ in Al-Dākhilah Oasis, some

distance west of Al-Khārijah Oasis. Egypt no longer controlled Lower Nubia, which was settled by the C Group and formed into political units of gradually increasing size, possibly as far as Karmah (Kerma), south of the Third Cataract. Karmah was the southern cultural successor of the Nubian A Group and became an urban centre in the late 3rd millennium BC, remaining Egypt's chief southern neighbour for seven centuries. To the north the Karmah state stretched as far as the Second Cataract and at times farther still. Its southern extent has not been determined, but sites of similar material culture are scattered over vast areas of the central Sudan.

The provincializing tendencies of the late 5th dynasty continued in the 6th, especially during the extremely long reign (up to 94 years) of Pepi II. Increasing numbers of officials resided in the provinces, amassed local offices, and emphasized local concerns, including religious leadership, in their inscriptions. At the capital the size and splendour of the cemeteries decreased, and some tombs of the end of the dynasty were decorated only in their subterranean parts, as if security could not be guaranteed aboveground. The pyramid complex of Pepi II at southern Ṣaqqārah, which was probably completed in the first 30 years of his reign, stands out against this background as the last major monument of the Old Kingdom, comparable to its predecessors in artistic achievement. Three of his queens were buried in small pyramids around his own; these are the only known queens' monuments inscribed with Pyramid Texts.

THE 7TH AND 8TH DYNASTIES (c. 2150–c. 2130 BC)

Pepi II was followed by several ephemeral rulers, who were in turn succeeded by the short-lived 7th dynasty of Manetho's history (from which no king's name is known) and the 8th, one of whose kings, Ibi, built a small pyramid at southern Ṣaqqārah. Several 8th-dynasty kings are known from inscriptions found in the temple of Min at Qifṭ (Coptos) in the south; this suggests that their rule was recognized throughout the country. The instability of the throne is, however, a sign of political decay, and the fiction of centralized rule may have been accepted only because there was no alternative style of government to kingship.

With the end of the 8th dynasty, the Old Kingdom system of control collapsed. About that time there were incidents of famine and local violence. The country emerged impoverished and decentralized from this episode, the prime cause of which may have been political failure, environmental disaster, or, more probably, a combination of the two. In that period the desiccation of northeastern Africa reached a peak, producing conditions similar to those of contemporary times, and a related succession of low inundations may have coincided with the decay of central political authority. These environmental changes are, however, only approximately dated, and their relationship with the collapse cannot be proved.

THE FIRST INTERMEDIATE PERIOD

After the end of the 8th dynasty, the throne passed to kings from Heracleopolis. These kings made Heracleopolis the capital, although Memphis continued to be important.

THE 9TH DYNASTY (c. 2130–2080 BC)

The 9th-dynasty kings were acknowledged throughout the country, but inscriptions of nomarchs (chief officials of nomes) in the south show that the kings' rule was nominal. At Dara, north of Asyūṭ, for example, a local ruler called Khety styled himself in a regal manner and built a pyramid with a surrounding "courtly" cemetery. At Al-Miʿalla, south of Luxor, Ankhtify, the nomarch of the al-Jabalayn region, recorded his annexation of the Idfū nome and extensive raiding in the Theban area. Ankhtify acknowledged an unidentifiable king Neferkare but campaigned with his own troops. Major themes of inscriptions of the period are the nomarch's provision of food supplies for his people in times of famine and his success in promoting irrigation works. Artificial irrigation had probably long been practiced, but exceptional poverty and crop failure made concern with it worth recording. Inscriptions of Nubian mercenaries employed by local rulers in the south indicate how entrenched military action was.

THE 10TH (c. 2080–c. 1970 BC) AND 11TH (2081–1938 BC) DYNASTIES

A period of generalized conflict focused on rival dynasties at Thebes and Heracleopolis. The latter, the 10th, probably continued the line of the 9th. The founder of the 9th or 10th dynasty was named Khety, and the dynasty as a whole was termed the House of Khety. Several Heracleopolitan kings were named Khety; another important name is Merikare. There was intermittent conflict, and the boundary between the two realms shifted around the region of Abydos. As yet, the course of events in this period cannot be reconstructed.

Several major literary texts purport to describe the upheavals of the First Intermediate period—the *Instruction for Merikare,* for example, being ascribed to one of the kings of Heracleopolis. These texts led earlier Egyptologists to posit a Heracleopolitan literary flowering, but there is now a tendency to date them to the Middle Kingdom, so that they would have been written with enough hindsight to allow a more effective critique of the sacred order.

Until the 11th dynasty made Thebes its capital, Armant (Greek, Hermonthis),

on the west bank of the Nile, was the centre of the Theban nome. The dynasty honoured as its ancestor the God's Father Mentuhotep, probably the father of its first king, Inyotef I (2081–65 BC), whose successors were Inyotef II and Inyotef III (2065–16 and 2016–08 BC, respectively). The fourth king, Mentuhotep II (2008–1957 BC, whose throne name was Nebhepetre), gradually reunited Egypt and ousted the Heracleopolitans, changing his titulary in stages to record his conquests. Around his 20th regnal year he assumed the Horus name Divine of the White Crown, implicitly claiming all of Upper Egypt. By his regnal year 42 this had been changed to Uniter of the Two Lands, a traditional royal epithet that he revived with a literal meaning. In later times Mentuhotep was celebrated as the founder of the epoch now known as the Middle Kingdom. His remarkable mortuary complex at Dayr al-Baḥrī, which seems to have had no pyramid, was the architectural inspiration for Hatshepsut's later structure built alongside.

In the First Intermediate period, monuments were set up by a slightly larger section of the population, and, in the absence of central control, internal dissent and conflicts of authority became visible in public records. Nonroyal individuals took over some of the privileges of royalty, notably identification with Osiris in the hereafter and the use of the Pyramid Texts; these were incorporated into a more extensive corpus inscribed on coffins (and hence termed the Coffin Texts) and continued to be inscribed during the Middle Kingdom. The unified state of the Middle Kingdom did not reject these acquisitions and so had a broader cultural basis than the Old Kingdom.

THE MIDDLE KINGDOM

Mentuhotep II campaigned in Lower Nubia, where he may have been preceded by the Inyotefs. His mortuary complex in Thebes contained some of the earliest known depictions of Amon-Re, the dynastic god of the Middle Kingdom and the New Kingdom. Mentuhotep II was himself posthumously deified and worshipped, notably in the Aswān area. In administration, he attempted to break the power of the nomarchs, but his policy was unsuccessful in the longer term.

Mentuhotep II's successors, Mentuhotep III (1957–45 BC) and Mentuhotep IV (1945–38 BC), also ruled from Thebes. The reign of Mentuhotep IV corresponds to seven years marked "missing" in the Turin Canon, and he may later have been deemed illegitimate. Records of a quarrying expedition to the Wadi Ḥammāmāt from his second regnal year were inscribed on the order of his vizier Amenemhet, who almost certainly succeeded to the throne and founded the 12th dynasty. Not all the country welcomed the 11th dynasty, the monuments and self-presentation of which remained local and Theban.

THE 12TH DYNASTY (1938–c. 1756 BC)

In a text probably circulated as propaganda during the reign of Amenemhet I (1938–08 BC), the time preceding his reign is depicted as a period of chaos and despair, from which a saviour called Ameny from the extreme south was to emerge. This presentation may well be stereotyped, but there could have been armed struggle before he seized the throne. Nonetheless, his mortuary complex at Al-Lisht contained monuments on which his name was associated with that of his predecessor. In style, his pyramid and mortuary temple looked back to Pepi II of the end of the Old Kingdom, but the pyramid was built of mud brick with a stone casing; consequently, it is now badly ruined.

Amenemhet I moved the capital back to the Memphite area, founding a residence named Itjet-towy, "she who takes possession of the Two Lands," which was for later times the archetypal royal residence. Itjet-towy was probably situated between Memphis and the pyramids of Amenemhet I and Sesostris I (at modern Al-Lisht), while Memphis remained the centre of population. From later in the dynasty there is the earliest evidence for a royal palace (not a capital) in the eastern delta. The return to the Memphite area was accompanied by a revival of Old Kingdom artistic styles, in a resumption of central traditions that contrasted with the local ones of the 11th dynasty. From the reign of Amenemhet major tombs of the first half of the dynasty, which display considerable local independence, are preserved at several sites, notably Beni Hasan, Meir, and Qau. After the second reign of the dynasty, no more important private tombs were constructed at Thebes, but several kings made benefactions to Theban temples.

In his 20th regnal year, Amenemhet I took his son Sesostris I (or Senwosret, reigned 1908–1875 BC) as his coregent, presumably in order to ensure a smooth transition to the next reign. This practice was followed in the next two reigns and recurred sporadically in later times. During the following 10 years of joint rule, Sesostris undertook campaigns in Lower Nubia that led to its conquest as far as the central area of the Second Cataract. A series of fortresses were begun in the region, and there was a full occupation, but the local C Group population was not integrated culturally with the conquerors.

Amenemhet I apparently was murdered during Sesostris's absence on a campaign to Libya, but Sesostris was able to maintain his hold on the throne without major disorder. He consolidated his father's achievements, but, in one of the earliest preserved inscriptions recounting royal exploits, he spoke of internal unrest. An inscription of the next reign alludes to campaigns to Syria-Palestine in the time of Sesostris; whether these were raiding expeditions and parades of strength, in what was then a seminomadic region, or whether a conquest was

intended or achieved is not known. It is clear, however, that the traditional view that the Middle Kingdom hardly intervened in the Middle East is incorrect.

In the early 12th dynasty the written language was regularized in its classical form of Middle Egyptian, a rather artificial idiom that was probably always somewhat removed from the vernacular. The first datable corpus of literary texts was composed in Middle Egyptian. Two of these relate directly to political affairs and offer fictional justifications for the rule of Amenemhet I and Sesostris I, respectively. Several that are ascribed to Old Kingdom authors or that describe events of the First Intermediate period but are composed in Middle Egyptian probably also date from around this time. The most significant of these is the *Instruction for Merikare,* a discourse on kingship and moral responsibility. It is often used as a source for the history of the First Intermediate period but may preserve no more than a memory of its events. Most of these texts continued to be copied in the New Kingdom.

Little is known of the reigns of Amenemhet II (1876–42 BC) and Sesostris II (1844–37 BC). These kings built their pyramids in the entrance to Al-Fayyūm while also beginning an intensive exploitation of its agricultural potential that reached a peak in the reign of Amenemhet III (1818–1770 BC). The king of the 12th dynasty with the most enduring reputation was Sesostris III (1836–18 BC), who extended Egyptian conquests to Semna,

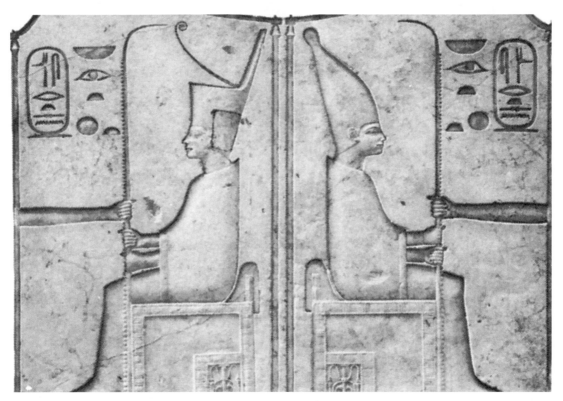

The crown of Lower Egypt (left) and the crown of Upper Egypt (right), both worn by King Sesostris III, Egypt, 19th century BC; in the Egyptian Museum, Cairo. Hirmer Fotoarchiv, Munich

at the south end of the Second Cataract, while also mounting at least one campaign to Palestine. Sesostris III completed an extensive chain of fortresses in the Second Cataract; at Semna he was worshipped as a god in the New Kingdom.

Frequent campaigns and military occupation, which lasted another 150 years, required a standing army. A force of this type may have been created early in the 12th dynasty but becomes better attested near the end. It was based on "soldiers"—whose title means literally "citizens"—levied by district and officers of several grades and types. It was separate from New Kingdom military organization and seems not to have enjoyed very high status.

The purpose of the occupation of Lower Nubia is disputed, because the size of the fortresses and the level of manpower needed to occupy them might seem disproportionate to local threats. An inscription of Sesostris III set up in the fortresses emphasizes the weakness of the Nubian enemy, while a boundary marker and fragmentary papyri show that the system channeled trade with the south through the central fortress of Mirgissa. The greatest period of the Karmah state to the south was still to come, but for centuries it had probably controlled a vast stretch of territory. The best explanation of the Egyptian presence is that Lower Nubia was annexed by Egypt for purposes of securing the southern trade route, while Karmah was a rival worth respecting and preempting; in addition, the physical scale of the fortresses may have become something of an end in itself. It is not known whether Egypt wished similarly to annex Palestine, but numerous administrative seals of the period have been found there.

Sesostris III reorganized Egypt into four regions corresponding to the northern and southern halves of the Nile valley and the eastern and western delta. Rich evidence for middle-ranking officials from the religious centre of Abydos and for administrative practice in documents from Al-Lāhūn conveys an impression of a pervasive, centralized bureaucracy, which later came to run the country under its own momentum. The prosperity created by peace, conquests, and agricultural development is visible in royal monuments and monuments belonging to the minor elite, but there was no small, powerful, and wealthy group of the sort seen in the Old and New Kingdoms. Sesostris III and his successor, Amenemhet III (1818–c. 1770 BC), left a striking artistic legacy in the form of statuary depicting them as aging, careworn rulers, probably

alluding to a conception of the suffering king known from literature of the dynasty. This departure from the bland ideal, which may have sought to bridge the gap between king and subjects in the aftermath of the attack on elite power, was not taken up in later times.

The reigns of Amenemhet III and Amenemhet IV (c. 1770–60 BC) and of Sebeknefru (c. 1760–56 BC), the first certainly attested female monarch, were apparently peaceful, but the accession of a woman marked the end of the dynastic line.

THE 13TH DYNASTY (c. 1756–c. 1630 BC)

Despite a continuity of outward forms and of the rhetoric of inscriptions between the 12th and 13th dynasties, there was a complete change in kingship. In little more than a century about 70 kings occupied the throne. Many can have reigned only for months, and there were probably rival claimants to the throne, but in principle the royal residence remained at Itjet-towy and the kings ruled the whole country. Egypt's hold on Lower Nubia was maintained, as was its position as the leading state in the Middle East. Large numbers of private monuments document the prosperity of the official classes, and a proliferation of titles is evidence of their continued expansion. In government the vizier assumed prime importance, and a single family held the office for much of a century.

Immigration from Asia is known in the late 12th dynasty and became more widespread in the 13th. From the late 18th century BC the northeastern Nile River delta was settled by successive waves of peoples from Palestine, who retained their own material culture. Starting with the *Instruction for Merikare*, Egyptian texts warn against the dangers of infiltration of this sort, and its occurrence shows a weakening of government. There may also have been a rival dynasty, called the 14th, at Xois in the north-central delta, but this is known only from Manetho's history and could have had no more than local significance.

Toward the end of this period, Egypt lost control of Lower Nubia, where the garrisons—which had been regularly replaced with fresh troops—settled and were partly assimilated. The Karmah state overran and incorporated the region. Some Egyptian officials resident in the Second Cataract area served the new rulers. The site of Karmah has yielded many Egyptian artifacts, including old pieces pillaged from their original contexts. Most were items of trade between the two countries, some probably destined for exchange against goods imported from sub-Saharan Africa. Around the end of the Middle Kingdom and during the Second Intermediate period, Medjay tribesmen from the Eastern Desert settled in the Nile valley from around Memphis to the Third Cataract. Their presence is marked by distinctive shallow graves with black-topped pottery, and they have traditionally been termed the "Pangrave" culture by archaeologists. They were assimilated culturally in the New Kingdom, but the word *Medjay* came to mean police or militia; they probably came as mercenaries.

THE SECOND INTERMEDIATE PERIOD

The increasing competition for power in Egypt and Nubia crystallized in the formation of two new dynasties: the 15th, called the Hyksos (*c.* 1630–*c.* 1523 BC), with its capital at Avaris (Tell el-Dabʻa) in the delta, and the 17th (*c.* 1630–1540 BC), ruling from Thebes. The word *Hyksos* dates to an Egyptian phrase meaning "ruler of foreign lands" and occurs in Manetho's narrative cited in the works of the Jewish historian Flavius Josephus (1st century AD), which depicts the new rulers as sacrilegious invaders who despoiled the land. They presented themselves—with the exception of the title Hyksos—as Egyptian kings and appear to have been accepted as such. The main line of Hyksos was acknowledged throughout Egypt and may have been recognized as overlords in Palestine, but they tolerated other lines of kings, both those of the 17th dynasty and the various minor Hyksos who are termed the 16th dynasty. The 15th dynasty consisted of six kings, the best known being the fifth, Apopis, who reigned for up to 40 years. There were many 17th-dynasty kings, probably belonging to several different families. The northern frontier of the Theban domain was at Al-Qūṣiyyah, but there was trade across the border.

Asiatic rule brought many technical innovations to Egypt, as well as cultural innovations such as new musical instruments and foreign loan words. The changes affected techniques from bronze working and pottery to weaving, and new breeds of animals and new crops were introduced. In warfare, composite bows, new types of daggers and scimitars, and above all the horse and chariot transformed previous practice, although the chariot may ultimately have been as important as a prestige vehicle as for tactical military advantages it conferred. The effect of these changes was to bring Egypt, which had been technologically backward, onto the level of southwestern Asia. Because of these advances and the perspectives it opened up, Hyksos rule was decisive for Egypt's later empire in the Middle East.

Whereas the 13th dynasty was fairly prosperous, the Second Intermediate period may have been impoverished. The regional centre of the cult of Osiris at Abydos, which has produced the largest quantity of Middle Kingdom monuments, lost importance, but sites such as Thebes, Idfū, and Al-Kawm al-Aḥmar have yielded significant, if sometimes crudely worked, remains. Aside from Avaris itself, virtually no information has come from the north, where the Hyksos ruled, and it is impossible to assess their impact on the economy or on high culture. The Second Intermediate period was the consequence of political fragmentation and immigration and was not associated with economic collapse, as in the early First Intermediate period.

Toward the end of the 17th dynasty (c. 1545 BC), the Theban king Seqenenre challenged Apopis, probably dying in battle against him. Seqenenre's successor, Kamose, renewed the challenge, stating in an inscription that it was intolerable to share his land with an Asiatic and a Nubian (the Karmah ruler). By the end of his third regnal year, he had made raids as far south as the Second Cataract (and possibly much farther) and in the north to the neighbourhood of Avaris, also intercepting in the Western Desert a letter sent from Apopis to a new Karmah ruler on his accession. By campaigning to the north and to the south, Kamose acted out his implicit claim to the territory ruled by Egypt in the Middle Kingdom. His exploits formed a vital stage in the long struggle to expel the Hyksos.

CHAPTER 4

THE NEW KINGDOM AND THE THIRD INTERMEDIATE PERIOD

T he New Kingdom is generally acknowledged to be the period of ancient Egypt's greatest material wealth and general prosperity. This period saw the rise of the military and the expansion of the kingdom into Syria and Palestine.

THE NEW KINGDOM: THE 18TH DYNASTY

Egypt's 18th dynasty is marked by a succession of rulers. The founder of the 18th dynasty, Ahmose, was the leader responsible for completing the expulsion of the Hyksos (Asiatic rulers of Egypt). He also invaded Palestine and re-exerted Egypt's hegemony over northern Nubia, to the south. The dynasty is considered to have concluded with the reign of Horemheb, a general under Tutankhamen who claimed the throne upon the death of Tutankhamen's successor, Ay.

AHMOSE

Although Ahmose (ruled c. 1539–14 BC) had been preceded by Kamose, who was his brother, Egyptian tradition regarded Ahmose as the founder of a new dynasty because he was the native ruler who reunified Egypt. Continuing a recently inaugurated practice, he married his full sister Ahmose-Nofretari. The queen was given the title of God's Wife of Amon. Like her predecessors of the 17th dynasty, Queen Ahmose-Nofretari was influential and highly honoured. A measure of her importance was her posthumous veneration at Thebes, where later pharaohs were depicted offering to her as a goddess among the gods.

Ahmose's campaigns to expel the Hyksos from the Nile River delta and regain former Egyptian territory to the south probably started around his 10th regnal year. Destroying the Hyksos stronghold at Avaris, in the eastern delta, he finally drove them beyond the eastern frontier and then besieged Sharuḥen (Tell el-Fār'ah) in southern Palestine; the full extent of his conquests may have been much greater. His penetration of the Middle East came at a time when there was no major established power in the region. This political gap facilitated the creation of an Egyptian "empire."

Ahmose's officers and soldiers were rewarded with spoil and captives, who became personal slaves. This marked the creation of an influential military class. Like Kamose, Ahmose campaigned as far south as Buhen. For the administration of the regained territory, he created a new office, overseer of southern foreign lands, which ranked second only to the vizier. Its incumbent was accorded the honorific title of king's son, indicating that he was directly responsible to the king as deputy.

The early New Kingdom bureaucracy was modeled on that of the Middle Kingdom. The vizier was the chief administrator and the highest judge of the realm. By the mid-15th century BC the office had been divided into two, one vizier for Upper and one for Lower Egypt. During the 18th dynasty some young bureaucrats were educated in temple schools, reinforcing the integration of civil and priestly sectors. Early in the dynasty many administrative posts were inherited, but royal appointment of capable officials, often selected from military officers who had served the king on his campaigns, later became the rule. The trend was thus away from bureaucratic families and the inheritance of office.

AMENHOTEP I

Ahmose's son and successor, Amenhotep I (ruled c. 1514–1493 BC), pushed the Egyptian frontier southward to the Third Cataract, near the capital of the Karmah (Kerma) state, while also gathering tribute from his Asiatic possessions and perhaps campaigning in Syria. The emerging kingdom of Mitanni in northern Syria, which is first mentioned on a stela of one of Amenhotep's soldiers and was also known by the name of Nahrin, may have threatened Egypt's conquests to the north.

The New Kingdom was a time of increased devotion to the state god Amon-Re, whose cult largely benefited as Egypt was enriched by the spoils of war. Riches were turned over to the god's treasuries, and as a sign of filial piety the king had sacred monuments constructed at Thebes. Under Amenhotep I the pyramidal form of royal tomb was abandoned in favour of a rock-cut tomb, and, except for Akhenaton, all subsequent New Kingdom rulers were buried in concealed tombs in

VALLEY OF THE KINGS

The Valley of the Kings is a long, narrow defile just west of the Nile River in Upper Egypt, in the western hills behind Dayr al-Bahri. Part of the ancient city of Thebes, it was the burial site of almost all the kings (pharaohs) of the 18th, 19th, and 20th dynasties (1539–1075 BC), from Thutmose I to Ramses X.

The plan of the tombs varies considerably but consists essentially of a descending corridor interrupted by deep shafts to baffle robbers and by pillared chambers or vestibules. At the farther end of the corridor is a burial chamber with a stone sarcophagus in which the royal mummy was laid and store chambers around which furniture and equipment were stacked for the king's use in the next world.

In many cases the walls were covered with sculptured and painted scenes depicting the dead king in the presence of deities, especially the gods of the underworld, and with illustrated magical texts similar to those found in funerary papyri, designed to help him on his journey through the nether regions. These texts represented differing but not necessarily conflicting views of the afterlife, in which the king had to undergo trials and surmount perils. Astronomical figures decorate the ceilings of several burial chambers.

Virtually all the tombs in the valley were cleared out in antiquity. Some had been partially robbed during the New Kingdom, but all were systematically denuded of their contents in the 21st dynasty, in an effort to protect the royal mummies and to recycle the rich funerary goods back into the royal treasury. Only the little tomb of Tutankhamen (reigned 1333–23 BC), located on the floor of the valley and protected by a pile of rock chippings thrown down from a later Ramesside tomb, escaped pillage.

the famous Valley of the Kings in western Thebes. Separated from the tombs, royal mortuary temples were erected at the edge of the desert. Perhaps because of this innovation, Amenhotep I later became the patron deity of the workmen who excavated and decorated the royal tombs. The location of his own tomb is unknown.

THUTMOSE I AND THUTMOSE II

Lacking a surviving heir, Amenhotep I was succeeded by one of his generals, Thutmose I (ruled 1493–*c.* 1482 BC), who married his own full sister Ahmose. In the south Thutmose destroyed the Karmah state. He inscribed a rock as a boundary marker, later confirmed by Thutmose III, near Kanisa-Kurgus, north of the Fifth Cataract. He then executed a brilliant campaign into Syria and across the Euphrates River, where he erected a victory stela near Carchemish.

Thus, in the reign of Thutmose I, Egyptian conquests in the Middle East and Africa reached their greatest extent, but they may not yet have been firmly held. His little-known successor, Thutmose II (c. 1482–79 BC), apparently continued his policies.

Hatshepsut and Thutmose III

At Thutmose II's death his queen and sister, Hatshepsut, had only a young daughter, but a minor wife had borne him a boy, who was apparently very young at his accession. This son, Thutmose III (ruled 1479–26 BC), later reconquered Egypt's Asian empire and became an outstanding ruler.

During his first few regnal years, Thutmose III theoretically controlled the land, but Hatshepsut governed as regent. Sometime between Thutmose III's second and seventh regnal years, she assumed the kingship herself. According to one version of the event, the oracle of Amon proclaimed her king at Karnak, where she was crowned. A more propagandistic account, preserved in texts and reliefs of her splendid mortuary temple at Dayr al-Baḥrī, ignores the reign of Thutmose II and asserts that her father, Thutmose I, proclaimed her his successor.

Upon becoming king, Hatshepsut became the dominant partner in a joint rule that lasted until her death in about 1458 BC. There are monuments dedicated by Hatshepsut that depict both kings. She had the support of various powerful personalities; the most notable among them was Senenmut, the steward and tutor of her daughter Neferure. In styling herself king, Hatshepsut adopted the royal titulary but avoided the epithet "mighty bull," regularly employed by other kings. Although in her reliefs she was depicted as a male, pronominal references in the texts usually reflect her womanhood. Similarly, much of her statuary shows her in male form, but there are rarer examples that render her as a woman. In less formal documents she was referred to as "King's Great Wife"— that is, "Queen"—while Thutmose III was "King." There is thus a certain ambiguity in the treatment of Hatshepsut as king.

Her temple reliefs depict pacific enterprises, such as the transporting of obelisks for Amon's temple and a commercial expedition to Punt; her art style looked back to Middle Kingdom ideals. Some warlike scenes are depicted, however, and she may have waged a campaign in Nubia. In one inscription she blamed the Hyksos for the supposedly poor state of the land before her rule, even though they had been expelled from the region more than a generation earlier.

During Hatshepsut's ascendancy Egypt's position in Asia may have deteriorated because of the expansion of Mitannian power in Syria. Shortly after her death, the prince of the Syrian city of Kadesh, stood with troops of 330 princes of a Syro-Palestinian coalition at Megiddo; such a force was more than merely defensive, and the intention may have been to advance against Egypt. The 330 must have represented all the places of any size in the region that were not subject to Egyptian rule and may be a schematic figure derived from a list of place-names. It is noteworthy that Mitanni itself was not directly involved.

Thutmose III proceeded to Gaza with his army and then to Yehem, subjugating rebellious Palestinian towns along the way. His annals relate how, at a consultation concerning the best route over the Mount Carmel ridge, the king overruled his officers and selected a shorter but more dangerous route through the 'Arūnah Pass and then led the troops himself. The march went smoothly, and, when the Egyptians attacked at dawn, they prevailed over the enemy troops and besieged Megiddo.

Thutmose III meanwhile coordinated the landing of other army divisions on the Syro-Palestinian littoral, whence they proceeded inland, so that the strategy resembled a pincer technique. The siege ended in a treaty by which Syrian princes swore an oath of submission to the king. As was normal in ancient diplomacy and in Egyptian practice, the oath was binding only upon those who swore it, not upon future generations.

By the end of the first campaign, Egyptian domination extended northward to a line linking Byblos and Damascus. Although the prince of Kadesh remained to be vanquished, Assyria sent lapis lazuli as tribute; Asian princes surrendered their weapons, including a large number of horses and chariots. Thutmose III took only a limited number of captives. He appointed Asian princes to govern the towns and took their brothers and sons to Egypt, where they were educated at the court. Most eventually returned home to serve as loyal vassals, though some remained in Egypt at court. In order to ensure the loyalty of Asian city-states, Egypt maintained garrisons that could quell insurrection and supervise the delivery of tribute. There never was an elaborate Egyptian imperial administration in Asia.

Thutmose III conducted numerous subsequent campaigns in Asia. The submission of Kadesh was finally achieved, but Thutmose III's ultimate aim was the defeat of Mitanni. He used the navy to transport troops to Asian coastal towns, avoiding arduous overland marches from Egypt. His great eighth campaign led him across the Euphrates; although the countryside around Carchemish was ravaged, the city was not taken, and the Mitannian prince was able to flee. The psychological gain of this campaign was perhaps greater than its military success, for Babylonia, Assyria, and the Hittites all sent tribute in recognition of Egyptian dominance. Although Thutmose III never subjugated Mitanni, he placed Egypt's conquests on a firm footing by constant campaigning that contrasts with the forays of his predecessors. Thutmose III's annals inscribed in the temple of Karnak are remarkably succinct and accurate, but his other texts, particularly one set in his newly founded Nubian capital of Napata, are more conventional in their rhetoric. He seems to have married three Syrian wives, which may represent diplomatic unions, marking Egypt's entry into the realm of international affairs of the ancient Middle East.

Thutmose III initiated a truly imperial Egyptian rule in Nubia. Much of the land became estates of institutions in Egypt, while local cultural traits disappear from the archaeological record. Sons of chiefs were educated at the Egyptian court; a few returned to Nubia to serve as administrators, and some were buried there in Egyptian fashion. Nubian fortresses lost their strategic value and became administrative centres. Open towns developed around them, and, in several temples outside their walls, the cult of the divine king was established. Lower Nubia supplied gold from the desert and hard and semiprecious stones. From farther south came tropical African woods, perfumes, oil, ivory, animal skins, and ostrich plumes. There is scarcely any trace of local population from the later New Kingdom, when many more temples were built in Nubia; by the end of the 20th dynasty, the region had almost no prosperous settled population.

Under Thutmose III the wealth of empire became apparent in Egypt. Many temples were built, and vast sums were donated to the estate of Amon-Re. There are many tombs of his high officials at Thebes. The capital had been moved to Memphis, but Thebes remained the religious centre.

The campaigns of kings such as Thutmose III required a large military establishment, including a hierarchy of officers and an expensive chariotry. The king grew up with military companions whose close connection with him enabled them to participate increasingly in government. Military officers were appointed to high civil and religious positions, and by the Ramesside period the influence of such people had come to outweigh that of the traditional bureaucracy.

AMENHOTEP II AND THUTMOSE IV

About two years before his death, Thutmose III appointed his 18-year-old son, Amenhotep II (ruled c. 1426–1400 BC), as coregent. Just prior to his father's death, Amenhotep II set out on a campaign to an area in Syria near Kadesh, whose city-states were now caught up in the power struggle between Egypt and Mitanni. (Amenhotep II killed seven princes and shipped their bodies back to Egypt to be suspended from the ramparts of Thebes and Napata.) In his seventh and ninth years, Amenhotep II made further campaigns into Asia, where the Mitannian king pursued a more vigorous policy. The revolt of the important coastal city of Ugarit was a serious matter, because Egyptian control over Syria required bases along the littoral for inland operations and the provisioning of the army. Ugarit was pacified, and the fealty of Syrian cities, including Kadesh, was reconfirmed.

Amenhotep II's son Thutmose IV (ruled 1400–1390 BC) sought to establish peaceful relations with the Mitannian king Artatama, who had been successful against the Hittites. Artatama gave his daughter in marriage, the prerequisite for which was probably the Egyptian

FOREIGN INFLUENCES DURING THE EARLY 18TH DYNASTY

Detail of a wall painting from a tomb in Thebes, Egypt, c. 1450 BC. Courtesy of the trustees of the British Museum

During the empire period Egypt maintained commercial ties with Phoenicia, Crete, and the Aegean islands. The Egyptians portrayed goods obtained through trade as foreign tribute. In the Theban tombs there are representations of Syrians bearing Aegean products and of Aegeans carrying Syrian bowls and amphorae—indicative of close commercial interconnections between Mediterranean lands. Egyptian ships trading with Phoenicia and Syria journeyed beyond to Crete and the Aegean, a route that explains the occasional confusion of products and ethnic types in Egyptian representations. The most prized raw material from the Aegean world was silver, which was lacking in Egypt, where gold was relatively abundant.

One result of the expansion of the empire was a new appreciation of foreign culture. Not only were foreign objets d'art imported into Egypt, but Egyptian artisans imitated Aegean wares as well. Imported textiles inspired the ceiling patterns of Theban tomb chapels, and Aegean art with its spiral motifs influenced Egyptian artists. Under Amenhotep II, Asian gods are found in Egypt: Astarte and Resheph became revered for their reputed potency in warfare, and Astarte was honoured also in connection with medicine, love, and fertility. Some Asian gods were eventually identified with similar Egyptian deities; thus, Astarte was associated with Sekhmet, the goddess of pestilence, and Resheph with Mont, the war god. Just as Asians resident in Egypt were incorporated into Egyptian society and could rise to important positions, so their gods, though represented as foreign, were worshipped according to Egyptian cult practices. The breakdown of Egyptian isolationism and an increased cosmopolitanism in religion are also reflected in hymns that praise Amon-Re's concern for the welfare of Asians.

cession of some Syrian city-states to the Mitannian sphere of influence.

AMENHOTEP III

Thutmose IV's son Amenhotep III (ruled 1390–53 BC) acceded to the throne at about age 12. He soon wed Tiy, who became his queen. Earlier in the dynasty military men had served as royal tutors, but Tiy's father was a commander of the chariotry, and through this link the royal line became even more directly influenced by the military. In his fifth year Amenhotep III claimed a victory over Cushite rebels, but the viceroy of Cush, the southern portion of Nubia, probably actually led the troops. The campaign may have led into the Butāna, west of the 'Aṭbarah River, farther south than any previous Egyptian military expedition had gone. Several temples erected under Amenhotep III in Upper Nubia between the Second and Third cataracts attest to the importance of the region.

Peaceful relations prevailed with Asia, where control of Egypt's vassals was successfully maintained. A commemorative scarab from the king's 10th year announced the arrival in Egypt of

The Colossi of Memnon, stone statues of Amenhotep III, near Thebes, Egypt, 14th century BC. Katherine Young/EB Inc.

the Mitannian princess Gilukhepa, along with 317 women; thus, another diplomatic marriage helped maintain friendly relations between Egypt and its former foe. Another Mitannian princess was later received into Amenhotep III's harem, and during his final illness the Hurrian goddess Ishtar of Nineveh was sent to his aid. At the expense of older bureaucratic families and the principle of inheritance of office, military men acquired high posts in the civil administration. Most influential was the aged scribe and commander of the elite troops, Amenhotep, son of Hapu, whose reputation as a sage survived into the Ptolemaic period.

Amenhotep III sponsored building on a colossal scale, especially in the Theban area. At Karnak he erected the huge third pylon, and at Luxor he dedicated a magnificent new temple to Amon. The king's own mortuary temple in western Thebes was unrivaled in its size. Little remains of it today, but its famous Colossi of Memnon testify to its proportions. He also built a huge harbour and palace complex nearby. Some colossal statues served as objects of public veneration, before which men could

Papyrus-cluster columns of the peristyle forecourt of the Temple of Luxor (seen from the southwest) in Thebes, Egypt. The 18th– to 19th-dynasty structure was built by Amenhotep III about 1390 BC and is sometimes called the Great Temple of Amon, though that name is normally reserved for the larger temple complex at nearby Karnak. Hirmer Fotoarchiv, München

appeal to the king's *ka*, which represented the transcendent aspect of kingship. In Karnak, statues of Amenhotep, son of Hapu, were placed to act as intermediaries between supplicants and the gods.

Among the highest-ranking officials at Thebes were men of Lower Egyptian background, who constructed large tombs with highly refined decoration. An eclectic quality is visible in the tombs, certain scenes of which were inspired by Old Kingdom reliefs. The earliest preserved important New Kingdom monuments from Memphis also date from this reign. Antiquarianism is evidenced in Amenhotep III's celebration of his *sed* festivals (rituals of renewal celebrated after 30 years of rule), which were performed at his Theban palace in accordance, it was claimed, with ancient writings. Tiy, whose role was much more prominent than that of earlier queens, participated in these ceremonies.

Amenhotep III's last years were spent in ill health. To judge from his mummy and less formal representations of him from Amarna, he was obese when, in his 38th regnal year, he died and was succeeded by his son Amenhotep IV (ruled 1353–36 BC), the most controversial of all the kings of Egypt.

AMENHOTEP IV (AKHENATON)

The earliest monuments of Amenhotep IV, who in his fifth regnal year changed his name to Akhenaton ("One Useful to Aton"), are conventional in their

Queen Nefertiti and King Akhenaton, Egypt, 14th century BC; courtesy of the Louvre, Paris.

iconography and style, but from the first he gave the sun god a didactic title naming Aton, the solar disk. This title was later written inside a pair of cartouches, as a king's name would be. The king declared his religious allegiance by the unprecedented use of "high priest of the sun god" as one of his own titles. The term *Aton* had long been in use, but under Thutmose IV the Aton had been referred to as a god, and under Amenhotep III those references became more frequent.

Thus, Akhenaton did not create a new god but rather singled out this aspect of the sun god from among others. He also carried further radical tendencies that had recently developed in solar religion, in which the sun god was freed from his traditional mythological context and presented as the sole beneficent provider for the entire world. The king's own divinity was emphasized. The Aton was said to be his father, of whom he alone had knowledge, and they shared the status of king and celebrated jubilees together.

In his first five regnal years, Akhenaton built many temples to the Aton, of which the most important were in the precinct of the temple of Amon-Re at Karnak. In these open-air structures was developed a new, highly stylized form of relief and sculpture in the round. The Aton was depicted not in anthropomorphic form but as a solar disk from which radiating arms extend the hieroglyph for "life" to the noses of the king and his family. During the construction of these temples, the cult of Amon and other gods was suspended, and the worship of the Aton in an open-air sanctuary superseded that of Amon, who had dwelt in a dark shrine of the Karnak temple. The king's wife Nefertiti, whom he had married before his accession, was prominent in the reliefs and had a complete shrine dedicated to her that included no images of the king. Her prestige continued to grow for much of the reign.

At about the time that he altered his name to conform with the new religion, the king transferred the capital to a virgin site at Amarna (Tell el-Amarna; Al-'Amārinah) in Middle Egypt. There he constructed a well-planned city—Akhetaton ("the Horizon of Aton")—comprising temples to the Aton, palaces, official buildings, villas for the high ranking, and extensive residential quarters. In the Eastern Desert cliffs surrounding the city, tombs were excavated for the courtiers, and deep within a secluded wadi the royal sepulchre was prepared. Reliefs in these tombs have been invaluable for reconstructing life at Amarna. The tomb reliefs and stelae portray the life of the royal family with an unprecedented degree of intimacy.

In Akhenaton's ninth year a more monotheistic didactic name was given to the Aton, and an intense persecution of the older gods, especially Amon, was undertaken. Amon's name was excised from many older monuments throughout the land, and occasionally the word *gods* was expunged.

Akhenaton's religious and cultural revolution was highly personal in that he seems to have had a direct hand in devising the precepts of the Aton religion and the conventions of Amarna art. In religion the accent was upon the sun's life-sustaining power, and naturalistic scenes adorned the walls and even the floors of Amarna buildings. The king's role in determining the composition of the court is expressed in epithets given to officials he selected from the lesser ranks of society, including the military. Few officials had any connection with the old ruling elite, and some courtiers who had been accepted at the beginning of the reign were purged. Even at Amarna the new religion was not widely accepted below the level of the elite; numerous small objects relating to traditional beliefs have been found at the site.

Akhenaton's revolutionary intent is visible in all of his actions. In representational art, many existing conventions were revised to emphasize the break with the past. Such a procedure is comprehensible because traditional values were consistently incorporated in cultural expression as a whole; in order to change one part, it was necessary to change the whole.

A vital innovation was the introduction of vernacular forms into the written language. This led in later decades to the appearance of current verbal forms in monumental inscriptions. The vernacular form of the New Kingdom, which is now known as Late Egyptian, appears fully developed in letters of the later 19th and 20th dynasties.

Akhenaton's foreign policy and use of force abroad are less well understood. He mounted one minor campaign in Nubia. In the Middle East, Egypt's hold on its possessions was not as secure as earlier, but the cuneiform tablets found at Amarna recording his diplomacy are difficult to interpret because the vassals who requested aid from him exaggerated their plight. One reason for unrest in the region was the decline of Mitanni and the resurgence of the Hittites. Between the reign of Akhenaton and the end of the 18th dynasty, Egypt lost control of much territory in Syria.

THE AFTERMATH OF AMARNA

Akhenaton had six daughters by Nefertiti and possibly a son, perhaps by a secondary wife Kiya. Either Nefertiti or the widow of Tutankhamen called on the Hittite king Suppiluliumas to supply a consort because she could find none in Egypt. A prince was sent, but he was murdered as he reached Egypt. Thus, Egypt never had a diplomatic marriage in which a foreign man was received into the country.

After the brief rule of Smenkhkare (1335–32 BC), possibly a son of Akhenaton, Tutankhaten, a nine-year-old child, succeeded and was married to the much older Ankhesenpaaten, Akhenaton's third daughter. Around his third regnal year, the king moved his capital to Memphis, abandoned the Aton cult, and changed his and the queen's names to Tutankhamen and Ankhesenamen. In an inscription recording Tutankhamen's actions for the gods, the Amarna period is described as one of misery and of the withdrawal of the gods from Egypt. This change, made in the name of the young king, was probably the work of high officials. The most influential were Ay, known by the title God's Father, who served as vizier and regent (his title indicates a close relationship to the royal family), and the general Horemheb, who functioned as royal deputy and whose tomb at Ṣaqqārah contains remarkable

Gold funerary mask of King Tutankhamen, Thebes, Egypt, 14th century BC; in the Egyptian Museum, Cairo. © Lee Boltin

scenes of Asiatic captives being presented to the King.

Just as Akhenaton had adapted and transformed the religious thinking that was current in his time, the reaction to the religion of Amarna was influenced by the rejected doctrine. In the new doctrine, all gods were in essence three: Amon, Re, and Ptah (to whom Seth was later added), and in some ultimate sense they too were one. The earliest evidence of this triad is on a trumpet of Tutankhamen and is related to the naming of the three chief army divisions after these gods; religious life and secular life were not separate. This concentration on a small number of essential deities may possibly be related to the piety of the succeeding Ramesside period, because both viewed the cosmos as being thoroughly permeated with the divine.

Under Tutankhamen a considerable amount of building was accomplished in Thebes. His Luxor colonnade bears detailed reliefs of the traditional beautiful festival of Opet. He decorated another structure (now only a series of disconnected blocks) with warlike scenes. He affirmed his legitimacy by referring back to Amenhotep III, whom he called his father. Tutankhamen's modern fame comes from the discovery of his rich burial in the Valley of the Kings. His tomb equipment was superior in quality to the fragments known from other royal burials, and the opulent display—of varying aesthetic value—represents Egyptian wealth at the peak of the country's power.

AY AND HOREMHEB

Tutankhamen's funeral in about 1323 BC was conducted by his successor, the aged Ay (ruled 1323–19 BC), who in turn was succeeded by Horemheb. The latter probably ruled from 1319 to c. 1292 BC, but the length of his poorly attested reign is not certain. Horemheb dismantled many monuments erected by Akhenaton and his successors and used the blocks as fill for huge pylons at Karnak. At Karnak and Luxor he appropriated Tutankhamen's reliefs by surcharging the latter's cartouches with his own. Horemheb appointed new officials and priests not from established families but from the army. His policies concentrated on domestic problems. He issued police regulations dealing with the misbehaviour of palace officials and personnel, and he reformed the judicial system, reorganizing the courts and selecting new judges.

THE RAMESSIDE PERIOD (19TH AND 20TH DYNASTIES)

Horemheb was the first post-Amarna king to be considered legitimate in the 19th dynasty, which looked to him as the founder of an epoch. The reigns of the Amarna pharaohs were eventually to be subsumed into his own, leaving no official record of what posterity deemed to be an unorthodox and distasteful interlude. Having no son, he selected his general and vizier, Ramses, to succeed him.

TUTANKHAMEN'S TOMB

Tutankhamen's tomb (lower left) in the Valley of the Kings, Thebes, Egypt, 14th century BC. © Robert Holmes

Tutankhamen unexpectedly died in his 19th year without designating an heir and was succeeded by Ay. He was buried in a small tomb hastily converted for his use in the Valley of the Kings (his intended sepulchre was probably taken over by Ay). Like other rulers associated with the Amarna period—Akhenaton, Smenkhkare, and Ay—he was to suffer the posthumous fate of having his name stricken from later king lists and his monuments usurped, primarily by his former general, Horemheb, who subsequently became king. Although Tutankhamen's tomb shows evidence of having been entered and briefly plundered, the location of his burial was clearly forgotten by the time of the 20th dynasty (1190–1075 BC), when craftsmen assigned to work on the nearby tomb of Ramses VI built temporary stone shelters directly over its entrance. The tomb was preserved until a systematic search of the Valley of the Kings by the English archaeologist Howard Carter revealed its location in 1922.

Inside his small tomb, the king's mummy lay within a nest of three coffins, the innermost of solid gold, the two outer ones of gold hammered over wooden frames. On the king's head was a magnificent golden portrait mask, and numerous pieces of jewelry and amulets lay upon the mummy and in its wrappings. The coffins and stone sarcophagus were surrounded by four text-covered shrines of hammered gold over wood, which practically filled the burial chamber. The other rooms were crammed with furniture, statuary, clothes, chariots, weapons, staffs, and numerous other objects.

But for his tomb, Tutankhamen has little claim to fame. As it is, he is perhaps better known than any of his longer-lived and better-documented predecessors and successors. His renown was secured after the highly popular "Treasures of Tutankhamun" exhibit traveled the world in the 1960s and '70s. The treasures, housed at the Egyptian Museum in Cairo, were the subject of another multiyear tour in Canada and the United States beginning in 2009.

RAMSES I AND SETI I

Ramses I (ruled 1292–90 BC) hailed from the eastern Nile River delta, and with the 19th dynasty there was a political shift into the delta. Ramses I was succeeded by his son and coregent, Seti I, who buried his father and provided him with mortuary buildings at Thebes and Abydos.

Seti I (ruled 1290–79 BC) was a successful military leader who reasserted authority over Egypt's weakened empire in the Middle East. The Mitanni state had been dismembered, and the Hittites had become the dominant Asian power. Before tackling them, Seti laid the groundwork for military operations in Syria by fighting farther south against nomads and Palestinian city-states. Then, following the strategy of Thutmose III, he secured the coastal cities and gained Kadesh. Although his engagement with the Hittites was successful, Egypt acquired only temporary control of part of the north Syrian plain. A treaty was concluded with the Hittites, who, however, subsequently pushed farther southward and regained Kadesh by the time of Ramses II. Seti I ended a new threat to Egyptian security when he defeated Libyans attempting to enter the delta. He also mounted a southern campaign, probably to the Fifth Cataract region.

Seti I's reign looked for its model to the mid-18th dynasty and was a time of considerable prosperity. Seti I restored countless monuments that had been defaced in the Amarna period, and the refined decoration of his monuments, particularly his temple at Abydos, shows a classicizing tendency. He also commissioned striking and novel reliefs showing stages of his campaigns, which are preserved notably on the north wall of the great hypostyle hall at Karnak. This diversity of artistic approach is characteristic of the Ramesside period, which was culturally and ethnically pluralistic.

RAMSES II

Well before his death, Seti I appointed his son Ramses II, sometimes called Ramses the Great, as crown prince. During the long reign of Ramses II (1279–13 BC), there was a prodigious amount of building, ranging from religious edifices throughout Egypt and Nubia to a new cosmopolitan capital, Pi Ramesse, in the eastern delta. His cartouches were carved ubiquitously, often on earlier monuments. Ramses II's penchant for decorating vast temple walls with battle scenes gives the impression of a mighty warrior king. His campaigns were, however, relatively few, and after the first decade his reign was peaceful. The most famous scenes record the battle of Kadesh, fought in his fifth regnal year. These and extensive accompanying texts present the battle as an Egyptian victory, but in fact the opposing Hittite coalition fared at least as well as the Egyptians. After this inconclusive struggle, his officers advised him to make peace, saying, "There is no reproach in reconciliation when you make it." In succeeding years Ramses II campaigned in Syria; after a

VALLEY OF THE QUEENS

The Valley of the Queens is a gorge in the hills along the western bank of the Nile River in Upper Egypt. It was part of ancient Thebes and served as the burial site of the queens and some royal children of the 19th and 20th dynasties (1292–1075 BC). The queens' necropolis is located about 1.5 miles (2.4 km) west of the mortuary temple of Ramses III (1187–56 BC) at Madīnat Habu. There are more than 90 known tombs, usually consisting of an entrance passage, a few short halls, and a sarcophagus chamber. The earliest may be that of Sitre, wife of Ramses I. The most notable are those of Nefertari, the favourite queen of Ramses II; of Princes Khaemwese and Amonhirkhopsef; and of a Ramesside queen called Titi. In 1979 UNESCO added the Valley of the Queens, the Valley of the Kings, Karnak, Luxor, and other sites of Thebes to the World Heritage List.

decade of stalemate, a treaty in his 21st year was concluded with Hattusilis III, the Hittite king.

The rise of Assyria and unrest in western Anatolia encouraged the Hittites to accept this treaty, while Ramses II may have feared a new Libyan threat to the western delta. Egyptian and Hittite versions of the treaty survive. It contained a renunciation of further hostilities, a mutual alliance against outside attack and internal rebellion, and the extradition of fugitives. The gods of both lands were invoked as witnesses. The treaty was further cemented 13 years later by Ramses II's marriage to a Hittite princess.

The king had an immense family by his numerous wives, among whom he especially honoured Nefertari. He dedicated a temple to her at Abū Simbel, in Nubia, and built a magnificent tomb for her in the Valley of the Queens.

For the first time in more than a millennium, princes were prominently represented on the monuments. Ramses II's fourth surviving son, Khaemwese, was famous as high priest of Ptah at Memphis. He restored many monuments in the Memphite area, including pyramids and pyramid temples of the Old Kingdom, and had buildings constructed near the Sarapeum at Ṣaqqārah. He was celebrated into Roman times as a sage and magician and became the hero of a cycle of stories.

MERNEPTAH AND THE LAST YEARS OF THE 19TH DYNASTY

Ramses II's 13th son, Merneptah (ruled 1213–04 BC), was his successor. Several of Merneptah's inscriptions, of unusual literary style, treat an invasion of the western delta in his fifth year by Libyans, supported by groups of Sea Peoples who had traveled from Anatolia to Libya in search of new homes. The Egyptians defeated this confederation and settled captives in military camps to serve as Egyptian mercenaries.

One of the inscriptions concludes with a poem of victory (written about another battle), famous for its words "Israel is desolated and has no seed." This is the earliest documented mention of Israel. It is generally assumed that the exodus of the Jews from Egypt took place under Ramses II.

Merneptah was able to hold most of Egypt's possessions, although early in his reign he had to reassert Egyptian suzerainty in Palestine, destroying Gezer in the process. Peaceful relations with the Hittites and respect for the treaty of Ramses II are indicated by Merneptah's dispatch of grain to them during a famine and by Egyptian military aid in the protection of Hittite possessions in Syria.

Upon the death of Merneptah, competing factions within the royal family contended for the succession. Merneptah's son Seti II (ruled 1204–1198 BC) had to face a usurper, Amenmeses, who rebelled in Nubia and was accepted in Upper Egypt. His successor, Siptah, was installed on the throne by a Syrian royal butler, Bay, who had become chancellor of Egypt. Siptah was succeeded by Seti II's widow Tausert, who ruled as king from 1193 to 1190 BC, counting her regnal years from the death of Seti II, whose name she restored over that of Siptah. A description in a later papyrus of the end of the dynasty alludes to a Syrian usurper, probably Bay, who subjected the land to harsh taxation and treated the gods as mortals with no offerings in their temples.

The Early 20th Dynasty: Setnakht and Ramses III

Order was restored by a man of obscure origin, Setnakht (ruled 1190–87 BC), the founder of the 20th dynasty, who appropriated Tausert's tomb in the Valley of the Kings. An inscription of Setnakht recounts his struggle to pacify the land, which ended in the second of his three regnal years.

Setnakht's son Ramses III (ruled 1187–56 BC) was the last great king of the New Kingdom. There are problems in evaluating his achievements because he emulated Ramses II and copied numerous scenes and texts of Ramses II in his mortuary temple at Madīnat Habu, one of the best-preserved temples of the empire period. Thus, the historicity of certain Nubian and Syrian wars depicted as his accomplishments is subject to doubt. He did, however, fight battles that were more decisive than any fought by Ramses II. In his fifth year Ramses III defeated a large-scale Libyan invasion of the delta in a battle in which thousands of the enemy perished.

A greater menace lay to the north, where a confederation of Sea Peoples was progressing by land and sea toward Egypt. This alliance of obscure tribes traveled south in the aftermath of the destruction of the Hittite empire. In his eighth regnal year Ramses III engaged them successfully on two frontiers—a land battle in Palestine and a naval engagement in one of the mouths of the delta. Because of these two victories, Egypt did not undergo the political turmoil or experience the rapid technical advance of the early Iron Age in the Near East. Forced away from the borders of Egypt, the Sea Peoples sailed farther westward, and some of their groups may have given their names to the Sicilians, Sardinians, and Etruscans. The Philistine and Tjekker peoples, who had come by land, were established in the southern Palestinian coastal district in an area where the overland trade route to Syria was threatened by attacks by nomads. Initially settled to protect Egyptian interests, these groups later became independent of Egypt. Ramses III used some of these peoples as mercenaries, even in battle against their own kinfolk. In his 11th year he successfully repulsed another great Libyan invasion by the Meshwesh tribes. Meshwesh prisoners of war, branded with the king's name, were settled in military camps in Egypt, and in later centuries their descendants became politically important because of their ethnic cohesiveness and their military role.

The economic resources of Egypt were in decline at that time. Under Ramses III the estate of Amon received only one-fifth as much gold as in Thutmose III's time. Even at the great temple of Madīnat Habu, the quality of the masonry betrays a decline. Toward the end of his reign, administrative inefficiency and the deteriorating economic situation resulted in the government's failure to deliver grain rations on time to necropolis workers, whose dissatisfaction was expressed in demonstrations and in the first recorded strikes in history. Such demonstrations continued sporadically throughout the dynasty. A different sort of internal trouble originated in the royal harem, where a minor queen plotted unsuccessfully to murder Ramses III so that her son might become king. Involved in the plot were palace and harem personnel, government officials, and army officers. A special court of 12 judges was formed to try the accused, who received the death sentence.

Many literary works date to the Ramesside period. Earlier works in Middle Egyptian were copied in schools and in good papyrus copies, and new texts were composed in Late Egyptian. Notable among the latter are stories, several with mythological or allegorical content, that look to folk models rather than to the elaborate written literary types of the Middle Kingdom.

RAMSES IV

Ramses III was succeeded by his son Ramses IV (ruled 1156–50 BC). In an act of piety that also reinforced his legitimacy, Ramses IV saw to the compilation of a long papyrus in which the deceased Ramses III confirmed the temple holdings throughout Egypt; Ramses III had provided the largest benefactions to the Theban temples, in terms of donations of both land and personnel. Most of these probably endorsed earlier donations, to which each king added his own gifts. Of the annual income to temples, 86 percent of the silver and 62 percent of the grain was awarded to Amon. The document demonstrates the economic power of the Theban temples, for the tremendous landholdings of Amon's estate throughout Egypt involved the labour of a considerable portion of the population; but the ratio of temple to state income is not known, and the two were not administratively separate. In addition, the temple of Amon, which figures prominently in the papyrus, included within its estates the king's own mortuary temple, for Ramses III was himself deified as a form of Amon-Re, known as Imbued with Eternity.

THE LATER RAMESSIDE KINGS

The Ramesside period saw a tendency toward the formation of high-priestly families, which kings sometimes tried to counter by appointing outside men to the high priesthood. One such family had developed at Thebes in the second half of the 19th dynasty, and Ramses IV tried to control it by installing Ramessesnakht, the son of a royal steward, as Theban high priest. Ramessesnakht participated in administrative as well as priestly affairs. He personally led an expedition to the Wadi Ḥammāmāt (present-day Wādī Rawḍ ʿĀʾid) quarries in the Eastern Desert, and at Thebes he supervised the distribution of rations to the workmen decorating the royal tomb.

Under Ramses V (ruled 1150–45 BC), Ramessesnakht's son not only served as steward of Amon, but also held the post of administrator of royal lands and chief taxing master. Thus, this family acquired extensive authority over the wealth of Amon and over state finances, but to what extent this threatened royal authority is uncertain. Part of the problem in evaluating the evidence is that Ramesside history is viewed from a Theban bias, because Thebes is the major source of information. Evidence from Lower Egypt, where the king normally resided, is meagre because conditions there were unfavourable for preserving monuments or papyri.

A long papyrus from the reign of Ramses V contains valuable information on the ownership of land and taxation. In Ramesside Egypt most of the land belonged to the state and the temples, while most peasants served as tenant farmers. Some scholars interpret this document as indicating that the state retained its right to tax temple property, at an estimated one-tenth of the crop.

Ramses VI (ruled 1145–37 BC), probably a son of Ramses III, usurped much of his two predecessors' work, including the tomb of Ramses V; a papyrus refers to a possible civil war at Thebes. Following the death of Ramses III and the disrupted migrations of the late Bronze Age, the Asian empire had rapidly withered away, and Ramses VI is the last king whose name appears at the Sinai turquoise mines. The next two Ramses (ruled

1137–26 BC) were obscure rulers, whose sequence has been questioned. During the reigns of Ramses IX (ruled 1126–08 BC) and Ramses X (1108–04 BC), there are frequent references in the papyri to the disruptions of marauding Libyans near the Theban necropolis.

By the time of Ramses IX the Theban high priest had attained great local influence, though he was still outranked by the king. By Ramses XI's 19th regnal year the new high priest of Amon, Herihor—who seems to have had a military background and also claimed the vizierate and the office of viceroy of Cush—controlled the Theban area. In reliefs at the temple of Khons at Karnak, Herihor was represented as high priest of Amon in scenes adjoining those of Ramses XI. This in itself was unusual, but subsequently he took an even bolder step in having himself depicted as king to the exclusion of the still-reigning Ramses XI. Herihor's limited kingship was restricted only to Thebes, where those years were referred to as a "repeating of [royal] manifestations," which lasted a decade.

With the shrinkage of the empire, the supply of silver and copper was cut off, and the amount of gold entering the economy was reduced considerably. During the reign of Ramses IX the inhabitants of western Thebes were found to have pillaged the tombs of kings and nobles (already a common practice in the latter case); the despoiling continued into the reign of Ramses XI, and even the royal mortuary temples were stripped of their valuable furnishings. Nubian troops, called in to restore order at Thebes, themselves contributed to the depredation of monuments. This pillaging brought fresh gold and silver into the economy, and the price of copper rose. The price of grain, which had become inflated, dropped.

The Ramesside growth of priestly power was matched by increasingly overt religiosity. Private tombs, the decoration of which had been mostly secular until then, came to include only religious scenes; oracles were invoked in many kinds of decisions; and private letters contain frequent references to prayer and to regular visits to small temples to perform rituals or consult oracles. The common expression used in letters, "I am all right today; tomorrow is in the hands of god," reflects the ethos of the age. This fatalism, which emphasizes that the god may be capricious and that his wishes cannot be known, is also typical of late New Kingdom Instruction Texts, which show a marked change from their Middle Kingdom forerunners by moving toward a passivity and quietism that suits a less expensive age.

Some of the religious material of the Ramesside period exhibits changes in conventions of display, and some categories have no parallel in the less abundant earlier record, but the shift is real as well as apparent. In its later periods, Egyptian society, the values of which had previously tended to be centralized, secular, and political, became more locally based and more thoroughly pervaded by religion, looking to the temple as the chief institution.

While Ramses XI was still king, Herihor died and was succeeded as high priest by Piankh, a man of similar military background. A series of letters from Thebes tell of Piankh's military venture in Nubia against the former viceroy of Cush while Egypt was on the verge of losing control of the south. With the death of Ramses XI, the governor of Tanis, Smendes, became king, founding the 21st dynasty (known as the Tanite).

THE THIRD INTERMEDIATE PERIOD

At the end of the New Kingdom, Egypt was divided. The north was inherited by the Tanite 21st dynasty (1075–c. 950 BC), and although much of the southern Nile River valley came under the control of the Theban priests (the northern frontier of their domain was the fortress town of Al-Hība), there is no indication of conflict between the priests and the Tanite kings. Indeed, the dating of documents, even at Thebes, was in terms of the Tanite reigns, and apparently there were close family ties between the kings and the Thebans. Piankh's son, Pinudjem I, who relinquished the office of high priest and assumed the kingship at Thebes, was probably the father of the Tanite king Psusennes I. Some members of both the Theban priestly and the Tanite royal lines had Libyan names. With the coming of the new dynasty, and possibly a little earlier, the Meshwesh Libyan military elite,

which had been settled mainly in the north by Ramses III, penetrated the ruling group, although it did not become dominant until the 22nd dynasty.

THE 21ST DYNASTY

Beginning with Herihor and continuing through the 21st dynasty, the high priests' activities included the pious rewrapping and reburial of New Kingdom royal mummies. The systematic removal of such goods from the royal tombs by royal order during the 20th dynasty necessitated the transfer of the royal remains in stages to two caches—the tomb of Amenhotep II and a cliff tomb at Dayr al-Baḥrī—where they remained undisturbed until modern times. Dockets pertaining to the reburial of these mummies contain important chronological data from the 21st dynasty.

The burials of King Psusennes I (ruled c. 1045–c. 997 BC) and his successor, Amenemope (ruled c. 998–c. 989 BC), were discovered at Tanis, but little is known of their reigns. This was a period when statuary was usurped and the material of earlier periods was reused. At Karnak, Pinudjem I, who decorated the facade of the Khons temple, usurped a colossal statue of Ramses II, and Psusennes I's splendid sarcophagus from Tanis had originally been carved for Merneptah at Thebes. Much of the remains from Tanis consists of material transported from other sites, notably from Pi Ramesse.

After the demise of Egypt's Asian empire, the kingdom of Israel eventually developed under the kings David and

Solomon. During David's reign, Philistia served as a buffer between Egypt and Israel; but after David's death the next to the last king of the 21st dynasty, Siamon, invaded Philistia and captured Gezer. If Egypt had any intention of attacking Israel, Solomon's power forestalled Siamon, who presented Gezer to Israel as a dowry in the diplomatic marriage of his daughter to Solomon. This is indicative of the reversal of Egypt's status in foreign affairs since the time of Amenhotep III, who had written the Babylonian king, "From of old, a daughter of the king of Egypt has not been given to anyone."

LIBYAN RULE: THE 22ND AND 23RD DYNASTIES

The fifth king of the 21st dynasty, Osorkon I (ruled *c.* 979–*c.* 973 BC), was of Libyan descent and probably was an ancestor of the 22nd dynasty, which followed a generation later. From Osorkon's time to the 26th dynasty, leading Libyans in Egypt kept their Libyan names and ethnic identity, but in a spirit of ethnicity rather than cultural separatism. Although political institutions were different from those of the New Kingdom, the Libyans were culturally Egyptian, retaining only their

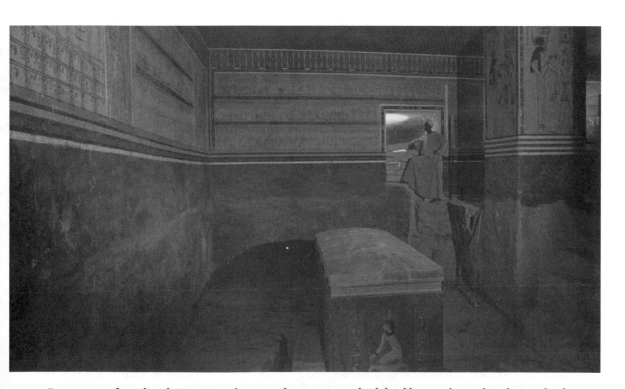

Documents found with New Kingdom royal mummies, which had been reburied in the tomb of 18th-century ruler Amenhotep II (pictured), provided several clues to Egyptian life in the 21st dynasty. Kenneth Garrett/National Geographic/Getty Images

group identity, names, and perhaps a military ethos. Toward the end of the 21st dynasty the Libyan leader of Bubastis, the great Meshwesh chief Sheshonk I (the biblical Shishak), secured special privileges from King Psusennes II (ruled c. 964–c. 950 BC) and the oracle of Amon for the mortuary cult of his father at Abydos. The oracle proffered good wishes not only for Sheshonk and his family but, significantly, also for his army. With a strong military backing, Sheshonk eventually took the throne. His reign (c. 950–929 BC) marks the founding of the 22nd dynasty (c. 950–c. 730 BC).

Military controls were established, with garrisons under Libyan commandants serving to quell local insurrections, so that the structure of the state became more feudalistic. The dynasty tried to cement relations with Thebes through political marriages with priestly families. King Sheshonk's son Osorkon married Psusennes II's daughter, and their son eventually became high priest at Karnak. By installing their sons as high priests and promoting such marriages, kings strove to overcome the administrative division of the country. But frequent conflicts arose over the direct appointment of the Theban high priest from among the sons of Libyan kings and over the inheritance of the post by men of mixed Theban and Libyan descent. This tension took place against a background of Theban resentment of the northern dynasty. During the reign of Takelot II, strife concerning the high priestship led

to civil war at Thebes. The king's son Osorkon was appointed high priest, and he achieved some semblance of order during his visits to Thebes, but he was driven from the post several times.

The initially successful 22nd dynasty revived Egyptian influence in Palestine. After Solomon's death (c. 936), Sheshonk I entered Palestine and plundered Jerusalem. Prestige from this exploit may have lasted through the reign of Osorkon II (ruled c. 929–c. 914 BC). In the reign of Osorkon III (ruled c. 888–c. 860 BC), Peywed Libyans posed a threat to the western delta, perhaps necessitating a withdrawal from Palestine.

The latter part of the dynasty was marked by fragmentation of the land: Libyan great chiefs ruled numerous local areas, and there were as many as six local rulers in the land at a time. Increased urbanization accompanied this fragmentation, which was most intense in the delta. Meanwhile, in Thebes, a separate 23rd dynasty was recognized.

From the 9th century BC a local Cushite state, which looked to Egyptian traditions from the colonial period of the New Kingdom, arose in the Sudan and developed around the old regional capital of Napata. The earliest ruler of the state known by name was Alara, whose piety toward Amon is mentioned in several inscriptions. His successor, Kashta, proceeded into Upper Egypt, forcing Osorkon IV (ruled c. 777–c. 750 BC) to retire to the delta. Kashta assumed the title of king and compelled Osorkon IV's daughter Shepenwepe I, the God's Wife of Amon at Thebes, to adopt his own daughter Amonirdis I as her successor. The Cushites stressed the role of the God's Wife of Amon, who was virtually the consecrated partner of Amon, and sought to bypass the high priests.

THE 24TH AND 25TH DYNASTIES

Meanwhile, the eastern capital in the Nile River delta, Tanis, lost its importance to Sais in the western delta. A Libyan prince of Sais, Tefnakhte, attempting to gain control over all Egypt, proceeded southward to Heracleopolis after acquiring Memphis. This advance was met by the Cushite ruler Piye (now the accepted reading of "Piankhi," ruled *c.* 750–*c.* 719 BC), who executed a raid as far north as Memphis and received the submission of the northern rulers (in about 730 BC). In his victory stela, Piye is portrayed as conforming strictly to Egyptian norms and reasserting traditional values against contemporary decay.

After Piye returned to Cush, Tefnakhte reasserted his authority in the north, where, according to Manetho, he was eventually succeeded by his son Bocchoris as the sole king of the 24th dynasty (*c.* 722–*c.* 715 BC). Piye's brother Shabaka meanwhile founded the rival 25th dynasty and brought all Egypt under

his rule (*c.* 719–703 BC). He had Bocchoris burned alive and removed all other claimants to the kingship.

In this period Egypt's internal politics were affected by the growth of the Assyrian Empire. In Palestine and Syria frequent revolts against Assyria were aided by Egyptian forces. Against the power of Assyria, the Egyptian and Nubian forces met with little success, partly because of their own fragmented politics and divided loyalties.

Although the earlier years of King Taharqa (ruled 690–664 BC), who as second son of Shabaka had succeeded his brother Shebitku (ruled 703–690 BC), were prosperous, the confrontation with Assyria became acute. In 671 BC the Assyrian king Esarhaddon entered Egypt and drove Taharqa into Upper Egypt. Two years later Taharqa regained a battered Memphis, but in 667 BC Esarhaddon's successor, Ashurbanipal, forced Taharqa to Thebes, where the Cushites held ground. Taharqa's successor, Tanutamon, defeated at Memphis a coalition of delta princes who supported Assyria, but Ashurbanipal's reaction to this was to humiliate Thebes, which the Assyrians plundered. By 656 the Cushites had withdrawn from the Egyptian political scene, although Cushite culture survived in the Sudanese Napatan and Meroitic kingdom for another millennium.

CHAPTER 5

THE LATE PERIOD AND BEYOND

Assyria, unable to maintain a large force in Egypt, supported several delta vassal princes, including the powerful Psamtik I of Sais. But the Assyrians faced serious problems closer to home, and Psamtik (or Psammetichus I, ruled 664–610 BC) was able to assert his independence and extend his authority as king over all Egypt without extensive use of arms, inaugurating the Saite 26th dynasty.

THE LATE PERIOD (664–332 BC)

In 656 Psamtik I compelled Thebes to submit. He allowed its most powerful man, who was Montemhat, the mayor and the fourth prophet of Amon, to retain his post, and, in order to accommodate pro-Cushite sentiments, he allowed the God's Wife of Amon and the Votaress of Amon (the sister and daughter of the late king Taharqa) to remain. Psamtik I's own daughter Nitocris was adopted by the Votaress of Amon and thus became heiress to the position of God's Wife. Essential to the settling of internal conflicts was the Saite dynasty's superior army, composed of Libyan soldiers, whom the Greeks called Machimoi ("Warriors"), and Greek and Carian mercenaries, who formed part of the great emigration from the Aegean in the 7th and 6th centuries BC. Greek pirates raiding the Nile delta coast were induced by Psamtik I to serve in his army and were settled like the Machimoi in colonies at the delta's strategically important northeastern border.

Trade developed between Egypt and Greece, and more Greeks settled in Egypt.

The Saite dynasty generally pursued a foreign policy that avoided territorial expansion and tried to preserve the status quo. Assyria's power was waning. In 655 BC Psamtik I marched into Philistia in pursuit of the Assyrians, and in 620 BC he apparently repulsed Scythians from the Egyptian frontier. During the reign of his son Necho II (610–595 BC), Egypt supported Assyria as a buffer against the potential threat of the Medes and the Babylonians. Necho was successful in Palestine and Syria until 605 BC, when the Babylonian Nebuchadrezzar inflicted a severe defeat on Egyptian forces at Carchemish. After withdrawing his troops from Asia, Necho concentrated on developing Egyptian commerce; the grain that was delivered to Greece was paid for in silver. He also built up the navy and began a canal linking the Nile with the Red Sea. Under Psamtik II (ruled 595–589 BC) there was a campaign through the Napatan kingdom involving the use of Greek and Carian mercenaries who left their inscriptions at Abu Simbel; at the same time, the names of the long-dead Cushite rulers were erased from their monuments in Egypt. Psamtik II also made an expedition to Phoenicia accompanied by priests; whether it was a military or a goodwill mission is unknown.

The next king, Apries (ruled 589–570 BC), tried unsuccessfully to end Babylonian domination of Palestine and Syria. With the withdrawal of Egyptian forces, Nebuchadrezzar destroyed the temple in Jerusalem in 586 BC. In the aftermath of his conquest, many Jews fled to Egypt, where some were enlisted as soldiers in the Persian army of occupation. Apries' army was then defeated in Libya when it attacked the Greek colony at Cyrene, some 620 miles (1,000 km) west of the Nile delta; this led to an army mutiny and to civil war in the delta. A new Saite king, Amasis (or Ahmose II; ruled 570–526 BC), usurped the throne and drove Apries into exile. Two years later Apries invaded Egypt with Babylonian support, but he was defeated and killed by Amasis, who nonetheless buried him with full honours. Amasis returned to a more conservative foreign policy in a long, prosperous reign. To reduce friction between Greeks and Egyptians, especially in the army, Amasis withdrew the Greeks from the military colonies and transferred them to Memphis, where they formed a sort of royal bodyguard. He limited Greek trade in Egypt to Sais, Memphis, and Naukratis, the latter becoming the only port to which Greek wares could be taken, so that taxes on imports and on business could be enforced. Naukratis prospered, and Amasis was seen by the Greeks as a benefactor. In foreign policy he supported a waning Babylonia, now threatened by Persia; but six months after his death in 526 BC the Persian Cambyses II (ruled as pharaoh 525–522 BC) penetrated Egypt, reaching Nubia in 525.

As was common in the Middle East in that period, the Saite kings used foreigners as mercenaries to prevent foreign invasions. An element within Egyptian culture, however, resisted any influence of the resident foreigners and gave rise to a nationalism that provided psychological security in times of political uncertainty. A cultural revival was initiated in the 25th dynasty and continued throughout the 26th. Temples and the priesthood were overtly dominant. In their inscriptions the elite displayed their priestly titles but did not mention the administrative roles that they probably also performed. Throughout the country, people of substance dedicated land to temple endowments that supplemented royal donations. The god Seth, who had been an antithetic element in Egyptian religion, came gradually to be proscribed as the god of foreign lands.

The revival of this period was both economic and cultural, but there is less archaeological evidence preserved than for earlier times because the economic centre of the country was now the delta, where conditions for the preservation of ancient sites were unfavourable. Prosperity increased throughout the 26th dynasty, reaching a high point in the reign of Amasis. Temples throughout the land were enhanced and expanded, often in hard stones carved with great skill. The chief memorials of private individuals were often temple statues, of which many fine examples were dedicated, again mostly in hard stones. In temple and tomb decoration and in statuary, the Late period rejected its immediate predecessors and looked to the great periods of the past for models.

There was, however, also significant innovation. In writing, the demotic script, the new cursive form, was introduced from the north and spread gradually through the country. Demotic was used to write a contemporary form of the language, and administrative Late Egyptian disappeared. Hieratic was, however, retained for literary and religious texts, among which very ancient material, such as the Pyramid Texts, was revived and inscribed in tombs and on coffins and sarcophagi.

The Late period was the time of the greatest development of animal worship in Egypt. This feature of religion, which was the subject of much interest and scorn among classical writers, had always existed but had been of minor importance. In the Late and Ptolemaic periods, it became one of the principal forms of popular religion in an intensely religious society. Many species of animals were mummified and buried, and towns sprang up in the necropolises to cater for the needs of dead animals and their worshipers. At Ṣaqqārah the Apis bull, which had been worshipped since the 1st dynasty, was buried in a huge granite sarcophagus in ceremonies in which royalty might take part. At least 10 species—from ibises, buried by the million, to dogs—were interred by the heterogeneous population of Memphis, Egypt's largest city.

EGYPT UNDER ACHAEMENID RULE

According to the Greek historian Herodotus, who visited Egypt in about 450

The remains of a mummified cat. Animals were frequently accorded many of the same burial rites as people during ancient Egypt's Late period. SSPL via Getty Images

BC, Cambyses II's conquest of Egypt was ruthless and sacrilegious. Contemporary Egyptian sources, however, treat him in a more favourable light. He assumed the full titulary of an Egyptian king and paid honour to the goddess Neith of Sais. His unfavourable later reputation probably resulted from adverse propaganda by Egyptian priests, who resented his reduction of temple income.

THE 27TH DYNASTY

Darius I, who succeeded Cambyses in 522 BC and ruled as pharaoh until 486 BC, was held in higher esteem because he was concerned with improving the temples and restored part of their income, and because he codified laws as they had been in the time of Amasis. These stances, which aimed to win over priests and learned Egyptians, were elements of his strategy to retain Egypt as a lasting part of the Persian Empire. Egypt, together with the Libyan oases and Cyrenaica, formed the sixth Persian satrapy (province), whose satrap resided at Memphis, while Persian governors under him held posts in cities throughout the land. Under Darius I the tax burden upon Egyptians was relatively light, and Persians aided Egypt's economy through irrigation projects and improved commerce, enhanced by the completion of the canal to the Red Sea.

The Persian defeat by the Athenians at Marathon in 490 BC had significant repercussions in Egypt. On Darius I's death in 486 BC, a revolt broke out in the delta, perhaps instigated by Libyans of its western region. The result was that the Persian king Xerxes reduced Egypt to the status of a conquered province. Egyptians dubbed him the "criminal Xerxes." He never visited Egypt and appears not to have utilized Egyptians in high positions in the administration. Xerxes' murder in 465 BC was the signal for another revolt in the western delta. It was led by a dynast, Inaros, who acquired control over the delta and was supported by Athenian forces against the Persians. Inaros was crucified by the Persians in 454 BC, when they regained control of most of the delta. In the later 5th century BC, under the rule of Artaxerxes I (ruled 465–425 BC) and Darius II Ochus (ruled 423–404 BC), conditions in Egypt were very unsettled, and scarcely any monuments of the period have been identified.

The 28th, 29th, and 30th Dynasties

The death of Darius II in 404 BC prompted a successful rebellion in the Nile delta, and the Egyptian Amyrtaeus formed a Saite 28th dynasty, of which he was the sole king (404–399 BC). His rule was recognized in Upper Egypt by 401 BC, at a time when Persia's troubles elsewhere forestalled an attempt to regain Egypt.

Despite growing prosperity and success in retaining independence, 4th-century Egypt was characterized by continual internal struggle for the throne. After a long period of fighting in the delta, a 29th dynasty (399–380 BC) emerged at Mendes. Achoris (ruled 393–380 BC), its third and final ruler, was especially vigorous, and the prosperity of his reign is indicated by many monuments in Upper and Lower Egypt. Once again Egypt was active in international politics, forming alliances with the opponents of Persia and building up its army and navy. The Egyptian army included Greeks both as mercenaries and as commanders; the mercenaries were not permanent residents of military camps in Egypt but native Greeks seeking payment for their services in gold. Payment was normally made in non-Egyptian coins, because as

yet Egypt had no coinage in general circulation; the foreign coins may have been acquired in exchange for exports of grain, papyrus, and linen. Some Egyptian coins were minted in the 4th century, but they do not seem to have gained widespread acceptance.

Aided by the Greek commander Chabrias of Athens and his elite troops, Achoris prevented a Persian invasion; but after Achoris's death in 380 BC his son Nepherites II lasted only four months before a general, Nectanebo I (Nekhtnebef; ruled 380–362 BC) of Sebennytos, usurped the throne, founding the 30th dynasty (380–343 BC). In 373 BC the Persians attacked Egypt, and, although Egyptian losses were heavy, disagreement between the Persian satrap Pharnabazus and his Greek commander over strategy, combined with a timely inundation of the delta, saved the day for Egypt. With the latent dissolution of the Persian Empire under the weak Artaxerxes II, Egypt was relatively safe from further invasion; it remained prosperous throughout the dynasty.

Egypt had a more aggressive foreign policy under Nectanebo's son Tachos (ruled c. 365–360 BC). Possessing a strong army and navy composed of Egyptian Machimoi and Greek mercenaries and supported by Chabrias and the Spartan king Agesilaus, Tachos (in Egyptian called Djeho) invaded Palestine. But friction between Tachos and Agesilaus and the cost of financing the venture proved to be Tachos's undoing. In an attempt to raise funds quickly, he had imposed taxes and seized temple property. Egyptians, especially the priests, resented this burden and supported Tachos's nephew Nectanebo II (Nekhtharehbe; ruled 360–343 BC) in his usurpation of the throne. The cost of retaining the allegiance of mercenaries proved too high for a nonmonetary economy.

Agesilaus supported Nectanebo in his defensive foreign policy, and the priests sanctioned the new king's building activities. Meanwhile, Persia enjoyed a resurgence under Artaxerxes III (Ochus), but a Persian attack on Egypt in 350 BC was repulsed. In 343 BC the Persians once again marched against Egypt. The first battle was fought at Pelusium and proved the superiority of Persia's strategy. Eventually the whole delta, and then the rest of Egypt, fell to Artaxerxes III, and Nectanebo fled to Nubia.

The 4th century BC was the last flourishing period of an independent Egypt and was a time of notable artistic and literary achievements. The 26th dynasty artistic revival evolved further toward more-complex forms that culminated briefly in a Greco-Egyptian stylistic fusion, as seen in the tomb of Petosiris at Tūnah al-Jabal from the turn of the 3rd century BC. In literature works continued to be transmitted, and possibly composed, in hieratic, but that tradition was to develop no further. Demotic literary works began to appear, including stories set in the distant past, mythological tales, and an acrostic text apparently designed to teach an order of sounds in the Egyptian language.

Artaxerxes dealt harshly with Egypt, razing city walls, rifling temple treasuries, and removing sacred books. Persia acquired rich booty in its determination to prevent Egypt from further rebelling. After the murder of Artaxerxes III, in 338 BC, there was a brief obscure period during which a Nubian prince, Khabbash, seems to have gained control over Egypt, but Persian domination was reestablished in 335 BC under Darius III Codommanus. It was to last only three years.

THE MACEDONIAN CONQUEST

In the autumn of 332 BC Alexander the Great invaded Egypt with his mixed army of Macedonians and Greeks and found the Egyptians ready to throw off the oppressive control of the Persians. Alexander was welcomed by the Egyptians as a liberator and took the country without a battle. He journeyed to Siwa Oasis in the Western Desert to visit the Oracle of Amon, renowned in the Greek world; it disclosed the information that Alexander was the son of Amon. There may also have been a coronation at the Egyptian capital, Memphis, which, if it occurred, would have placed him firmly in the tradition of the kings (pharaohs); the same purpose may be seen in the later dissemination of the romantic myth that gave him an Egyptian parentage by linking his mother, Olympias, with the last king, Nectanebo II.

Alexander left Egypt in the spring of 331 BC, dividing the military command between Balacrus, son of Amyntas, and Peucestas, son of Makartatos. The earliest known Greek documentary papyrus, found at Ṣaqqārah in 1973, reveals the sensitivity of the latter to Egyptian religious institutions in a notice that reads: "Order of Peucestas. No one is to pass. The chamber is that of a priest." The civil administration was headed by an official with the Persian title of satrap, one Cleomenes of Naukratis. When Alexander died in 323 BC and his generals divided his empire, the position of satrap was claimed by Ptolemy, son of a Macedonian nobleman named Lagus. The senior general Perdiccas, the holder of Alexander's royal seal and prospective regent for Alexander's posthumous son, might well have regretted his failure to take Egypt. He gathered an army and marched from Asia Minor to wrest Egypt from Ptolemy in 321 BC; but Ptolemy had Alexander's corpse, Perdiccas's army was not wholehearted in support, and the Nile crocodiles made a good meal from the flesh of the invaders.

THE PTOLEMAIC DYNASTY

Until the day when he openly assumed an independent kingship as Ptolemy I Soter, on Nov. 7, 305 BC, Ptolemy used only the title satrap of Egypt, but the great hieroglyphic Satrap stela, which he had inscribed in 311 BC, indicates a degree of self-confidence that transcends his viceregal role. It reads, "I, Ptolemy the satrap, I restore to Horus, the avenger of his father, the lord of Pe and to Buto, the lady

of Pe and Dep, the territory of Patanut, from this day forth for ever, with all its villages, all its towns, all its inhabitants, all its fields." The inscription emphasizes Ptolemy's own role in wresting the land from the Persians (though the epithet of Soter, meaning "Saviour," resulted not from his actions in Egypt but from the gratitude of the people of Rhodes for his having relieved them from a siege in 315 BC) and links him with Khabbash, who had laid claim to the kingship during the last Persian occupation in about 338 BC.

Egypt was ruled by Ptolemy's descendants until the death of Cleopatra VII on Aug. 12, 30 BC. The kingdom was one of several that emerged in the aftermath of Alexander's death and the struggles of his successors. It was the wealthiest, however, and for much of the next 300 years

Portrait of Ptolemy I Soter on a silver tetradrachm coin, Alexandria, Egypt, 3rd century BC. Courtesy of the trustees of the British Museum

the most powerful politically and culturally, and it was the last to fall directly under Roman dominion. In many respects, the character of the Ptolemaic monarchy in Egypt set a style for other Hellenistic kingdoms; this style emerged from the Greeks' and Macedonians' awareness of the need to dominate Egypt, its resources, and its people and at the same time to turn the power of Egypt firmly toward the context of a Mediterranean world that was becoming steadily more Hellenized.

THE PTOLEMIES (305–145 BC)

The first 160 years of the Ptolemaic dynasty are conventionally seen as its most prosperous era. Little is known of the foundations laid in the reign of Ptolemy I Soter (304–282 BC), but the increasing amount of documentary, inscriptional, and archaeological evidence from the reign of his son and successor, Ptolemy II Philadelphus (285–246 BC), shows that the kingdom's administration and economy underwent a thorough reorganization. A remarkable demotic text of the year 258 BC refers to orders for a complete census of the kingdom that was to record the sources of water; the position, quality, and irrigation potential of the land; the state of cultivation; the crops grown; and the extent of priestly and royal landholdings. There were important agricultural innovations in this period. New crops were introduced, and massive irrigation works brought under cultivation a great deal of new land, especially in Al-Fayyūm, where many of the immigrant Greeks were settled.

The Macedonian-Greek character of the monarchy was vigorously preserved. There is no more emphatic sign of this than the growth and importance of the city of Alexandria. It had been founded, on a date traditionally given as April 7, 331 BC (but often cited as 332 BC), by Alexander the Great on the site of the insignificant Egyptian village of Rakotis in the northwestern Nile River delta, and it ranked as the most important city in the eastern Mediterranean until the foundation of Constantinople in the 4th century AD. The importance of the new Greek city was soon emphasized by contrast to its Egyptian surroundings when the royal capital was transferred, within a few years of Alexander's death, from Memphis to Alexandria. The Ptolemaic court cultivated extravagant luxury in the Greek style in its magnificent and steadily expanding palace complex, which occupied as much as a third of the city by the early Roman period. Its grandeur was emphasized in the reign of Ptolemy II Philadelphus by the foundation of a quadrennial festival, the Ptolemaieia, which was intended to enjoy a status equal to that of the Olympic Games. The festival was marked by a procession of amazingly elaborate and ingeniously constructed floats, with scenarios illustrating Greek religious cults.

Ptolemy II gave the dynasty another distinctive feature when he married his full sister, Arsinoe II, one of the most

Arsinoe II, Egyptian coin, 270–250 BC. Courtesy of the trustees of the British Museum

powerful and remarkable women of the Hellenistic age. They became, in effect, co-rulers, and both took the epithet Philadelphus ("Brother-Loving" and "Sister-Loving"). The practice of consanguineous marriage was followed by most of their successors and imitated by ordinary Egyptians too, even though it had not been a standard practice in the pharaonic royal houses and had been unknown in the rest of the native Egyptian population. Arsinoe played a prominent role in the formation of royal policy. She was displayed on the coinage and was eventually worshipped, perhaps even before her death, in the distinctively Greek style of ruler cult that developed in this reign.

From the first phase of the wars of Alexander's successors the Ptolemies had harboured imperial ambitions. Ptolemy I won control of Cyprus and Cyrene and quarreled with his neighbour over control of Palestine. In the course of the 3rd century a powerful Ptolemaic empire developed, which, for much of the period, laid claim to sovereignty in the Levant, in many of the cities of the western and southern coast of Asia Minor, in some of the Aegean islands, and in a handful of towns in Thrace, as well as in Cyprus and Cyrene. Family connections and dynastic alliances, especially between the Ptolemies and the neighbouring Seleucids, played an important role in these imperialistic ambitions. Such links were far from able to preserve harmony between the royal houses (between 274 and 200 BC five wars were fought with the Seleucids over possession of territory in Syria and the Levant), but they did keep the ruling houses relatively compact, interconnected, and more true to their Macedonian-Greek origins.

When Ptolemy II Philadelphus died in 246 BC, he left a prosperous kingdom to his successor, Ptolemy III Euergetes (246–221 BC). His reign saw a very successful campaign against the Seleucids in Syria, occasioned by the murder of Euergetes' sister, Berenice, who had been married to the Seleucid Antiochus II. To avenge Berenice, Euergetes marched into Syria, where he won a great victory. He gained popularity at home by recapturing statues of Egyptian gods originally taken by the Persians. The decree promulgated at Canopus in the delta on March 7, 238 BC, attests both this event and the many great benefactions conferred on Egyptian temples throughout the land. It was during Euergetes' reign, for instance, that the rebuilding of the great Temple of Horus at Idfū (Apollinopolis Magna) was begun.

Euergetes was succeeded by his son Ptolemy IV Philopator (221–205 BC), whom the Greek historians portray as a weak and corrupt ruler, dominated by a powerful circle of Alexandrian Greek courtiers. The reign was notable for another serious conflict with the Seleucids, which ended in 217 BC in a great Ptolemaic victory at Raphia in southern Palestine. The battle is notable for the fact that large numbers of native Egyptian soldiers fought alongside the Macedonian and Greek contingents. Events surrounding the death of Philopator and the succession of the youthful Ptolemy V Epiphanes (205–180 BC) are obscured by court intrigue. Before Epiphanes had completed his first decade of rule, serious difficulties arose. Native revolts in the south, which had been sporadic in the second half of the 3rd century BC, became serious and weakened the hold of the monarch on a vital part of the kingdom. These revolts, which produced native claimants to the kingship, are generally attributed to the native Egyptians' realization, after their contribution to the victory at Raphia, of their potential power. Trouble continued to break out for several more decades. By about 196 BC a great portion of the Ptolemaic overseas empire had been permanently lost (though there may have been a brief revival in the Aegean islands in about 165–145 BC). To shore up and advertise the strength of the ruling house at home and abroad, the administration adopted a series of grandiloquent honorific titles for its officers. To conciliate Egyptian feelings, a religious synod that met in 196 BC to crown Epiphanes at Memphis (the first occasion on which a Ptolemy is certainly known to have been crowned at the traditional capital) decreed extensive privileges for the Egyptian temples, as recorded on the Rosetta Stone.

The reign of Ptolemy VI Philometor (180–145 BC), a man of pious and magnanimous character, was marked by renewed conflict with the Seleucids after the death of his mother, Cleopatra I, in 176 BC. In 170/169 BC Antiochus IV of Syria invaded Egypt and established a protectorate; in 168 BC he returned, accepted coronation at Memphis, and installed a Seleucid governor. But he had failed to reckon with the more powerful interests of Rome. In the summer of 168 BC a Roman ambassador, Popillius Laenas, arrived at Antiochus's headquarters near Pelusium in the Delta and staged an awesome display of Roman power. He ordered Antiochus to withdraw from Egypt. Antiochus asked for time to consult his advisers. Laenas drew a circle around the king with his stick and told him to answer before he stepped out of the circle. Only one answer was possible, and by the end of July Antiochus had left Egypt. Philometor's reign was further troubled by rivalry with his brother, later Ptolemy VIII Euergetes II Physcon. The solution, devised under Roman advice, was to remove Physcon to Cyrene, where he remained until Philometor died in 145

BC; but it is noteworthy that in 155 BC Physcon took the step of bequeathing the kingdom of Cyrene to the Romans in the event of his untimely death.

DYNASTIC STRIFE AND DECLINE (145–30 BC)

Physcon was able to rule in Egypt until 116 BC with his sister Cleopatra II (except for a period in 131–130 BC when she was in revolt) and her daughter Cleopatra III. His reign was marked by generous benefactions to the Egyptian temples, but he was detested as a tyrant by the Greeks, and the historical accounts of the reign emphasize his stormy relations with the Alexandrian populace.

During the last century of Ptolemaic rule, Egypt's independence was exercised under Rome's protection and at Rome's discretion. For much of the period Rome was content to support a dynasty that had no overseas possession except Cyprus after 96 BC (the year in which Cyrene was bequeathed to Rome by Ptolemy Apion) and no ambitions threatening Roman interests or security. After a series of brief and unstable reigns, Ptolemy XII Auletes acceded to the throne in 80 BC. He maintained his hold for 30 years, despite the attractions that Egypt's legendary wealth held for avaricious Roman politicians. In fact, Auletes had to flee Egypt in 58 BC and was restored by Pompey's friend Gabinius in 55 BC, no doubt after spending so much in bribes that he had to bring back Rabirius Postumus, one of his Roman creditors, to Egypt with him to manage his financial affairs.

In 52 BC, the year before his death, Auletes associated with himself on the throne his daughter Cleopatra VII and his elder son Ptolemy XIII (who died in 47 BC). The reign of Cleopatra was that of a vigorous and exceptionally able queen who was ambitious, among other things, to revive the prestige of the dynasty by cultivating influence with powerful Roman commanders and using their capacity to aggrandize Roman clients and allies. Julius Caesar pursued Pompey to Egypt in 48 BC. After learning of Pompey's murder at the hands of Egyptian courtiers, Caesar stayed long enough to enjoy a sightseeing tour up the Nile in the queen's company in the summer of 47 BC. When he left for Rome, Cleopatra was pregnant with a child she claimed was Caesar's. The child, a son, was named Caesarion ("Little Caesar"). Cleopatra and Caesarion later followed Caesar back to Rome, but, after his assassination in 44 BC, they returned hurriedly to Egypt. Cleopatra tried for a while to play a neutral role in the struggles between the Roman generals and their factions.

Her long liaison with Mark Antony began when she visited him at Tarsus in 41 BC and he returned to Egypt with her. Between 36 and 30 BC the famous romance between the Roman general and the eastern queen was exploited to great effect by Antony's political rival Octavian (the future emperor Augustus).

The visage of Cleopatra, on display in London in 2001. Cleopatra's reign marked the end of Ptolemic leadership in Egypt. Adrian Dennis/AFP/Getty Images

By 34 BC Caesarion was officially co-ruler with Cleopatra, but his rule clearly was an attempt to exploit the popularity of Caesar's memory. In the autumn Cleopatra and Antony staged an extravagant display in which they made grandiose dispositions of territory in the east to their children, Alexander Helios, Ptolemy, and Cleopatra Selene. Cleopatra and Antony were portrayed to the Roman public as posing for artists in the guise of Dionysus and Isis, or whiling away their evenings in rowdy and decadent banquets that kept the citizens of Alexandria awake all night.

This propaganda war was merely the prelude to armed conflict, and the issue was decided in September 31 BC in a naval battle at Actium in western Greece. When the battle was at its height Cleopatra and her squadron withdrew, and Antony eventually followed suit. They fled to Alexandria but could do little more than await the arrival of the victorious Octavian 10 months later. Alexandria was captured and Antony and Cleopatra committed suicide—he by falling on his sword, she probably by the bite of an asp—in August of 30 BC. It is reported that when Octavian reached the city he visited and touched the preserved corpse of Alexander the Great, causing a piece of the nose to fall off. He refused to gaze upon the remains of the Ptolemies, saying "I wished to see a king, not corpses."

GOVERNMENT AND CONDITIONS UNDER THE PTOLEMIES

The changes brought to Egypt by the Ptolemies were momentous. The land's resources were harnessed with unparalleled efficiency with the result that Egypt became the wealthiest of the Hellenistic kingdoms. Land under cultivation was increased, new crops were introduced (especially important was the introduction of naked tetraploid wheat, *Triticum durum*, to replace the traditional husked emmer, *Triticum dicoccum*). The population, estimated at perhaps three to four million in the late Dynastic period, may have more than doubled by the early Roman period to a level not reached again until the late 19th century. Some of the increase was due to immigration.

Particularly during the 2nd and 3rd centuries many settlers were attracted from cities in Anatolia (Asia Minor) and the Greek islands, and large numbers of Jews came from Palestine. The flow may have decreased later in the Ptolemaic period, and it is often suggested, on slender evidence, that there was a serious decline in prosperity in the 1st century BC. If so, there may have been some reversal of this trend under Cleopatra VII.

ADMINISTRATION

The foundation of the prosperity was the governmental system devised to exploit the country's economic resources. Directly below the monarch were a handful of powerful officials whose authority extended over the entire land: a chief finance minister, a chief accountant, and a chancery of ministers in charge of records, letters, and decrees. A level below them lay the broadening base of a pyramid of subordinate officials with authority in limited areas, which extended down to the chief administrator of each individual village (*kōmarchēs*). Between the chief ministers and the village officials stood those such as the nome-steward (*oikonomos*) and the *stratēgoi*, whose jurisdiction extended over one of the more than 30 nomes of Egypt, the long-established geographic divisions. In theory this bureaucracy could regulate and control the economic activities of every subject in the land, its smooth operation guaranteed by the multiplicity of officials capable of checking each upon the other. In practice, it is difficult to see a rigid civil-service mentality at work, involving clear demarcation of departments. Specific functions might well have been performed by different officials according to local need and the availability of a person competent to take appropriate action.

By the same token, rigid lines of separation between military, civil, legal, and administrative matters are difficult to perceive. The same official might perform duties in one or all of these areas. The military was inevitably integrated into civilian life because its soldiers were also farmers who enjoyed royal grants of land, either as Greek cleruchs (holders of allotments) with higher status and generous grants, or as native Egypt *machimoi* with small plots. Interlocking judiciary institutions, in the form of Greek and Egyptian courts (*chrēmatistai* and *laokritai*), provided the means for Greeks and Egyptians to regulate their legal relationships according to the language in which they conducted their business. The bureaucratic power was heavily weighted in favour of the Greek speakers, the dominant elite. Egyptians were nevertheless able to obtain official posts in the bureaucracy, gradually infiltrating to the highest levels, but in order to do so they had to Hellenize.

ECONOMY

The basis of Egypt's legendary wealth was the highly productive land, which technically remained in royal ownership. A considerable portion was kept under the control of temples, and the remainder was leased out on a theoretically revocable basis to tenant-farmers. A portion also was available to be granted as gifts to leading courtiers. One of these was Apollonius, the finance minister of Ptolemy II Philadelphus, who had an estate of 10,000 *arourae* (about 6,500 acres [2,630 hectares]) at Philadelphia in Al-Fayyūm. Tenants and beneficiaries were able to behave very much as if these leases and grants were private property. The revenues in cash and kind were enormous, and royal control extended to the manufacture and marketing of almost all important products, including papyrus, oil, linen, and beer. An extraordinarily detailed set of revenue laws, promulgated under Ptolemy II Philadelphus, laid down

Bowl of pressed mosaic glass, believed to be from Alexandria, Egypt, 1st century AD; in the Victoria and Albert Museum, London. Courtesy of Victoria and Albert Museum

rules for the way in which officials were to monitor the production of such commodities. In fact, the Ptolemaic economy was very much a mixture of direct royal ownership and exploitation by private enterprise under regulated conditions.

One fundamental and far-reaching Ptolemaic innovation was the systematic monetarization of the economy. The monarchy also controlled this from top to bottom by operating a closed monetary system, which permitted only the royal coinage to circulate within Egypt. A sophisticated banking system underpinned this practice, operating again with a mixture of direct royal control and private enterprise and handling both private financial transactions and those that directed money into and out of the royal coffers. One important concomitant of this change was an enormous increase in the volume of trade, both within Egypt and abroad, which eventually reached its climax under the peaceful conditions of Roman rule. There the position and role of Alexandria as the major port and trading entrepôt was crucial. The city handled a great volume of Egypt's domestic produce, as well as the import and export of luxury goods to and from the East and the cities of the eastern Mediterranean. It developed its own importance as an artistic centre, the products of which found ready markets throughout the Mediterranean. Alexandrian glassware and jewelry were particularly fine, Greek-style sculpture of the late Ptolemaic period shows especial excellence, and it is likely that the city was

also the major production centre for high-quality mosaic work.

Religion

The Ptolemies were powerful supporters of the native Egyptian religious foundations, the economic and political power of which was, however, carefully controlled. A great deal of the late building and restoration work in many of the most important Egyptian temples is Ptolemaic, particularly from the period of about 150–50 BC, and the monarchs appear on temple reliefs in the traditional forms of the Egyptian kings. The native traditions persisted in village temples and local cults, many having particular associations with species of sacred animals or birds. At the same time, the Greeks created their own identifications of Egyptian deities, identifying Amon with Zeus, Horus with Apollo, Ptah with Hephaestus, and so on. They also gave some deities, such as Isis, a more universal significance that ultimately resulted in the spread of her mystery cult throughout the Mediterranean world. The impact of the Greeks is most obvious in two phenomena. One is the formalized royal cult of Alexander and the Ptolemies, which evidently served both a political and a religious purpose. The other is the creation of the cult of Sarapis, which at first was confined to Alexandria but soon became universal. The god was represented as a Hellenized deity and the form

Apis, the ancient Egyptian bull deity, painted on the bottom of a wooden coffin, c. 700 BC; in the Roemer-Pelizaeus Museum, Hildesheim, Ger. Bavaria-Verlag

of cult is Greek, but its essence is the old Egyptian notion that the sacred Apis bull merged its divinity in some way with the god Osiris when it died.

CULTURE

The continuing vitality of the native Egyptian artistic tradition is clearly and abundantly expressed in the temple architecture and the sculpture of the Ptolemaic period. The Egyptian language continued to be used in its hieroglyphic and demotic forms until late in the Roman period, and it survived through the Byzantine period and beyond in the form of Coptic. The Egyptian literary tradition flourished vigorously in the Ptolemaic period and produced a large number of works in demotic. The genre most commonly represented is the romantic tale, exemplified by several story cycles, which are typically set in the native, Pharaonic milieu and involve the gods, royal figures, magic, romance, and the trials and combats of heroes.

Another important category is the Instruction Text, the best known of the period being that of Ankhsheshonq, which consists of a list of moralizing maxims, composed, as the story goes, when Ankhsheshonq was imprisoned for having failed to inform the king (pharaoh) of an assassination plot. Another example, known as Papyrus Insinger, is a more narrowly moralizing text. But the arrival of a Greek-speaking elite had an enormous impact on cultural patterns. The Egyptian story cycles were probably affected by Greek influence, literary and technical works were translated into Greek, and under royal patronage an Egyptian priest named Manetho of Sebennytos wrote an account of the kings of Egypt in Greek. Most striking is the diffusion of the works of the poets and playwrights of classical Greece among the literate Greeks in the towns and villages of the Nile River valley.

Thus there are clear signs of the existence of two interacting but distinct cultural traditions in Ptolemaic Egypt. This was certainly reflected in a broader

ALEXANDRIAN MUSEUM

The Alexandrian Museum, or Museum of Alexandria, in Egypt was an ancient centre of classical learning. Especially noted as a research facility containing much scientific and literary scholarship, the Alexandrian Museum was built near the royal palace about 280 BC by Ptolemy I Soter (reigned 323–285/283 BC). The best surviving description of the museum is by the Greek geographer and historian Strabo, who mentions that it was a large complex of buildings and gardens with richly decorated lecture and banquet halls linked by porticos, or colonnaded walks. It was organized in faculties with a president-priest at the head. The salaries of the scholars on the staff were paid by the Egyptian king and later by the Roman emperor. The renowned Library of Alexandria formed a part of the museum.

The Alexandrian library and museum were maintained by the long succession of Ptolemies in Egypt. The library's initial organization was the work of Demetrius of Phaleron, who was familiar with the achievements of the library at Athens. A subsidiary "daughter library" was established about 235 BC by Ptolemy III (Euergetes) in the Temple of Serapis, the main museum and library being located in the palace precincts, in the district known as the Brucheium. It is not known how far the ideal of an international library—incorporating not only all Greek literature but also translations into Greek from the other languages of the Mediterranean, the Middle East, and India—was realized. It is certain that the library was in the main Greek. The only translation recorded was the Septuagint, the earliest extant Greek translation of the Hebrew Bible from the original Hebrew.

The library's editorial program included the establishment of the Alexandrian canon of Greek poets, the division of works into "books" as they are now known (probably to suit the standard length of rolls), and the gradual introduction of systems of punctuation and accentuation. The compilation of a national bibliography was entrusted to Callimachus. Though now lost, it survived into the Byzantine period as a standard reference work of Greek literature. The museum and library survived for many centuries but were destroyed in the civil war that occurred under the Roman emperor Aurelian in the late 3rd century AD. The daughter library was destroyed by Christians in AD 391. In 2002 the Egyptian government inaugurated a new library, the Bibliotheca Alexandrina, near the site of the ancient institution.

social context. The written sources offer little direct evidence of ethnic discrimination by Greeks against Egyptians, but Greek and Egyptian consciousness of the Greeks' social and economic superiority comes through strongly from time to time. Intermarriage was one means, though not the only one, by which Egyptians could better their status and Hellenize. Many native Egyptians learned to speak Greek, some to write it as well; some even went so far as to adopt Greek names in an attempt to assimilate themselves to the elite group.

Alexandria occupied a unique place in the history of literature, ideas, scholarship, and science for almost a millennium after the death of its founder. Under the royal patronage of the Ptolemies and in an environment almost oblivious to its Egyptian surroundings, Greek culture was preserved and developed. Early in the Ptolemaic period, probably in the reign of Ptolemy I Soter, the Alexandrian Museum (Greek: *Mouseion*, "Seat of the Muses") was established within the palace complex. The geographer and historian Strabo, who saw it early in the Roman period, described it as having a covered walk, an arcade with recesses and seats, and a large house containing the dining hall of the members of the Museum, who lived a communal existence. The Library of Alexandria (together with its offshoot in the Sarapeum) was indispensable to the functioning of the scholarly community in the Museum. Books were collected voraciously under the Ptolemies, and at its height the library's collection probably numbered 500,000 or more papyrus rolls, most of them containing more than one work.

The major poets of the Hellenistic period, Theocritus, Callimachus, and Apollonius of Rhodes, all took up residence and wrote there. Scholarship flourished, preserving and ordering the manuscript traditions of much of the classical literature from Homer onward. Librarian-scholars such as Aristophanes of Byzantium and his pupil Aristarchus made critical editions and wrote commentaries and works on grammar. Also

notable was the cultural influence of Alexandria's Jewish community, which is inferred from the fact that the Pentateuch was first translated into Greek at Alexandria during the Ptolemaic period. One by-product of this kind of activity was that Alexandria became the centre of the book trade, and the works of the classical authors were copied there and diffused among a literate Greek readership scattered in the towns and villages of the Nile valley.

The Alexandrian achievement in scientific fields was also enormous. Great advances were made in pure mathematics, mechanics, physics, geography, and medicine. Euclid worked in Alexandria in about 300 BC and achieved the systematization of the whole existing corpus of mathematical knowledge and the development of the method of proof by deduction from axioms. Archimedes was there in the 3rd century BC and is said to have invented the Archimedean screw when he was in Egypt. Eratosthenes calculated the Earth's circumference and was the first to attempt a map of the world based on a system of lines of latitude and longitude. And the school of medicine founded in the Ptolemaic period retained its leading reputation into the Byzantine era. Late in the Ptolemaic period Alexandria began to develop as a great centre of Greek philosophical studies as well. In fact, there was no field of literary, intellectual, or scientific activity to which Ptolemaic Alexandria failed to make an important contribution.

CHAPTER 6

ROMAN AND BYZANTINE EGYPT

"I added Egypt to the Empire of the Roman people." With these words the emperor Augustus (as Octavian was known from 27 BC) summarized the subjection of Cleopatra's kingdom in the great inscription that records his achievements.

EGYPT AS A PROVINCE OF ROME

The Roman province of Egypt was to be governed by a viceroy, a prefect with the status of a Roman knight (eques) who was directly responsible to the emperor. The first viceroy was the Roman poet and soldier Gaius Cornelius Gallus, who boasted too vaingloriously of his military achievements in the province and paid for it first with his position and then with his life. Roman senators were not allowed to enter Egypt without the emperor's permission, because this wealthiest of provinces could be held militarily by a very small force, and the threat implicit in an embargo on the export of grain supplies, vital to the provisioning of the city of Rome and its populace, was obvious. Internal security was guaranteed by the presence of three Roman legions (later reduced to two), each about 6,000 strong, and several cohorts of auxiliaries.

In the first decade of Roman rule the spirit of Augustan imperialism looked farther afield, attempting expansion to the east and to the south. An expedition to Arabia by the prefect Aelius Gallus in about 26–25 BC was undermined by the treachery of the Nabataean Syllaeus, who led the Roman fleet astray in uncharted waters. Arabia was to remain an independent though friendly client of Rome until AD 106, when the emperor Trajan (ruled AD 98–117) annexed it, making it possible to reopen Ptolemy II's canal from the Nile to the head of the Gulf of Suez. To the south the Meroitic people beyond the First Cataract had taken advantage of Gallus's preoccupation with Arabia and mounted an attack on the Thebaid.

The next Roman prefect, Petronius, led two expeditions into the Meroitic kingdom (c. 24–22 BC), captured several towns, forced the submission of the formidable queen, who was characterized by Roman writers as "the one-eyed Queen Candace," and left a Roman garrison at Primis (Qaṣr Ibrīm). But thoughts of maintaining a permanent presence in Lower Nubia were soon abandoned, and within a year or two the limits of Roman occupation had been set at Hiera Sykaminos, some 50 miles (80 km) south of the First Cataract. The mixed character of the region is indicated, however, by the continuing popularity of the goddess Isis among the people of Meroe and by the Roman emperor Augustus's foundation of a temple at Kalabsha dedicated to the local god Mandulis.

Egypt achieved its greatest prosperity under the shadow of the Roman peace, which, in effect, depoliticized it. Roman emperors or members of their families visited Egypt—Tiberius's nephew and adopted son, Germanicus; Vespasian and his elder son, Titus; Hadrian; Septimius Severus; Diocletian—to see the famous sights, receive the acclamations of the Alexandrian populace, attempt to ensure the loyalty of their volatile subjects, or initiate administrative reform. Occasionally its potential as a power base was realized. Vespasian, the most successful of the imperial aspirants in the "Year of the Four Emperors," was first proclaimed emperor at Alexandria on July 1, AD 69, in a maneuver contrived by the prefect of Egypt, Tiberius Julius Alexander.

Others were less successful. Gaius Avidius Cassius, the son of a former prefect of Egypt, revolted against Marcus Aurelius in AD 175, stimulated by false rumours of Marcus's death, but his attempted usurpation lasted only three months. For several months in AD 297/298 Egypt was under the dominion of a mysterious usurper named Lucius Domitius Domitianus. The emperor Diocletian was present at the final capitulation of Alexandria after an eight-month siege and swore to take revenge by slaughtering the populace until the river of blood reached his horse's knees. The threat was mitigated when his mount stumbled as he rode into the city. In gratitude, the citizens of Alexandria erected a statue of the horse.

The only extended period during the turbulent 3rd century AD in which Egypt was lost to the central imperial authority was 270–272, when it fell into the hands of the ruling dynasty of the Syrian city of Palmyra. Fortunately for Rome, the military strength of Palmyra proved to be the major obstacle to the overrunning of the Eastern Empire by the powerful Sāsānian monarchy of Persia.

Internal threats to security were not uncommon but normally were dissipated without major damage to imperial control. These included rioting between Jews and Greeks in Alexandria in the reign of Caligula (Gaius Caesar Germanicus; ruled AD 37–41), a serious Jewish revolt under Trajan (ruled AD 98–117), a revolt in the Nile delta in AD 172 that was quelled by Avidius Cassius, and a revolt centred on the town of Coptos (Qifṭ) in AD 293/294 that was put down by Galerius, Diocletian's imperial colleague.

ADMINISTRATION AND ECONOMY UNDER ROME

The Romans introduced important changes in the administrative system, aimed at achieving a high level of efficiency and maximizing revenue. The duties of the prefect of Egypt combined responsibility for military security through command of the legions and cohorts, for the organization of finance and taxation, and for the administration of justice. This involved a vast mass of detailed paperwork: one document from AD 211 notes that in a period of three days 1,804 petitions were handed into the prefect's office. But the prefect was assisted by a hierarchy of subordinate equestrian officials with expertise in particular areas. There were three or four *epistratēgoi* in charge of regional subdivisions. Special officers were in charge of the emperors' private account, the administration of justice, religious institutions, and so on. Subordinate to them were the local officials in the nomes (*stratēgoi* and royal scribes) and finally the authorities in the towns and villages.

It was in these growing towns that the Romans made the most far-reaching changes in administration. They introduced colleges of magistrates and officials who were to be responsible for running the internal affairs of their own communities on a theoretically autonomous basis and, at the same time, were to guarantee the collection and payment of tax quotas to the central government. This was backed up by the development of a range of "liturgies," compulsory public services that were imposed on individuals according to rank and property to ensure the financing and upkeep of local facilities. These institutions were the Egyptian counterpart of the councils and magistrates that oversaw the Greek cities in the eastern Roman provinces. They had been ubiquitous in other Hellenistic kingdoms, but in Ptolemaic Egypt they had existed only in the so-called Greek cities (Alexandria, Ptolemais in Upper Egypt, Naukratis, and later Antinoöpolis, founded by Hadrian in AD 130). Alexandria lost the right to have a council, probably in the Ptolemaic period. When it recovered its right in AD 200, the privilege was diluted by being extended to the nome capitals (*mētropoleis*) as well. This extension of privilege represented an attempt to shift more of the burden and expense of administration onto the local propertied classes, but it was eventually to prove too heavy. The consequences were the impoverishment of many of the councillors and their families and serious problems in administration that led to an increasing degree of central government interference and, eventually, more direct control.

The economic resources that this administration existed to exploit had not changed since the Ptolemaic period, but the development of a much more complex and sophisticated taxation system was a hallmark of Roman rule. Taxes in both cash and kind were assessed on land, and a bewildering variety of small taxes in cash, as well as customs dues and the like, was collected by appointed officials. A massive amount of Egypt's grain was shipped downriver both to feed the population of Alexandria and for export to Rome. Despite frequent complaints of oppression and extortion from the taxpayers, it is not obvious that official tax rates were all that high. In fact the Roman government had actively encouraged the privatization of land and the increase of private enterprise in manufacture, commerce, and trade, and low tax rates favoured private owners and entrepreneurs. The poorer people gained their livelihood as tenants of state-owned land or property belonging to the emperor or to wealthy private landlords, and they were relatively much more heavily burdened by rentals, which tended to remain at a fairly high level.

Overall, the degree of monetarization and complexity in the economy, even at the village level, was intense. Goods were moved around and exchanged through the medium of coin on a large scale and, in the towns and the larger villages, a high level of industrial and commercial activity developed in close conjunction with the exploitation of the predominant agricultural base. The volume of trade, both internal and external, reached its peak in the 1st and 2nd centuries AD. However, by the end of the 3rd century AD, major problems were evident. A series of debasements of the imperial currency had undermined confidence in the coinage, and even the government itself was contributing to this by demanding increasing amounts of irregular tax payments in kind, which it channeled directly to the main consumers—army personnel. Local administration by the councils was careless, recalcitrant, and inefficient. The evident need for firm and purposeful reform had to be squarely faced in the reigns of Diocletian and Constantine.

SOCIETY, RELIGION, AND CULTURE

One of the more noticeable effects of Roman rule was the clearer tendency toward classification and social control of the populace. Thus, despite many years of intermarriage between Greeks and Egyptians, lists drawn up in AD 4/5 established the right of certain families to class themselves as Greek by descent and to claim privileges attaching to their status as members of an urban aristocracy, known as the gymnasial class. Members of this group were entitled to lower rates of poll tax, subsidized or free distributions of food, and maintenance at the public expense when they grew old. If they or their descendants were upwardly mobile, they might gain Alexandrian citizenship, Roman citizenship, or even equestrian status, with correspondingly greater prestige and privileges. The preservation of such distinctions was implicit in the spread of Roman law and was reinforced by elaborate codes of social and fiscal regulations such as the *Rule-Book of the Emperors' Special Account*. The *Rule-Book* prescribed conditions under which people of different status might marry, for instance, or bequeath property and fixed fines, confiscations, and other penalties for transgression. When an edict of the emperor Caracalla conferred Roman citizenship on practically all of the subjects of the empire in AD 212, the distinction between citizens and noncitizens became meaningless. But it was gradually replaced by an equally important distinction between *honestiores* and *humiliores* (meaning, roughly, "upper classes" and "lower classes," respectively), groups that, among other distinctions, were subjected to different penalties in law.

Naturally, it was the Greek-speaking elite that continued to dictate the visibly dominant cultural pattern, though Egyptian culture was not moribund or insignificant. One proof of its continued survival can be seen in its reemergent importance in the context of Coptic Christianity in the Byzantine period. An important reminder of the mixing of the traditions comes from a family of Panopolis in the 4th century, whose members included both teachers of

Greek oratory and priests in Egyptian cult tradition. The towns and villages of the Nile valley have preserved thousands of papyri that show what the literate Greeks were reading (e.g., the poems of Homer and the lyric poets, works of the classical Greek tragedians, and comedies of Menander). The pervasiveness of the Greek literary tradition is strikingly demonstrated by evidence left by an obscure and anonymous clerk at Al-Fayyūm village of Karanis in the 2nd century AD. In copying out a long list of taxpayers, the clerk translated an Egyptian name in the list by an extremely rare Greek word that he could only have known from having read the Alexandrian Hellenistic poet Callimachus. He must have understood the etymology of the Egyptian name as well.

Alexandria continued to develop as a spectacularly beautiful city and to foster Greek culture and intellectual pursuits, though the great days of Ptolemaic court patronage of literary figures had passed. But the flourishing interest in philosophy, particularly Platonic philosophy, had important effects. The great Jewish philosopher and theologian of the 1st century, Philo of Alexandria (Philo Judaeus), brought a training in Greek philosophy to bear on his commentaries on the Old Testament. This anticipates by a hundred years the period after the virtual annihilation of the great Jewish community of Alexandria in the revolt of AD 115–117, when the city was the intellectual crucible in which Christianity developed a theology that took it away from the influence of the Jewish exegetical tradition and toward that of Greek philosophical ideas. There the foundations were laid for teaching the heads of the Christian catechetical school, such as Clement of Alexandria. And in the 3rd century there was the vital textual and theological work of Origen, the greatest of the Christian Neoplatonists, without which there would hardly have been a coherent New Testament tradition at all.

Outside the Greek ambience of Alexandria, traditional Egyptian religious institutions continued to flourish

Philo Judaeus. Library of Congress Prints and Photographs Division

in the towns and villages; but the temples were reduced to financial dependence on a state subvention (*syntaxis*), and they became subject to stringent control by secular bureaucrats. Nevertheless, like the Ptolemies before them, Roman emperors appear in the traditional form as Egyptian kings on temple reliefs until the mid-3rd century. Five professional hieroglyph cutters were still employed at the town of Oxyrhynchus in the 2nd century. The animal cults continued to flourish, despite Augustus's famous sneer that he was accustomed to worship gods, not cattle. As late as the reign of Diocletian (285–305), religious stelae preserved the fiction that in the cults of sacred bulls (best known at Memphis and at Hermonthis [Armant]) the successor of a dead bull was "installed" by the monarch. Differences between cults of the Greek type and the native Egyptian cults were still highly marked, in the temple architecture as in the status of the priests. Priests of Egyptian cults formed, in effect, a caste distinguished by their special clothing, whereas priestly offices in Greek cults were much more like magistracies and tended to be held by local magnates. Cults of Roman emperors, living and dead, became universal after 30 BC, but their impact is most clearly to be seen in the foundations of Caesarea (Temples of Caesar) and in religious institutions of Greek type, where divine emperors were associated with the resident deities.

One development that did have an important effect on this religious amalgam, though it was not decisive until the

4th century, was the arrival of Christianity. The tradition of the foundation of the church of Alexandria by St. Mark cannot be substantiated, but a fragment of a text of the *Gospel According to John* provides concrete evidence of Christianity in the Nile valley in the second quarter of the 2nd century AD. Inasmuch as Christianity remained illegal and subject to persecution until the early 4th century, Christians were reluctant to advertise themselves as such, and it is therefore difficult to know how numerous they were, especially because later pro-Christian sources may often be suspected of exaggerating the zeal and the numbers of the early Christian martyrs. But several papyri survive of the *libelli*—certificates in which people swore that they had performed sacrifices to Greek, Egyptian, or Roman divinities in order to prove that they were not Christians—submitted in the first official state-sponsored persecution of Christians, under the emperor Decius (ruled 249–251). By the 290s, a decade or so before the great persecution under Diocletian, a list of buildings in the sizeable town of Oxyrhynchus, some 125 miles (200 km) south of the apex of the delta, included two Christian churches, probably of the house-chapel type.

EGYPT'S ROLE IN THE BYZANTINE EMPIRE

Diocletian was the last reigning Roman emperor to visit Egypt, in AD 302. Within about 10 years of his visit, the persecution of Christians ceased. The end of

persecution had such far-reaching effects that from this point on it is necessary to think of the history of Egypt in a very different framework. No single point can be identified as the watershed between the Roman and Byzantine period, as the divide between a brighter era of peace, culture, and prosperity and a darker age, supposedly characterized by more-oppressive state machinery in the throes of decline and fall. The crucial changes occurred in the last decade of the 3rd century and the first three decades of the 4th. With the end of persecution of Christians came the restoration of the property of the church. In 313 a new system of calculating and collecting taxes was introduced, with 15-year tax cycles, called indictions, inaugurated retrospectively from the year 312. Many other important administrative changes had already taken place. In 296 the separation of the Egyptian coinage from that of the rest of the empire had come to an end when the Alexandrian mint stopped producing its tetradrachms, which had been the basis of the closed-currency system.

One other event that had an enormous effect on the political history of Egypt was the founding of Constantinople (now Istanbul) on May 11, 330. First, Constantinople was established as an imperial capital and an eastern counterpart to Rome itself, thus undermining Alexandria's traditional position as the first city of the Greek-speaking East. Second, it diverted the resources of Egypt away from Rome and the West. Henceforth, part of the surplus of the

Egyptian grain supply, which was put at 8 million *artabs* (about 300 million litres) of wheat (one *artab* was roughly equivalent to one bushel) in an edict of the emperor Justinian of about 537 or 538, went to feed the growing population of Constantinople. This created an important political and economic link. The cumulative effect of these changes was to knit Egypt more uniformly into the structure of the empire and to give it, once again, a central role in the political history of the Mediterranean world.

The key to understanding the importance of Egypt in that period lies in seeing how the Christian church came rapidly to dominate secular as well as religious institutions, and to acquire a powerful interest and role in every political issue. The corollary of this was that the head of the Egyptian Church, the patriarch of Alexandria, became the most influential figure within Egypt, as well as the person who could give the Egyptian clergy a powerful voice in the councils of the Eastern Church. During the course of the 4th century, Egypt was divided for administrative purposes into a number of smaller units but the patriarchy was not, and its power thus far outweighed that of any local administrative official. Only the governors of groups of provinces (*vicarii* of dioceses) were equivalent and the praetorian prefects and emperors were superior. When a patriarch of Alexandria was given civil authority as well, as happened in the case of Cyrus, the last patriarch under Byzantine rule, the combination was very powerful indeed.

The turbulent history of Egypt in the Byzantine period can largely be understood in terms of the struggles of the successive (or, after 570, coexisting) patriarchs of Alexandria to maintain their position both within their patriarchy and outside it in relation to Constantinople. What linked Egypt and the rest of the Eastern Empire was the way in which the imperial authorities, when strong (as, for instance, in the reign of Justinian), tried to control the Egyptian Church from Constantinople, while at the same time assuring the capital's food supply and, as often as not, waging wars to keep their empire intact. Conversely, when weak, they failed to control the church. For the patriarchs of Alexandria, it proved impossible to secure the approval of the imperial authorities in Constantinople and at the same time maintain the support of their power base in Egypt. The two made quite different demands, and the ultimate result was a social, political, and cultural gulf between Alexandria and the rest of Egypt and between Hellenism and native Egyptian culture, which found a powerful new means of expression in Coptic Christianity. The gulf was made more emphatic after the Council of Chalcedon in 451 established the official doctrine that Christ was to be seen as existing in two natures, inseparably united. The council's decision in effect sent the Egyptian Coptic (now Coptic Orthodox) Church off on its own path of Monophysitism, which centred around a firm insistence on the singularity of the nature of Christ.

Despite the debilitating effect of internal quarrels between rival churchmen, and despite the threats posed by the hostile tribes of Blemmyes and Nubade in the south (until their conversion to Christianity in the mid-6th century), emperors of Byzantium still could be threatened by the strength of Egypt if it were properly harnessed. The last striking example is the case of the emperor Phocas, a tyrant who was brought down in 609 or 610. Nicetas, the general of the future emperor Heraclius, made for Alexandria from Cyrene, intending to use Egypt as his power base and cut off Constantinople's grain supply. By the spring of 610 Nicetas's struggle with Bonosus, the general of Phocas, was won, and the fall of the tyrant duly followed.

The difficulty of defending Egypt from a power base in Constantinople was forcefully illustrated during the last three decades of Byzantine rule. First, the old enemy, the Persians, advanced to the Nile delta and captured Alexandria. Their occupation was completed early in 619 and continued until 628, when Persia and Byzantium agreed to a peace treaty and the Persians withdrew. This had been a decade of violent hostility to the Egyptian Coptic Christians. Among other oppressive measures, the Persians are said to have refused to allow the normal ordination of bishops and to have massacred hundreds of monks in their cave monasteries. The Persian withdrawal hardly heralded the return of peace to Egypt.

In Arabia events were taking place that would soon bring momentous changes for Egypt. These were triggered by the flight of the Prophet Muḥammad from Mecca to Medina and by his declaration in AD 632 of a holy Islamic war against Byzantium. A decade later, by Sept. 29, 642, the Arab general 'Amr ibn al-'Āṣ was able to march into Alexandria, and the Arab conquest of Egypt, which had begun with an invasion three years earlier, ended in peaceful capitulation. The invasion itself had been preceded by several years of vicious persecution of Coptic Christians by Cyrus, the Chalcedonian patriarch of Alexandria, and it was he who is said to have betrayed Egypt to the forces of Islam.

The Islamic conquest was not bloodless. There was desultory fighting at first in the eastern delta, then Al-Fayyūm was lost in battle in 640. A great battle took place at Heliopolis (now a suburb of Cairo) in July 640 in which 15,000 Arabs engaged 20,000 Egyptian defenders. The storming and capture of Trajan's old fortress at Babylon (on the site of the present-day quarter called Old Cairo) on April 6, 641, was crucial. By Sept. 14, Cyrus, who had been recalled from Egypt 10 months earlier by the emperor Heraclius, was back with authority to conclude a peace. Byzantium signed Egypt away on Nov. 8, 641, with provision for an 11-month armistice to allow ratification of the treaty of surrender by the emperor and the caliph. In December 641 heavily laden ships were dispatched to carry Egypt's wealth to its new masters. Nine months later the last remnants of Byzantine forces had left Egypt in ships bound for Cyprus, Rhodes, and Constantinople, and 'Amr ibn al-'Āṣ had taken Alexandria in the name of the caliph. The new domination by the theocratic Islamic caliphate was strikingly different from anything that had happened in Egypt since the arrival of Alexander the Great almost a thousand years earlier.

BYZANTINE GOVERNMENT OF EGYPT

The reforms of the early 4th century had established the basis for another 250 years of comparative prosperity in Egypt, at a cost of perhaps greater rigidity and more-oppressive state control. Egypt was subdivided for administrative purposes into a number of smaller provinces, and separate civil and military officials were established (the *praeses* and the *dux*, respectively). By the middle of the 6th century the emperor Justinian was eventually forced to recognize the failure of this policy and to combine civil and military power in the hands of the *dux* with a civil deputy (the *praeses*) as a counterweight to the power of the church authorities.

All pretense of local autonomy had by then vanished. The presence of the soldiery was more noticeable, its power and influence more pervasive in the routine of town and village life. Taxes were perhaps not heavier than they had been earlier, but they were collected ruthlessly, and strong measures were sanctioned against those who tried to escape from their fiscal or legal obligations. The wealthier landowners probably enjoyed increased prosperity, especially as a result of the opportunity to buy now state-owned land that had once been sold into private ownership in the early 4th century. The great landlords were powerful enough to offer their peasant tenants a significant degree of collective fiscal protection against the agents of the state, the rapacious tax collector, the officious bureaucrat, or the brutal soldier. But, if the life of the average peasant did not change much, nevertheless the rich probably became richer, and the poor became poorer and more numerous as the moderate landholders were increasingly squeezed out of the picture.

THE ADVANCE OF CHRISTIANITY

The advance of Christianity had just as profound an effect on the social and cultural fabric of Byzantine Egypt as on the political power structure. It brought to the surface the identity of the native Egyptians in the Coptic Church, which found a medium of expression in the development of the Coptic language—basically Egyptian written in Greek letters with the addition of a few characters. Coptic Christianity also developed its own distinctive art, much of it pervaded by the long-familiar motifs of Greek mythology. These motifs coexisted with representations of the Virgin and Child and with Christian parables and were expressed in decorative styles that owed a great deal to both Greek and Egyptian precedents.

Although Christianity had made great inroads into the populace by 391 (the year in which the practice of the local polytheistic religions was officially made illegal), it is hardly possible to quantify it or to trace a neat and uniform progression. In the first half of the 5th century a polytheistic literary revival occurred, centred on the town of Panopolis, and there is evidence that fanatical monks in the area attacked non-Christian temples and stole statues and magical texts. Outside the rarefied circles in which doctrinal disputes were discussed in philosophical terms, there was a great heterogeneous mass of commitment and belief. For example, both the Gnostics, who believed in redemption through knowledge, and the Manichaeans, followers of the Persian prophet Mani, clearly thought of themselves as Christians. In the 4th century a Christian community, the library of which was discovered at Naj' Ḥammādī in 1945, was reading both canonical and apocryphal gospels as well as mystical revelatory tracts. At the lower levels of

A Coptic monk against the backdrop of religious artwork on the walls of Egypt's ancient St. Anthony's monastery. Kenneth Garrett/National Geographic/Getty Images

society magical practices remained ubiquitous and were simply transferred to a Christian context.

By the mid-5th century Egypt's landscape was dominated by the great churches, such as the magnificent Church of St. Menas (Abū Mīna), south of Alexandria, and by the monasteries. The latter were Egypt's distinctive contribution to the development of Christianity and were particularly important as strongholds of native loyalty to the Monophysite Church. The origins of Antonian communities, named for the founding father of monasticism, St. Anthony of Egypt (c. 251–356), lay in the desire of individuals to congregate about the person of a celebrated ascetic in a desert location, building their own cells, adding a church and a refectory, and raising towers and walls to enclose the unit. Other monasteries, called Pachomian—for Pachomius, the founder of cenobitic monasticism—were planned from the start as walled complexes with communal facilities. The provision of water cisterns, kitchens, bakeries, oil presses, workshops, stables, and cemeteries and the ownership and cultivation of land in the vicinity made these communities self-sufficient to a high degree, offering their residents peace and protection against the oppression of the tax collector and the brutality of the soldier. But it does not follow that they were divorced from contact with nearby towns and villages. Indeed, many monastics were important local figures, and many monastery churches were probably open to the local public for worship.

The economic and social power of the Christian church in the Nile River valley and delta is the outstanding development of the 5th and 6th centuries. By the time of the Arab invasion, in the mid-7th century, the uncomplicated message of Islam might have seemed attractive and drawn attention to the political and religious rifts that successive and rival patriarchs of the Christian church had so violently created and exploited. But the advent of Arab rule did not suppress Christianity in Egypt. Some areas remained heavily Christian for several more centuries.

CHAPTER 7

EGYPTIAN RELIGION

Over the centuries Egyptian religion contained polytheism, henotheism, pluriform monotheism, trinitary speculations, and even a kind of monotheism. Especially in the time of the New Kingdom (16th–11th century BC) and later, there arose theological speculations about many gods and the one god, involving concepts that belong to the realm of pluriform monotheism. These ideas are especially interesting when related to trinitarian conceptions, as they sometimes are. In a New Kingdom hymn to Amon are the words: "Three are all gods: Amon, Re and Ptah . . . he who hides himself for them [mankind] as Amon, he is Re to be seen, his body is Ptah." As Amon he is the "hidden god" (deus absconditus). In Re, the god of the sun, he becomes visible. As Ptah, one of the gods of the earth, he is immanent (indwelling, an activating spirit) in this world.

NATURE AND SIGNIFICANCE

Egyptian religious beliefs and practices were closely integrated into Egyptian society of the historical period (from c. 3000 BC). Although there were probably many survivals from prehistory, these may be relatively unimportant for understanding later times, because the transformation that established the Egyptian state created a new context for religion.

Religious phenomena were pervasive, so much so that it is not meaningful to view religion as a single entity that cohered as a system. Nevertheless, religion must be seen against a background of potentially nonreligious human activities and values. During its more than 3,000 years of development, Egyptian religion underwent significant changes of emphasis and practice, but in all periods religion had a clear consistency in character and style.

It is inappropriate to define religion narrowly, as consisting only in the cult of the gods and in human piety. Religious behaviour encompassed contact with the dead, practices such as divination and oracles, and magic, which mostly exploited divine instruments and associations.

There were two essential foci of public religion: the king and the gods. Both are among the most characteristic features of Egyptian civilization. The king had a unique status between humanity and the gods, partook in the world of the gods, and constructed great, religiously motivated funerary monuments for his afterlife. Egyptian gods are renowned for their wide variety of forms, including animal forms and mixed forms with an animal head on a human body. The most important deities were the sun god, who had several names and aspects and was associated with many supernatural beings in a solar cycle modeled on the alternation of night and day, and Osiris, the god of the dead and ruler of the underworld. With his consort, Isis, Osiris became dominant in many contexts during the 1st millennium BC, when solar worship was in relative decline.

The Egyptians conceived of the cosmos as including the gods and the present world—whose centre was, of course, Egypt—and as being surrounded by the realm of disorder, from which order had arisen and to which it would finally revert. Disorder had to be kept at bay. The task of the king as the protagonist of human society was to retain the benevolence of the gods in maintaining order against disorder. This ultimately pessimistic view of the cosmos was associated principally with the sun god and the solar cycle. It formed a powerful legitimation of king and elite in their task of preserving order.

Despite this pessimism, the official presentation of the cosmos on the monuments was positive and optimistic, showing the king and the gods in perpetual reciprocity and harmony. This implied contrast reaffirmed the fragile order. The restricted character of the monuments was also fundamental to a system of decorum that defined what could be shown, in what way it could be shown, and in what context. Decorum and the affirmation of order reinforced each other.

These beliefs are known from monuments and documents created by and for the king and the small elite. The beliefs and practices of the rest of the people are poorly known. While there is no reason to believe that there was a radical opposition between the beliefs of the elite and those of others, this possibility cannot be ruled out.

SOURCES AND LIMITATIONS OF ANCIENT AND MODERN KNOWLEDGE

The only extensive contemporaneous descriptions of ancient Egyptian culture from the outside were made by Classical Greek and Roman writers. Their works include many important observations about Egyptian religion, which particularly interested the writers and which until late antiquity was not fundamentally different in type from their own religions. Herodotus (5th century BC) remarked that the Egyptians were the most religious of people, and the comment is apt because popular religious practices proliferated in the 1st millennium BC. Other significant Classical sources include Plutarch's essay on Isis and Osiris (1st century AD), which gives the only known connected narrative of their myth, and the writings of Apuleius (2nd century AD) and others about the Isis cult as it spread in the Greco-Roman world.

In other respects, ancient Egypt has been recovered archaeologically. Excavation and the recording of buildings have produced a great range of material, from large monuments to small objects and texts on perishable papyrus. Egyptian monuments are almost unique in the amount of inscription they bear. Vast numbers of texts and representations with religious content are preserved, especially from the later 2nd and 1st millennia BC. Much of this material is religious or has religious implications. This dominance may be misleading, partly because many monuments were in the desert, where they are well preserved, and partly because the lavishing of great resources on religious monuments for the king and the gods need not mean that people's lives were dominated by religion.

In addition to favouring large monuments and the elite, the archaeological record has other important biases. The formal cults of major deities and the realm of the dead are far better known than everyday religious activities, particularly those occurring in towns and villages, very few of which have been excavated. The absence of material deriving from the religious practice of most people in itself constitutes evidence suggesting both the inequality of society and the possibility, confirmed by other strands of evidence, that many people's religious life did not focus on official cult places and major temples.

Many official works of art present standard conceptions of the divine world and of the king's role in this world and in caring for the gods. Much religious evidence is at the same time artistic, and the production of works of art was a vital prestige concern of king and elite. Religious activities and rituals are less well known than this formalized artistic presentation of religious conceptions. The status of personal religion in the context of official cults is poorly understood.

Official forms were idealizing, and the untoward, which is everywhere an important focus of religion, was excluded almost entirely from them. The world of the monuments is that of Egypt alone, even though the Egyptians had normal, sometimes reciprocal, relations with other peoples. Decorum affected what was shown. Thus, the king was almost always depicted as the person offering to the gods, although temple rituals were performed by priests. Scenes of offering and of the gods conferring benefits on the king may not depict specific rituals, while the equal form in which king and gods are depicted bears no direct relation to real cult actions, which were performed on small cult images kept inside shrines.

An additional limitation is that knowledge of many central concerns was restricted. The king was stated to be alone in knowing aspects of the solar cycle. Knowledge of some religious texts was reserved to initiates, who would benefit from them both in this life and in the next. Magic evoked the power of the exotic and esoteric. Evidence for some restricted material is preserved, but it is not known who had access to it, while in other cases the restricted knowledge is only alluded to and is now inaccessible.

Death and the next world dominate both the archaeological record and popular modern conceptions of Egyptian religion. This dominance is determined to a great extent by the landscape of the country, since tombs were placed if possible in the desert. Vast resources were expended on creating prestigious burial places for absolute rulers or wealthy officials. Tombs contained elaborate grave goods (mostly plundered soon after deposition), representations of "daily life," or less commonly of religious subjects, and some texts that were intended to help the deceased attain the next world and prosper there. The texts came increasingly to be inscribed on coffins and stone sarcophagi or deposited in burials on papyrus. Some royal tombs included long passages from religious texts, many of them drawn from nonmortuary contexts and hence more broadly valuable as source material.

One crucial area where religion extended beyond narrow bounds was in the ethical instructions, which became the principal genre of Egyptian literature. These are known from the Middle Kingdom (c. 1900–1600 BC) to the Roman period (1st century AD). As with other sources, the later texts are more overtly religious, but all show inextricable connections between proper conduct, the order of the world, and the gods.

KING, COSMOS, AND SOCIETY

The king was the centre of human society, the guarantor of order for the gods, the recipient of god-given benefits including life itself, and the benevolent ruler of the world for humanity. He was ultimately responsible for the cults of the dead, both for his predecessors in office and for the dead in general. His dominance in religion corresponded to his central political role. From late predynastic times (c. 3100 BC), state organization was based on kingship and on the service of officials for the king. For humanity, the

Horus offering a libation, bronze statue, 22nd dynasty (c. 800 BC); in the Louvre, Paris. Giraudon/Art Resource, New York

king had a superhuman role, being a manifestation of a god or of various deities on earth.

The king's principal original title, the Horus name, proclaimed that he was an aspect of the chief god Horus, a sky god who was depicted as a falcon. Other identifications were added to this one, notably "Son of Re" (the sun god) and "Perfect God," both introduced in the 4th dynasty (c. 2575–2465 BC), when the great pyramids were constructed. The epithet "Son of Re" placed the king in a close but dependent relation with the leading figure in the pantheon. "Perfect God" (often rendered "Good God") indicated that the king had the status of a minor deity, for which he was "perfected" through accession to his office. It restricted the extent of his divinity and separated him from full deities.

In his intermediate position between humanity and the gods, the king could receive the most extravagant divine adulation and was in some ways more prominent than any single god. In death he aspired to full divinity but could not escape the human context. Although royal funerary monuments differed in type from other tombs and were vastly larger, they too were pillaged and vandalized, and few royal mortuary cults were long-lasting. Some kings, notably Amenhotep III (1390–53 BC), Ramses II (1279–13 BC), and several of the Ptolemies, sought deification during their own lifetime, while others, such as Amenemhet III (1818–c. 1770 BC), became minor gods after their death, but these developments show how restricted royal divinity was. The divinized king coexisted with his mortal self, and as many nonroyal individuals as kings became deified after death.

The gods, the king, humanity, and the dead existed together in the cosmos, which the creator god had brought into being from the preexistent chaos. All living beings, except perhaps the creator, would die at the end of time. The sun god became aged and needed to be rejuvenated and reborn daily. The ordered cosmos was surrounded by and shot through with disorder, which had to be kept at bay. Disorder menaced most strongly at such times of transition as the passage from one year to the next or the death of a king. Thus, the king's role in maintaining order was cosmic and not merely social. His exaction of service from people was necessary to the cosmos.

The concept of *maat* ("order") was fundamental in Egyptian thought. The king's role was to set *maat* in place of *isfet* ("disorder"). *Maat* was crucial in human life and embraced notions of reciprocity, justice, truth, and moderation. *Maat* was personified as a goddess and the creator's daughter and received a cult of her own. In the cult of other deities, the king's offering of *maat* to a deity encapsulated the relationship between humanity, the king, and the gods. As the representative of humanity, he returned to the gods the order that came from them and of which they were themselves part. *Maat* extended into the world of the dead: in the weighing of the heart after death, shown on papyri deposited in burials, the person's heart occupies one side of the scales and a representation of *maat* the other. The meaning of this image is deepened in the accompanying text, which asserts that the deceased behaved correctly on earth and did not overstep the boundaries of order, declaring that he or she did not "know that which is not"—that is, things that were outside the created and ordered world.

This role of *maat* in human life created a continuity between religion, political action, and elite morality. Over the centuries, private religion and morality drew apart from state concerns, paralleling a gradual separation of king and temple. It cannot be known whether religion and morality were as closely integrated for the people as they were for the elite, or even how fully the elite subscribed to these beliefs. Nonetheless, the integration of cosmos, king, and *maat* remained fundamental.

THE GODS

Egyptian religion was polytheistic. The gods who inhabited the bounded and ultimately perishable cosmos varied in nature and capacity. The word *netjer* ("god") described a much wider range of beings than the deities of monotheistic religions, including what might be termed demons. As is almost necessary in polytheism, gods were neither all-powerful nor all-knowing. Their power was immeasurably greater than that of human beings, and they had the ability to live almost indefinitely, to survive fatal wounds, to be in more than one place at once, to affect people in visible and invisible ways, and so forth.

Most gods were generally benevolent, but their favour could not be counted on, and they had to be propitiated and encouraged to inhabit their cult images so that they could receive the cult and further the reciprocity of divine and human. Some deities, notably such goddesses as Neith, Sekhmet, and Mut, had strongly ambivalent characters. The god Seth embodied the disordered aspects of the ordered world, and in the 1st millennium BC he came to be seen as an enemy who had to be eliminated (but would remain present).

The characters of the gods were not neatly defined. Most had a principal association, such as that of Re with the sun or that of the goddess Hathor with women, but there was much overlap, especially among the leading deities. In general, the more closely circumscribed a deity's character, the less powerful that deity was. All the main gods acquired the characteristics of creator gods. A single figure could have many names; among those of the sun god, the most important were Khepri (the morning form), Re-Harakhty (a form of Re associated with Horus), and Atum (the old, evening form). There were three principal "social" categories of deity: gods, goddesses, and youthful deities, mostly male.

Gods had regional associations, corresponding to their chief cult places. The sun god's cult place was Heliopolis, Ptah's

Mut, wearing the double crown and vulture's head on forehead, bronze statuette, c. 650–350 BC. Courtesy of the Oriental Institute, the University of Chicago

was Memphis, and Amon's was Thebes. These were not necessarily their original cult places. The principal cult of Khnum, the creator god who formed people from clay like a potter, was Elephantine, and he was the lord of the nearby First Cataract.

Thoth, represented in human form with ibis head, detail from the Greenfield Papyrus, c. 950 BC; in the British Museum, London. Copyright British Museum

His cult is not attested there before the New Kingdom, however, even though he was important from the 1st dynasty (c. 2925–2775 BC). The main earlier sanctuary there belonged to the goddess Satet, who became Khnum's companion. Similarly, Mut, the partner of Amon at Thebes, seems to have originated elsewhere.

Deities had principal manifestations, and most were associated with one or more species of animal. For gods the most important forms were the falcon and bull, and for goddesses the cow, cobra, vulture, and lioness. Rams were widespread, while some manifestations were as modest as the millipede of the god Sepa. Some gods were very strongly linked to particular animals, as Sebek was with the crocodile and Khepri with the scarab beetle. Thoth had two animals, the ibis and the baboon. Some animal cults were only partly integrated with specific gods, notably the Ram of Mendes in the Delta and the Apis and Mnevis bulls at Memphis and Heliopolis, respectively. Animals could express aspects of a deity's nature: some goddesses were lionesses in their fiercer aspect but were cats when mild.

These variable forms relate to aspects of the person that were common to gods and people. The most significant of these were the *ka*, which was the vital essence of a person that was transmitted from one generation to the next, the *ba*, which granted freedom of movement and the ability to take on different forms, principally in the next world, and the *akh*, the transfigured spirit of a person in the next world.

The chief form in which gods were represented was human, and many deities had only human form. Among these deities were very ancient figures such as the fertility god Min and the creator and craftsman Ptah. The cosmic gods Shu, of the air and sky, and Geb, of the earth, had human form, as did Osiris, Isis, and Nephthys, deities who provided a model of human society. In temple reliefs the gods were depicted in human form, which was central to decorum. Gods having animal manifestations were therefore shown with a human body and the head of their animal. The opposite convention, a human head and an animal body, was used for the king, who was shown as a sphinx with a lion's body. Sphinxes could receive other heads, notably those of rams and falcons, associating the form with Amon and Re-Harakhty. Demons were represented in more extravagant forms and combinations. These became common in the 1st millennium BC. Together with the cult of animals, they were mocked by Greek and Roman writers.

Apart from major deities—gods who received a cult or had a significant cosmic role—there were important minor figures. Several of these marginal beings had grotesque forms and variable names. The most prominent were Bes, a helpful figure with dwarf form and a masklike face, associated especially with women and children, and Taurt, a goddess with similar associations whose physical form combined features of a hippopotamus and a crocodile. Among demons, the most important figure was Apopis, shown as a colossal snake, who was the enemy of the sun god in his daily cycle through the cosmos. Apopis existed outside the ordered realm. He had to be defeated daily, but, since he did not belong to the sphere of existence, he could not be destroyed.

GROUPINGS OF DEITIES

The number of deities was large and was not fixed. New ones appeared, and some ceased to be worshipped. Deities were grouped in various ways. The most ancient known grouping is the ennead, which is probably attested from the 3rd dynasty (c. 2650–2575 BC). Enneads were groups of nine deities, nine being the "plural" of three (in Egypt the number three symbolized plurality in general); not all enneads consisted of nine gods.

The principal ennead was the Great Ennead of Heliopolis. This was headed by the sun god and creator Re or Re-Atum, followed by Shu and Tefnut, deities of air and moisture; Geb and Nut, who represented earth and sky; and Osiris, Isis, Seth, and Nephthys. This ordering incorporated a myth of creation, to which was joined the myth of Osiris, whose deeds and attributes ranged from the founding of civilization to kinship, kingship, and succession to office. The ennead excluded the successor figure, Horus, son of Osiris, who is essential to the meaning of the myth. Thus, the ennead has the appearance of a grouping that brought together existing religious conceptions but was rather arbitrary and inflexible, perhaps because of the significance of the number nine.

Other numerical ordering schemas included the Ogdoad (group of eight gods) of Hermopolis, which embodied the inchoate world before creation and consisted of four pairs of male and female deities with abstract names such as Darkness, Absence, and Endlessness. Here too the number was significant in itself, because at least six different pairs of names are known although eight deities are listed in any occurrence. The major god Amon, whose name can mean "He who is hidden," was often one of the ogdoad with his female counterpart, Amaunet.

The most common grouping, principally in the New Kingdom and later, was the triad. The archetypal triad of Osiris, Isis, and Horus exhibits the normal pattern of a god and a goddess with a youthful deity, usually male. Most local centres came to have triads, the second

King Seti I offering a figure of maat *to Osiris, Isis, and Horus; relief in the temple of King Seti I, Abydos, early 13th century* BC. Courtesy of the Egypt Exploration Society; photograph, The Oriental Institute, Chicago

and third members of which might be devised for the sake of form. Thus, one triad worshipped in the Greco-Roman-period temple at Kawm Umbū (Kôm Ombo) consisted of Haroeris (the "elder Horus"), the goddess Tsenetnofret ("the perfect companion"), and the youthful god Pnebtawy ("the lord of the two lands"). The last name, which is an epithet of kings, is revealing, because youthful gods had many attributes of kings. As this case indicates, triads resemble a minimal nuclear family, but deities were rarely spouses. The notion of plurality and the bringing together of the essential types of deity may have been as important to the triads as the family analogy.

Another important ordering of deities was syncretism, a term with a special meaning for Egyptian religion. Two or more names of gods were often combined to form a composite identity. Many combinations included the name of Re. Prominent examples are Amon-Re, a fusion of Amon and Re, and Osiris-Apis, a fusion of Osiris with the Apis Bull. Although composite forms such as Amon-Re became the principal identities of some gods, the separate deities continued to exist and sometimes, as in the case of Re, to receive a cult. In part, these syncretisms expressed the idea of Amon in his aspect as Re. They were thus analogous to the multiple manifestations of individual deities. Through syncretism many major deities came to resemble one another more closely.

MYTH

Myths are poorly known. Religious discourse was recorded in hymns, rituals, temple scenes, and specialized texts but rarely in narrative, which only slowly became a common written genre and never had the highest literary prestige. In addition, much religious activity focused on constant reiteration or repetition rather than on development. A central example of this tendency is the presentation of the cycle of the sun god through the sky and the underworld, which was an analogy for the creation, maturity, decay, and regeneration of an individual life and of the cosmos. This is strikingly presented in the underworld books. These pictorial and textual compositions, which probably imparted secret knowledge, were inscribed in the tombs of New Kingdom kings. They describe the solar cycle in great detail, including hundreds of names of demons and of deities and other beings who accompanied the sun god in his barque on his journey through night and day. The texts are in the present tense and form a description and a series of tableaux rather than a narrative.

The fact that mythical narratives are rare does not imply that myths or narratives did not exist. There is reason to think that some myths underlay features of enneads and therefore had originated by the Early Dynastic period (c. 3000 BC). Mythical narratives preserved from the New Kingdom and later include episodes of the rule of the sun god on earth, tales of the childhood of Horus in the delta marshes, and stories with themes similar to the Osiris myth but with differently named protagonists. The rule of the sun god was followed by his withdrawal into the sky, leaving people on earth. The withdrawal was motivated by his age and by the lack of tranquility in the world. One narrative recounts how Isis obtained a magical substance from Re's senile dribbling and fashioned from it a snake that bit him. To make her still the agony of the snakebite, he finally revealed to her the secret of his "true" name. A myth with varied realizations recounts how Re grew weary of humanity's recalcitrance and dispatched his daughter or "Eye" to destroy them. Regretting his action later, he arranged to have the bloodthirsty goddess tricked into drunkenness by spreading beer tinted the colour of blood over the land. This myth provides an explanation for the world's imperfection and the inaccessibility of the gods. In Greco-Roman times it was widespread in Lower Nubia, where it seems to have been related to the winter retreat of the sun to the Southern Hemisphere and its return in the spring.

THE CULT

Most cults centred on the daily tending and worship of an image of a deity and were analogous to the pattern of human life. The shrine containing the image was opened at dawn, and then the deity was purified, greeted and praised, clothed,

and fed. There were several further services, and the image was finally returned to its shrine for the night. Apart from this activity, which took place within the temple and was performed by a small group of priests, there were numerous festivals at which the shrine and image were taken out from the sanctuary on a portable barque, becoming visible to the people and often visiting other temples. Thus, the daily cult was a state concern, whose function was to maintain reciprocity between the human and the divine, largely in isolation from the people. This reciprocity was fundamental because deities and humanity together sustained the cosmos. If the gods were not satisfied, they might cease to inhabit their images and retreat to their other abode, the sky. Temples were constructed as microcosms whose purity and wholeness symbolized the proper order of the larger world outside.

The priesthood became increasingly important. In early periods there seem to have been no full-time professional priests. People could hold part-time high priestly offices, or they could have humbler positions on a rotating basis, performing duties for one month in four. The chief officiant may have been a professional. While performing their duties, priests submitted to rules of purity and abstinence. One result of this system was that more people were involved in the cult and had access to the temple than would have been the case if there had been a permanent staff. Although most priestly positions were for men, women were involved in the cult of the goddess Hathor, and in the New Kingdom and later many women held the title of "chantress" of a deity (perhaps often a courtesy title). They were principally involved in musical cult performances.

Festivals allowed more-direct interaction between people and the gods. Questions were often asked of a deity, and a response might be given by a forward or backward movement of the barque carried on the priests' shoulders. Oracles, of which this was one form, were invoked by the king to obtain sanction for his plans, including military campaigns abroad and important appointments. Although evidence is sparse, consultation with deities may have been part of religious interaction in all periods and for all levels of society.

Apart from this interaction between deities and individual people or groups, festivals were times of communal celebration, and often of the public reenactment of myths such as the death and vindication of Osiris at Abydos or the defeat of Seth by Horus at Idfū. They had both a personal and a general social role in the spectrum of religious practice.

Nonetheless, the main audience for the most important festivals of the principal gods of state held in capital cities may have been the ruling elite rather than the people as a whole. In the New Kingdom these cities were remodeled as vast cosmic stages for the enactment of royal-divine relations and rituals.

PIETY, PRACTICAL RELIGION, AND MAGIC

Despite the importance of temples and their architectural dominance, the evidence for cult does not point to mass participation in temple religion. The archaeological material may be misleading, because in addition to major temples there were many local sanctuaries that may have responded more directly to the concerns and needs of those who lived around them. From some periods numerous votive offerings are preserved from a few temples. Among these are Early Dynastic and Old Kingdom provincial temples, but the fullest evidence is from New Kingdom temples of Hathor at Thebes and several frontier sites and from the Late and Ptolemaic periods (664–30 BC).

Although votive offerings show that significant numbers of people took gifts to temples, it is difficult to gauge the social status of donors, whose intentions are seldom indicated, probably in part for reasons of decorum. Two likely motives are disinterested pious donation for the deity and offering in the hope of obtaining a specific benefit. Many New Kingdom offerings to Hathor relate to human fertility and thus belong to the second of these categories. Late period bronze statuettes are often inscribed with a formula requesting that the deity represented should "give life" to the donor, without stating a specific need. These may be more generally pious donations, among which can also be counted non-royal dedications of small parcels of land to temples. These donations are recorded on stelae from the New Kingdom onward. They parallel the massive royal endowments to temples of land and other resources, which resulted in their becoming very powerful economic and political institutions.

Apart from the donation of offerings to conventional cult temples, there was a vast Late period expansion in animal cults. These might be more or less closely related to major deities. They involved a variety of practices centring on the mummification and burial of animals. The principal bull cults, which gave important oracles, focused on a single animal kept in a special shrine. The burial of an Apis bull was a major occasion involving vast expenditure. Some animals, such as the sacred ibis (connected with Thoth), were kept, and buried, in millions. The dedication of a burial seems to have counted as a pious act. The best-known area for these cults and associated practices is the necropolis of northern Ṣaqqārah, which served the city of Memphis. Numerous species were buried there, and people visited the area to consult oracles and to spend the night in a temple area and receive healing dreams. A few people resided permanently in the animal necropolis in a state akin to monastic seclusion.

There are two further important groups of evidence for pious and reciprocal relations between people and gods.

One is proper names of all periods, the majority of which are meaningful utterances with religious content. For example, names state that deities "show favour" to or "love" a child or its parents. From the end of the New Kingdom (c. 1100 BC), names commonly refer to consultation of oracles during pregnancy, alluding to a different mode of human-divine relations. The second source is a group of late New Kingdom inscriptions recounting episodes of affliction that led to people's perceiving that they had wronged a god. These texts, which provide evidence of direct pious relations, are often thought to show a transformation of religious attitudes in that period, but allusions to similar relations in Middle Kingdom texts suggest that the change was as much in what was written down as in basic attitudes.

Piety was one of many modes of religious action and relations. Much of religion concerned attempts to comprehend and respond to the unpredictable and the unfortunate. The activities involved often took place away from temples and are little known. In later periods, there was an increasing concentration of religious practice around temples; for earlier times evidence is sparse. The essential questions people asked, as in many religious traditions, were why something had happened and why it had happened to them, what would be an appropriate response, what agency they should turn to, and what might happen in the future. To obtain answers to these

Book of the Dead

The ancient Egyptian collection of mortuary texts made up of spells or magic formulas is known as the Book of the Dead. It was placed in tombs and believed to protect and aid the deceased in the hereafter. Probably compiled and reedited during the 16th century BC, the collection included Coffin Texts dating from c. 2000 BC, Pyramid Texts dating from c. 2400 BC, and other writings. Later compilations included hymns to Re, the sun god. Numerous authors, compilers, and sources contributed to the work. Scribes copied the texts on rolls of papyrus, often colourfully illustrated, and sold them to individuals for burial use. Many copies of the book have been found in Egyptian tombs, but none contains all of the approximately 200 known chapters. The collection, literally titled "The Chapters of Coming-Forth-by-Day," received its present name from Karl Richard Lepsius, the German Egyptologist who published the first collection of the texts in 1842.

questions, people turned to oracles and to other forms of divination, such as consulting seers or calendars of lucky and unlucky days. From the New Kingdom and later, questions to oracles are preserved, often on such mundane matters as whether someone should cultivate a particular field in a given year. These cannot have been presented only at festivals, and priests must have addressed oracular questions to gods within their sanctuaries. Oracles of gods also played an important part in dispute settlement and litigation in some communities.

A vital focus of questioning was the world of the dead. The recently deceased might exert influence on the living for good or for bad. Offerings to the dead, which were required by custom, were intended, among other purposes, to make them well disposed. People occasionally deposited with their offerings a letter telling the deceased of their problems and asking for assistance. A few of these letters are complaints to the deceased person, alleging that he or she is afflicting the writer. This written communication with the dead was confined to the very few literate members of the population, but it was probably part of a more widespread oral practice. Some tombs of prominent people acquired minor cults that may have originated in frequent successful recourse to them for assistance.

Offerings to the dead generally did not continue long after burial, and most tombs were robbed within a generation or so. Thus, relations with dead kin probably focused on the recently deceased. Nonetheless, the dead were respected and feared more widely. The attitudes attested are almost uniformly negative. The dead were held accountable for much misfortune, both on a local and domestic level and in the broader context of the state. People were also concerned that, when they died, those in the next world would oppose their entry to it as newcomers who might oust the less recently dead. These attitudes show that, among many possible modes of existence after death, an important conception was one in which the dead remained near the living and could return and disturb them. Such beliefs are rare in the official mortuary literature.

A prominent aspect of practical religion was magic. There is no meaningful distinction between Egyptian religion and magic. Magic was a force present in the world from the beginning of creation and was personified as the god Heka, who received a cult in some regions. Magic could be invoked by using appropriate means and was generally positive, being valuable for counteracting misfortune and in seeking to achieve ends for which unseen help was necessary. Magic also formed part of the official cult. It could, however, be used for antisocial purposes as well as benign ones. There is a vast range of evidence for magical practice, from amulets to elaborate texts. Much magic from the Greco-Roman period mixed Egyptian and foreign materials and invoked new and exotic beings. Preserved magical texts record elite magic rather than general practice. Prominent among magical practitioners, both in folklore and, probably, in real life, were "lector priests," the officiants in temple cults who had privileged access to written texts. Most of the vast corpus of funerary texts was magical in character.

THE WORLD OF THE DEAD

The majority of evidence from ancient Egypt comes from funerary monuments and burials of royalty, of the elite, and, for the Late period, of animals. Relatively little is known of the mortuary practices of the mass of the population. Reasons for this dominance of the tomb include both the desert location of burials and the use of mortuary structures for display among the living. Alongside the fear of the dead, there was a moral community between the living and the dead, so that the dead were an essential part of society, especially in the 3rd and 2nd millennia BC.

The basic purpose of mortuary preparation was to ensure a safe and successful passage into the hereafter. Belief in an afterlife and a passage to it is evident in predynastic burials, which are oriented to the west, the domain of the dead, and which include pottery grave goods as well as personal possessions of the deceased. The most striking development of later mortuary practice was mummification, which was related to a belief that the body must continue intact for the deceased to live in the next world. Mummification evolved gradually from the Old Kingdom to the early 1st millennium BC, after which it declined. It was too elaborate and costly ever to be available to the majority.

Mummy and mummy case of a Tanite princess, 21st dynasty (1075–c. 950 BC); in the British Museum, London. © Photos.com/Jupiterimages

This decline of mortuary practice was part of the more general shift in the focus of religious life toward the temples and toward more communal forms. It has been suggested tentatively that belief in the afterlife became less strong in the 1st millennium BC. Whether or not this is true, it is clear that in various periods some people voiced skepticism about the existence of a blessed afterlife and the necessity for mortuary provision, but the provision nevertheless continued to the end.

It was thought that the next world might be located in the area around the tomb (and consequently near the living); on the "perfect ways of the West," as it is expressed in Old Kingdom invocations; among the stars or in the celestial regions with the sun god; or in the underworld, the domain of Osiris. One prominent notion was that of the "Elysian Fields," where the deceased could enjoy an ideal agricultural existence in a marshy land of plenty. The journey to the next world was fraught with obstacles. It could be imagined as a passage by ferry past a succession of portals, or through an "Island of Fire." One crucial test was the judgment after death, a subject often depicted from the New Kingdom onward. The date of origin of this belief is uncertain, but it was probably no later than the late Old Kingdom. The related text, Chapter 125 of the Book of the Dead, responded magically to the dangers of the judgment, which assessed the deceased's conformity with *maat*. Those who failed the judgment would "die a second time" and would be cast outside the ordered cosmos. In the demotic story of Setna (3rd century BC), this notion of moral retribution acquired overtones similar to those of the Christian judgment after death.

INFLUENCE ON OTHER RELIGIONS

Egyptian culture, of which religion was an integral part, was influential in Nubia as early as predynastic times and in Syria in the 3rd millennium BC. During the New Kingdom, Egypt was very receptive to cults from the Middle East, while Egyptian medical and magical expertise was highly regarded among the Hittites, Assyrians, and Babylonians. The chief periods of Egyptian influence were, however, the 1st millennium BC and the Roman period. Egypt was an important centre of the Jewish diaspora starting in the 6th century BC, and Egyptian literature influenced the Hebrew Bible. With Greek rule there was significant cultural interchange between Egyptians and Greeks. Notable among Egyptian cults that spread abroad were those of Isis, which reached much of the Roman world as a mystery religion, and of Serapis, a god whose name probably derives from Osiris-Apis, who was worshipped widely in a non-Egyptian iconography and cultural milieu. With Isis went Osiris and Horus the child, but Isis was the dominant figure. Many Egyptian monuments were imported to Rome to provide a setting for the principal Isis temple in the 1st century AD.

MUMMIFICATION

The process of mummification varied from age to age in Egypt, but it always involved removing the internal organs (though in a late period they were replaced after treatment), treating the body with resin, and wrapping it in linen bandages. Among the many other peoples who practiced mummification were the people living along the Torres Strait, between Papua New Guinea and Australia, and the Incas of South America.

There was a widespread belief that Egyptian mummies were prepared with bitumen (the word comes from the Arabic mūmiyah, "bitumen"), which was supposed to have medicinal value. Throughout the Middle Ages, a substance called "mummy," made by pounding mummified bodies, was a standard product of apothecary shops. In course of time it was forgotten that the virtue of mummy lay in the bitumen, and spurious mummy was made from the bodies of felons and suicides. The traffic in mummy continued in Europe until the 18th century.

The cult of Isis was probably influential on another level. The myth of Osiris shows some analogies with the Gospel story and, in the figure of Isis, with the role of the Virgin Mary. The iconography of the Virgin and Child has evident affinities with that of Isis and the infant Horus. Thus, one aspect of Egyptian religion may have contributed to the background of early Christianity, probably through the cultural centre of Alexandria. Egypt also was an influential setting for other religious and philosophical developments of late antiquity such as Gnosticism, Manichaeism, Hermetism, and Neoplatonism, some of which show traces of traditional Egyptian beliefs. Some of these religions became important in the intellectual culture of the Renaissance. Finally, Christian monasticism seems to have originated in Egypt and could look back to a range of native practices, among which were seclusion in temple precincts and the celibacy of certain priestesses. Within Egypt, there are many survivals from earlier times in popular Christianity and Islam.

CHAPTER 8

EGYPTIAN LANGUAGE AND WRITING

Egyptian is an extinct language of the Nile valley. It constitutes a branch of the Afro-Asiatic language phylum. The Semitic, Cushitic, Chadic, Omotic, and Amazigh (Berber) language groups constitute the remaining members of Afro-Asiatic languages. The writing system was both logographic and phonetic.

EGYPTIAN LANGUAGE

On the basis of ancient texts, scholars generally divide the history of Egyptian language into five periods: Old Egyptian (from before 3000 to about 2200 BC), Middle Egyptian (*c.* 2200–*c.* 1600 BC), Late Egyptian (*c.* 1550–*c.* 700 BC), Demotic (*c.* 700 BC–*c.* AD 400), and Coptic (*c.* 2nd century AD until at least the 17th century). Thus, five literary dialects are differentiated. These language periods refer to the written language only, which often differed greatly from the spoken dialects. Coptic is still in ecclesiastical use (along with Arabic) among the Arabic-speaking Monophysite Christians of Egypt.

Word formation in Egyptian is similar to the "root and pattern" system found across the Afro-Asiatic language phylum. In such systems, consonantal "roots" that indicate the general meaning of a word join with vocalic "patterns" that create more specific meaning. An example in English would be the difference between the words *wake* and *woke*, in which the root *wk* provides a basic notion of "being awake" and combines with the patterns -*a-e* and -*o-e* to create verbs of a particular tense. In ancient Egyptian texts, roots were predominantly composed of three consonants, and vowels were omitted.

Of the original Afro-Asiatic verb system, only the stative (that is, those verbs that express a state or condition) survived. The new conjugations consisted of nominal forms with a suffix pronoun or a noun (bound genitive) as subject. Suffixes indicated tense and voice. Later these conjugations were replaced by adverbial predicates (e.g., preposition plus infinitive).

Stem modifications were limited. An *s-* causative stem corresponds to the Semitic causatives, but it was no longer productive by Late Egyptian. The pronouns are close to those of Semitic. Some nouns of place or instrument were formed with the prefix *m-*. The masculine singular noun had no ending or was *-aw*, feminine singular *-at*, masculine plural *-āw*, and feminine plural *-āwāt*.

Syntax was governed by a rigid word order, with modifiers occurring in second position. Genitival constructions are of two types in all phases of Egyptian: noun with reduced stress bound to the possessor or noun plus the genitival adjective *n(y)* 'of' followed by the possessor.

EGYPTIAN WRITING

Logographic signs represent words, and phonetic signs represent one to three consonants (vowels not being of concern). Phonetic signs are used without regard for their original meaning. Thus, because the logograph for 'house' also signifies the sound *pr*, it is used to write the word *prn* 'to go out.' Because vowels are not represented in writing, the logograph for *prn* is differentiated from that for *pr* 'house' by the addition of the sign 'walking legs.' This type of addition is known as a "semantic determinative" because it indicates the part of speech (and thus the meaning) of the word in question.

HIEROGLYPHIC WRITING

Hieroglyphic writing employs characters in the form of pictures. These individual signs, called hieroglyphs, may be read either as pictures, as symbols for pictures, or as symbols for sounds.

The name *hieroglyphic* (from the Greek word for "sacred carving") is first encountered in the writings of Diodorus Siculus (1st century BC). Earlier, other Greeks had spoken of sacred signs when referring to Egyptian writing. Among the Egyptian scripts, the Greeks labeled as hieroglyphic the script that they found on temple walls and public monuments, in which the characters were pictures sculpted in stone. It was the Greeks who distinguished this script from hieratic, which was still employed during the time of the ancient Greeks for religious texts, and the demotic, the cursive script used for ordinary documents.

Hieroglyphic, in the strict meaning of the word, designates only the writing on Egyptian monuments. The word has,

COPTIC LANGUAGE

The Coptic language, which was spoken in Egypt from about the 2nd century AD, represents the final stage of the ancient Egyptian language. In contrast to earlier stages of Egyptian, which used hieroglyphic writing, hieratic script, or demotic script, Coptic was written in the Greek alphabet, supplemented by seven letters borrowed from demotic writing. Coptic also replaced the religious terms and expressions of earlier Egyptian with words borrowed from Greek.

Coptic is usually divided by scholars into six dialects, four of which were spoken in Upper Egypt and two in Lower Egypt. These differ from one another chiefly in their sound systems. The Fayyūmic dialect of Upper Egypt, spoken along the Nile River valley chiefly on the west bank, survived until the 8th century. Asyūṭic, or Sub-Akhmīmic, spoken around Asyūṭ, flourished in the 4th century. In it are preserved a text of the Gospel According to John and of the Acts of the Apostles, as well as a number of Gnostic documents. Akhmīmic was spoken in and around the Upper Egyptian city of Akhmīm. Sahidic (from Arabic, aṣ-Ṣaʿīd [Upper Egypt]) was originally the dialect spoken around Thebes. After the 5th century it was the standard Coptic of all of Upper Egypt. It is one of the best-documented and well-known dialects.

The dialects of Lower Egypt were Bashmūric, about which little is known (only a few glosses in the dialect are extant), and Bohairic (from Arabic, al-Buḥayrah), originally spoken in the western part of Lower Egypt including the cities of Alexandria and Memphis. Bohairic has been used for religious purposes since the 11th century by all Coptic Christians. The latest Coptic texts date from the 14th century.

however, been applied since the late 19th century to the writing of other peoples, insofar as it consists of picture signs used as writing characters. For example, the name *hieroglyphics* is always used to designate the monumental inscriptions of the Indus civilization and of the Hittites, who also possessed other scripts, in addition to the Mayan, the Incan, and Easter Island writing forms and also the signs on the Phaistos Disk on Crete.

Because of their pictorial form, hieroglyphs were difficult to write and were used only for monument inscriptions. They were usually supplemented in the writing of a people by other, more convenient scripts. Among living writing systems, hieroglyphic scripts are no longer used.

DEVELOPMENT OF EGYPTIAN HIEROGLYPHIC WRITING

The most ancient hieroglyphs date from the end of the 4th millennium BC and comprise annotations incised onto pottery jars and ivory plaques deposited in tombs, presumably for the purpose of identification of the dead. Although by no means can all of these earliest signs be read today, it is nonetheless probable that these forms are based on the same

Hieroglyphics adorning a temple wall. Primarily meant to describe sacred writings on monuments, the term "hieroglyphics" has become synonymous with any language system that uses pictures and symbols. Eliot Elisofon/Time & Life Pictures/Getty Images

system as the later classical hieroglyphs. In individual cases, it can be said with certainty that it is not the copied object that is designated but rather another word phonetically similar to it. This circumstance means that hieroglyphs were from the very beginning phonetic symbols. An earlier stage consisting exclusively of picture writing using actual illustrations of the intended words cannot be shown to have existed in Egypt. Indeed, such a stage can with great probability be ruled out. No development from pictures to letters took place. Hieroglyphic writing was never solely a system of picture writing. It can also be said with certainty that the jar marks (signs on the bottom of clay vessels) that occur at roughly the same period do not represent a primitive form of the script. Rather, these designs developed in parallel fashion to hieroglyphic writing and were influenced by it.

It is not possible to prove the connection of hieroglyphs to the cuneiform characters used by the Sumerians in southern Mesopotamia. Such a relationship is improbable because the two scripts are based on entirely different systems. What is conceivable is a general tendency toward words being fixed by the use of signs, without transmission of particular systems.

INVENTION AND USES OF HIEROGLYPHIC WRITING

The need to identify a pictorial representation with a royal individual or a specific, unique event, such as a hunt or a particular battle, led to the application of hieroglyphic writing to a monumental context. Hieroglyphs added to a scene signified that this illustration represented a particular war rather than an unspecified one or war in general. The writing reflected a new attitude toward time and a view of history as unique events in time. Beginning in the 1st dynasty (c. 2925–c. 2775 BC), images of nonroyal persons were also annotated with their names or titles, a further step toward expressing individuality and uniqueness. The so-called annalistic ivory tablets of the first two dynasties were pictorial representations of the events of a year with specifically designated personal names, places, and incidents. For example, accompanying a scene of the pharaoh's triumph over his enemies is the annotation "the first occasion of the defeat of the Libyans." Simultaneously, the writing of the Egyptians began to appear unaccompanied by pictorial representations, especially on cylinder seals. These roller-shaped incised stones were rolled over the moist clay of jar stoppers. Their inscription prevented the sealed jar from being covertly opened and at the same time described its contents and designated the official responsible for it. In the case of wine, its origin from a specific vineyard and often also the destination of the shipment were designated, and, as a rule, so was the name of the reigning king.

From the stone inscriptions of the 1st dynasty, only individual names are known, these being mainly the names of kings. In the 2nd dynasty, titles and names of offerings appear, and, at the end of this dynasty, sentences occur for the first time. The discovery of a blank papyrus scroll in the grave of a high official, however, shows that longer texts could have been written much earlier—i.e., since the early part of the 1st dynasty.

RELATIONSHIP OF WRITING AND ART

The form of these hieroglyphs of the Archaic period (the 1st to 2nd dynasty) corresponds exactly to the art style of this age. Although definite traditions or conventions were quickly formed with respect to the choice of perspective—e.g., a hand was depicted only as a palm, an eye or a mouth inscribed only in front view—the proportions remained flexible. The prerequisite of every writing system is a basic standardization, but such a standardization is not equivalent to a canon (an established body of rules and principles) in the degree of stylistic conformity that it requires. A recognized canon of Egyptian hieroglyphic writing arose in the 3rd dynasty and was maintained until the end of the use of the script.

In that hieroglyphic signs represented pictures of living beings or inanimate objects, they retained a close connection to the fine arts. The same models formed the basis of both writing and art, and the style of the writing symbols usually changed with the art style. This correspondence occurred above all because the same craftsmen painted or incised both the writing symbols and the pictures. Deviations from the fine arts occurred when the writing, which was more closely bound to convention, retained patterns that the fine arts had eliminated. The face in front view is an example of this. This representation, apart from very special instances, was eventually rejected as an artistic form, the human face being shown only in profile. The front view of the face was, however, retained as a hieroglyph from the Archaic period to the end of the use of hieroglyphic writing. Similar cases involve the depiction of various tools and implements. Although some of the objects themselves fell out of use in the course of history—e.g., the general use of clubs as weapons—their representations, mainly misunderstood, were preserved in the hieroglyphic script. The hieroglyphs corresponding to objects that had disappeared from daily life were therefore no longer well known and were occasionally distorted beyond recognition. But the style of representation in the hieroglyphs still remained closely bound to the art of the respective epoch. Thus, there appeared taut, slender hieroglyphic forms or sensuous, fleshy ones or even completely bloated characters, according to the art style of the period.

MEDIA FOR HIEROGLYPHIC WRITING

In historical times (2800 BC–AD 300), hieroglyphic writing was used for inscribing stone monuments and appears in Egyptian relief techniques, both high relief and bas-relief; in painted form; on metal, sometimes in cast form and sometimes incised; and on wood. In addition, hieroglyphs appear in the most varied kinds of metal and wood inlay work. All these applications correspond exactly with the techniques used in fine art.

Hieroglyphic texts are found primarily on the walls of temples and tombs, but they also appear on memorials and gravestones, on statues, on coffins, and on all sorts of vessels and implements. Hieroglyphic writing was used as much for secular texts—historical inscriptions, songs, legal documents, scientific documents—as for religious subject matter—cult rituals, myths, hymns, grave inscriptions of all kinds, and prayers. These inscriptions were, of course, only a decorative monumental writing, unsuitable for everyday purposes. For popular use, hieratic script was developed, an abbreviated form of the picture symbols such as would naturally develop in writing with brush and ink on smooth surfaces such as papyrus, wood, and limestone.

WRITING AND RELIGION

The influence of religious concepts upon hieroglyphic writing is attested in at least two common usages. First, in the 3rd millennium, certain signs were avoided or were used in garbled form in grave inscriptions for fear that the living beings represented by these signs could harm the deceased who lay helpless in the grave. Among these taboo symbols were human figures and dangerous animals, such as scorpions and snakes. Second, in all periods and for all uses of the writing, symbols to which a positive religious significance was attached were regularly placed in front of other signs, even if they were to be read after them. Among these were hieroglyphs for God or individual gods as well as those for the king or the palace. Thus, for example, the two signs,

denoting the word combination "servant of God" (priest), are written so that the symbol for God,

stands in front of that for servant,

although the former is to be read last. Moreover, theology traced the invention of hieroglyphic writing back to the god Thoth, although this myth of its divine origin did not have an effect on the development of the script. In the late period, Egyptian texts referred to hieroglyphic inscriptions as "writing of God's words." Earlier, in contrast, they were simply called "pictures."

LITERACY AND KNOWLEDGE OF HIEROGLYPHIC WRITING

At all periods only a limited circle understood the hieroglyphic script. Only those

Ankh

The ankh, an ancient Egyptian hieroglyph signifying "life," is represented as a cross surmounted by a loop. It is known in Latin as a crux ansata (ansate, or handle-shaped, cross). As a vivifying talisman, the ankh is often held or offered by gods and pharaohs. The form of the symbol derives from a sandal strap. As a cross, it has been extensively used in the symbolism of the Coptic Orthodox Church.

Crux ansata *(ankh cross).* Encyclopædia Britannica, Inc.

who needed the knowledge in their professions acquired the arts of writing and reading. These people were, for example, officials and priests (insofar as they had to be able to read rituals and other sacred texts), as well as craftsmen whose work included the making of inscriptions. Under Greek and especially under Roman rule, the knowledge declined and was entirely confined to temples where priests instructed their pupils in the study of hieroglyphic writing. From the time of the rule of the Ptolemies (305 to 30 BC), national consciousness became more and more narrowly bound up with religion, and the tradition-filled hieroglyphic writing was an outward sign of pharaonic civilization—in the fullest sense, a symbol. There was no lack of attempts to replace the hieroglyphic writing, cumbersome and ever more divergent from the spoken language, with the simpler and more convenient Greek script. Such experiments, however, remained ineffective precisely because of the emotional value that the old writing system had when the country was under the foreign domination of the Macedonian Greeks and the Romans.

Christianity and the Greek Alphabet

The situation was altered with the conversion of Egypt to Christianity in the 2nd and 3rd centuries AD. The new religion fought against the Egyptian polytheism and traditions, and with its victory the Greek script triumphed. From the beginning, Egyptian Christians used the Greek alphabet for writing their spoken Egyptian language. This practice involved enlarging the Greek alphabet with seven supplementary letters for Egyptian sounds not present in Greek. As a consequence, the knowledge of hieroglyphic writing quickly declined. The last datable evidence of the writing system is a graffito from the island of Philae, from Aug. 24, 394, during the reign of the emperor Theodosius I. The language, as well as the writing system, of the Egyptian Christians is called Coptic.

CHARACTERISTICS OF HIEROGLYPHIC WRITING

The hieroglyphic writing system consists almost entirely of signs that represent recognizable objects in the natural or constructed world, and these can be grouped into three categories. The first is the logogram, in which a word is written (and read) by means of a single sign, providing both sound and meaning in itself. Ideograms can be read as the object they represent, such as ⤝, "wood, stick," or can have extended meanings, such as the sun disk, , which can be understood as "sun or (the solar god) Re" (in its phonetic reading "day" (read as $H + r + w$).

The second category is the phonogram, which represents a sound (or series of sounds) in the language. This group includes not only simple phonemes, which usually derive from logograms of the objects they depict but which acquired purely phonetic character, but also a much larger corpus of biliteral and triliteral signs (that is, signs that denote two or three sounds). Biliterals and triliterals, as well as logograms themselves, are often accompanied by the simple phonetic signs as a reading aid.

The third category of signs consists of determinatives, which carry no phonetic significance but are employed to specify meaning and assist in word division. For example, the phonetic writing $p + r + t$ can signify the infinitive of the verb "to go," the name of the winter season, or the word for "fruit, seed." The meaning of the word is signaled by a terminal determinative that also acts as a word marker: the walking legs ( ), the sun disk (☉), or the pellet sign (°), respectively. Generic determinatives are those that are denoting walking, running, or movement; the man with a hand to his mouth signifies words for eating, drinking, feeling, and perception; and the book roll is used for nouns pertaining to books, writing, and abstract concepts.

Egyptian inscriptions usually employed a combination of all three categories of signs, with liberal allowance for variation in spelling and in the grouping of signs. Egyptian generally avoided the writing of vowels aside from the semivowels i, y, and w; thus, the hieroglyphic system represents for the most part only the consonants of words. Pronunciation of Egyptian, therefore, is imperfectly reflected in the hieroglyphic writing system.

NUMBER OF SYMBOLS

In the classical period of Egyptian writing, the number of hieroglyphs totaled approximately 700. Their number multiplied considerably in the late period (which began about 600 BC); this proliferation occurred because scholars began to invent new forms or signs. The additional hieroglyphs were, however, always in accordance with the principles that had governed Egyptian writing from its beginnings. The hieroglyphic system remained flexible throughout all periods, always open to innovation, even though, as with every writing system, convention played a preponderant role.

Direction of Writing

Hieroglyphic inscriptions were preferentially written from right to left, with the direction of reading indicated by the orientation of the signs, which normally face toward the beginning of the text. The right-to-left orientation in writing was scrupulously observed in the cursive form of the script, called hieratic. Reversals of orientation in the writing of individual signs are relatively rare and were incorporated for either religious or decorative purposes.

Because Egyptian monuments were decorated according to strict conventions of symmetry, temples and tombs are usually adorned with hieroglyphic texts that face in both directions, to provide a visual sense of axial balance. Inscriptions could be written either in horizontal rows or in vertical columns, a feature that was ideally suited for the decoration of monumental walls, doorways, and lintels. In two-dimensional scenes containing human or divine figures, hieroglyphic texts are closely associated with the figures to which they pertain. That is, the identifying name, epithet, and utterance of an individual are oriented in the same direction in which the figure itself faces. And as one might expect for a distinctly pictorial script, the preferential right-to-left orientation of the Egyptian writing system had an effect on the development of three-dimensional art as well. For example, the striding male stance used for statuary requires that the left foot be placed forward, a visual pose that derives from the prescribed stance of the human hieroglyphic figure in preferred right-oriented inscriptions.

Cryptographic Hieroglyphic Writing

That knowledge of the hieroglyphic system and the principles upon which it was devised had not become diluted with time is attested by two phenomena: cryptography and the development of the hieroglyphic writing during the last millennium of its existence. From the middle of the 3rd millennium but more frequently in the New Kingdom (from c. 1539 to c. 1075 BC), hieroglyphic texts are encountered that have a very strange appearance. The absence of familiar word groups and the presence of many signs not found in the canon characterize these texts at first glance as cryptographic, or encoded, writing. This kind of hieroglyphic writing was probably intended as an eye-catcher, to entice people to seek the pleasure of deciphering it. Composed according to the original principles of the script, these inscriptions differed only in that certain features excluded when the original canon was formulated were now exploited. The new possibilities involved not only the forms of the signs but also their selection. For example, the mouth was not drawn in front view (⟨═⟩), as in the classical script, but in profile (⟨☌⟩), although it had the same phonetic value. An example of a change in the choice of signs is the case in which a man carrying a basket on his head

,

a determinative without phonetic value in the classical script, was later to be read as *f* and was used in lieu of the familiar sign having this phonetic value, that of the horned viper. In the new selection of the sign, the phonetic value is obtained from the word *f + š + i* "to carry" (neglecting its two weak consonants), in accordance with a principle that the inventors of the writing had applied in 3000 BC. These cryptographic inscriptions prove that alongside the method of instruction in the schools, which was based on memorization or recognition, not upon analytical understanding, there was another tradition that transmitted knowledge of the basic principles of the hieroglyphic script. A command of the principles of hieroglyphics similar to that which the composers of the cryptic inscriptions had was presupposed for the puzzle-happy decipherers.

THE LATER DEVELOPMENT OF HIEROGLYPHIC WRITING

About the middle of the 1st millennium BC, Egyptian writing experienced new developments and a revival of interest. Again the inscriptions abounded with new signs and sign groups unknown in the classical period, all generated according to the same principles as the classical Egyptian script and the cryptographic texts. The writing of this late period was distinguished from the cryptograms in that this script, like every normal system of writing, developed a fixed tradition, being intended not to conceal but to be read easily, whereas the cryptography strove for originality.

The development of hieroglyphic writing thus proceeded approximately as follows: at first only the absolutely necessary symbols were invented, without a canonization of their artistic form. In a second stage, easier readability (i.e., increased rapidity of reading) was achieved by increasing the number of signs (thereby eliminating some doubts) and by employing determinatives. Finally, after the second stage had endured, essentially unaltered, for about 2,000 years, the number of symbols increased to several thousand about 500 BC. This rampant growth process occurred through the application of hitherto unused possibilities of the system. With the triumph of Christianity, the knowledge of hieroglyphic writing was extinguished along with the ancient Egyptian religion.

PAPYRUS

Both the writing material of ancient Egypt and the plant from which it was derived are called papyrus. The papyrus plant (Cyperus papyrus, sometimes called the paper plant) was long-cultivated in the Nile delta region in Egypt and was collected for its stalk or stem, whose central pith was cut into thin strips, pressed together, and dried to form a smooth, thin writing surface.

Papyrus is a grasslike aquatic plant that has woody, bluntly triangular stems and grows up to about 15 feet (4.6 m) high in quietly flowing water up to 3 feet (90 cm) deep. The triangular stem can grow to a width of as much as 6 cm (2.3 inches). The papyrus plant is now often used as a pool ornamental in warm areas or in conservatories. The dwarf papyrus (C. isocladus, also given as C. papyrus 'Nanus'), up to 60 cm (23.6 inches) tall, is sometimes potted and grown indoors.

The ancient Egyptians used the stem of the papyrus plant to make sails, cloth, mats, cords, and, above all, paper. Paper made from papyrus was the chief writing material in ancient Egypt, was adopted by the Greeks, and was used extensively in the Roman Empire. It was used not only for the production of books (in roll or scroll form) but also for correspondence and legal documents. Pliny the Elder gave an account of the manufacture of paper from papyrus. The fibrous layers within the stem of the plant were removed, and a number of these longitudinal strips were placed side by side and then crossed at right angles with another set of strips. The two layers formed a sheet, which was then dampened and pressed. Upon drying, the gluelike sap of the plant acted as an adhesive and cemented the layers together. The sheet was finally hammered and dried in the sun. The paper thus formed was pure white in colour and, if well-made, was free of spots, stains, or other defects. A number of these sheets were then joined together with paste to form a roll, with usually not more than 20 sheets to a roll.

Papyrus was cultivated and used for writing material by the Arabs of Egypt down to the time when the growing manufacture of paper from other plant fibres in the 8th and 9th centuries AD rendered papyrus unnecessary. By the 3rd century AD, papyrus had already begun to be replaced in Europe by the less-expensive vellum, or parchment, but the use of papyrus for books and documents persisted sporadically until about the 12th century.

TOOLS

The tools used by the craftsmen for writing hieroglyphic symbols consisted of chisels and hammers for stone inscriptions and brushes and colours for wood and other smooth surfaces. A modified form of hieroglyphic writing (called cursive hieroglyphs), in which certain details of the monumental signs were abbreviated, was used for the decorative and minor arts—that is, for inscriptions chased into metals, incised in wood, or lavishly painted onto papyrus. Only for the truly cursive scripts, hieratic and demotic, were special materials developed. Leather and papyrus became writing surfaces, and the stems of rushes in lengths of 6 to 13 inches (15 to 33 cm), cut obliquely at the writing end and chewed to separate the fibres into a brushlike tip, functioned as writing implements. The split calamus reed used as a writing implement was introduced into Egypt by the Greeks in the 3rd century BC.

HIERATIC SCRIPT

The Egyptian cursive script, called hieratic writing, received its name from the Greek *hieratikos* ("priestly") at a time during the late period when the script was used only for sacred texts, whereas everyday secular documents were written in another style, the demotic script (from Greek *dēmotikos*, "for the people" or "in common use"). Hieratic, the cursive form of Egyptian hieroglyphs, was in fact employed throughout the pharaonic period for administrative and literary purposes, as a faster and more convenient method of writing; thus, its Greek designation is a misnomer.

The structure of the hieratic script corresponds with that of hieroglyphic writing. Changes occurred in the characters of hieratic simply because they could be written rapidly with brush or rush and ink on papyrus. Often the original pictorial form is not, or not easily, recognizable. Because their models were well known and in current use throughout Egyptian history, the hieratic symbols never strayed too far from them. Nevertheless, the system differs from the hieroglyphic script in some important respects:

1. Hieratic was written in one direction only, from right to left. In earlier times the lines were arranged vertically and later, about 2000 BC, horizontally. Subsequently the papyrus scrolls were written in columns of changing widths.

2. There were ligatures in hieratic so that two or more signs could be written in one stroke.

3. As a consequence of its decreased legibility, the spelling of the hieratic script tended to be more rigid and more complete than that of hieroglyphic writing. Variations from uniformity at a given time were minor; but, during the course of the various historical periods, the spelling developed and changed. As a result, hieratic texts do not correspond exactly to contemporary hieroglyphic texts, either in the placing of signs or in the spelling of words.

4. Hieratic used diacritical additions to distinguish between two signs that had grown similar to one another because of cursive writing. For example, the cow's leg received a supplementary distinguishing cross, because in hieratic it had come to resemble the sign for a human leg. Certain hieratic signs were taken into the hieroglyphic script.

Egyptian hieratic numerals (mathematical papyrus, c. 1600 BC)

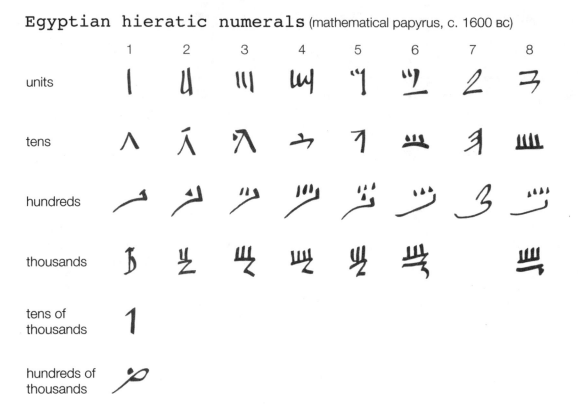

	1	2	3	4	5	6	7	8
units								
tens								
hundreds								
thousands								
tens of thousands								
hundreds of thousands								

Egyptian hieratic numerals. Encyclopædia Britannica, Inc.

All commonplace documents—e.g., letters, catalogs, and official writs—were written in hieratic script, as were literary and religious texts. In the life of the Egyptians, hieratic script played a larger role than hieroglyphic writing and was taught earlier in the schools. In offices, hieratic was replaced by demotic in the 7th century BC, but it remained in fashion until much later for religious texts of all sorts. The latest hieratic texts stem from the end of the 1st century or the beginning of the 2nd century AD.

DEMOTIC SCRIPT

Demotic script is first encountered at the beginning of the 26th dynasty, about 660 BC. The writing signs plainly demonstrate its connection with the hieratic script, although the exact relationship is not yet clear. It appears that demotic was originally developed expressly for government office

THE DISCOVERY AND DECIPHERMENT OF THE ROSETTA STONE

The Rosetta Stone, with Egyptian hieroglyphs in the top section, demotic characters in the middle, and Greek at the bottom; in the British Museum. Courtesy of the trustees of the British Museum

In August 1799, an ancient Egyptian stone bearing inscriptions in several languages and scripts was discovered by members of Napoleon's expedition. After the French surrender of Egypt in 1801, this stone—known as the Rosetta Stone because it was found near the town of Rosetta (Rashīd), about 35 miles (56 km) northeast of Alexandria—passed into British hands and is now in the British Museum in London. An irregularly shaped stone of black granite 3 feet 9 inches (114 cm) long and 2 feet 4.5 inches (72 cm) wide, the Rosetta Stone was broken in antiquity. Its decipherment led to the understanding of hieroglyphic writing.

The stone was inscribed in two languages, Egyptian and Greek, and three writing systems, hieroglyphics, demotic script, and the Greek alphabet. The Greek text stated clearly that the document set forth the same text in the sacred script, the folk or popular script, and Greek. The stone was promptly made known to all interested scholars.

Important partial successes in the effort of decipherment were achieved by the Swede Johan David Åkerblad and English physicist Thomas Young, who mainly studied the demotic text, beginning with the false hypothesis that the hieroglyphs were symbols. Young succeeded in proving that they were not symbols—at least that the proper names were not—and that the demotic seemed to derive from the hieroglyphs. He was the first to isolate correctly some single-consonant hieroglyphic signs. The hieroglyphic text on the Rosetta Stone contains six identical cartouches (oval figures enclosing hieroglyphs). Young deciphered the cartouche as the name of Ptolemy and proved a long-held assumption that the cartouches found in other inscriptions were the names of royalty. By examining the direction in which the bird and animal characters faced, Young also discovered the way in which hieroglyphic signs were to be read.

Jean-François Champollion of France took up the study where Young left off. In 1821–22 Champollion began to publish papers on the decipherment of hieratic and hieroglyphic writing based on study of the Rosetta Stone and eventually established an entire list of signs with their Greek equivalents. He was the first Egyptologist to realize that some of the signs were alphabetic, some syllabic, and some determinative, standing for the whole idea or object previously expressed. He also established that the hieroglyphic text of the Rosetta Stone was a translation from the Greek, not, as had been thought, the reverse. The inscriptions, apparently composed by the priests of Memphis, summarize benefactions conferred by Ptolemy V Epiphanes (205–180 bc) and were written in the ninth year of his reign in commemoration of his accession to the throne.

Starting, as had his predecessors, from the names Ptolemy and Cleopatra (both of which were enclosed in cartouches, or rings, used to set off royal names) and adding the hieroglyphic spelling of Ramses's name, Champollion determined, essentially correctly, the phonetic values of the signs. Research undertaken since that time has confirmed and refined Champollion's approach and most of his results.

use—that is, for documents in which the language was extensively formalized and thus well suited for the use of a standardized cursive script. Only some time after its introduction was demotic used for literary texts in addition to documents and letters; much later it was employed for religious texts as well. The latest dated demotic text, from Dec. 2, 425, consists of a rock inscription at Philae. In contrast to hieratic, which is almost without exception written in ink on papyrus or other flat surfaces, demotic inscriptions are not infrequently found engraved in stone or carved in wood.

The demotic system corresponds to the hieratic and hence ultimately to the hieroglyphic system. Alongside the traditional spelling, however, there was another spelling that took account of the markedly altered phonetic form of the words by appropriate respelling. This characteristic applied especially to a large number of words that did not occur in the older language and for which no written form had consequently been passed down. The nontraditional spelling could also be used for old, familiar words.

CHAPTER 9

Egyptian Art and Architecture

The course of art in Egypt paralleled to a large extent the country's political history, but it depended as well on the entrenched belief in the permanence of the natural, divinely ordained order. Artistic achievement in both architecture and representational art aimed at the preservation of forms and conventions that were held to reflect the perfection of the world at the primordial moment of creation and to embody the correct relationship between humankind, the king, and the pantheon of the gods. For this reason, Egyptian art appears outwardly resistant to development and the exercise of individual artistic judgment, but Egyptian artisans of every historical period found different solutions for the conceptual challenges posed to them.

Geographical factors were predominant in forming the particular character of Egyptian art. By providing Egypt with the most predictable agricultural system in the ancient world, the Nile afforded a stability of life in which arts and crafts readily flourished. Equally, the deserts and the sea, which protected Egypt on all sides, contributed to this stability by discouraging serious invasion for almost 2,000 years. The desert hills were rich in minerals and fine stones, ready to be exploited by artists and craftsmen. Only good wood was lacking, and the need for it led the Egyptians to undertake foreign expeditions to Lebanon, to Somalia, and, through intermediaries, to tropical Africa. In general, the search for useful and precious materials determined the direction of foreign policy and the establishment of trade routes and led ultimately to the enrichment of Egyptian material culture.

PREDYNASTIC PERIOD

In the 6th millennium BC there began to emerge patterns of civilization that displayed characteristics deserving to be called Egyptian. The accepted sequence of predynastic cultures is based on the excavations of British archaeologist Sir Flinders Petrie at Naqādah, at Al-ʿĀmirah (El-ʿÂmra), and at Al-Jīzah (El-Giza). Another earlier stage of predynastic culture has been identified at Al-Badārī in Upper Egypt.

From graves at Al-Badārī, Dayr Tasa, and Al-Mustaqiddah evidence of a relatively rich and developed artistic and industrial culture has been retrieved. Pottery of a fine red polished ware with blackened tops already shows distinctive Egyptian shapes. Copper was worked into small ornaments, and beads of steatite (soapstone) show traces of primitive glazing. Subsequently, in the Naqādah I and Naqādah II stages predynastic civilization developed steadily. Pottery remains the distinctive product, showing refinement of technique and the development of adventurous decoration. Shapes already found in Badarian graves were produced in Naqādah I with superior skill and decorated with geometric designs of white-filled lines and even simple representations of animals. Later, new clays were exploited, and fine buff-coloured wares were decorated in dark

red pigment with scenes of ships, figures, and a wide variety of symbols.

The working of hard stones also began in earnest in the later Predynastic period. At first craftsmen were devoted to the fashioning of fine vessels based on existing pottery forms and to the making of jewelry incorporating semiprecious stones.

Sculpture found its best beginnings not so much in representations of the human form (although figurines, mostly female, were made from Badarian times) as in the carving of small animal figures and the making of schist (slate) palettes (intended originally for the preparation of eye paint) and ivory knife handles. The Hunters and Battlefield palettes show sophisticated two-dimensional representation.

The basic techniques of two-dimensional art—drawing and painting—are exemplified in Upper Egyptian rock drawings and in the painted tomb at Hierakonpolis, now lost. Scenes of animals, boats, and hunting (the common subjects of rock drawings) were more finely executed in paint in the tomb, and additional themes, probably of conquest, presaged those found in dynastic art.

DYNASTIC EGYPT

Evidence suggests that the unification of Upper and Lower Egypt drew together the various threads of what was to become the rich tapestry of Egyptian culture and started the intricate weave on the loom of time. Many of the new artistic developments undoubtedly can be traced back to the Naqādah II period; but the abundant evidence from the great tombs of the 1st dynasty at Abydos and Ṣaqqārah far outweighs what was found in the modest burials of earlier times. The impression is certainly one of an extraordinary efflorescence of civilization. The motif of conquest is dramatically characterized in the scenes shown on the Narmer Palette, where Narmer (better known as Menes), probably the last ruler of predynastic Egypt, is depicted as the triumphant ruler.

The Narmer representations display much of what is typical of Egyptian art of the Dynastic period. Here is the characteristic image of the king smiting his enemy, depicted with the conventions that distinguish Egyptian two-dimensional art. The head is shown in profile, but the eye in full; the shoulders are frontally represented, while the torso is at three-quarters view; the legs again are in profile. To render each part of the human form from its most characteristic viewpoint was the principal intention of the artist—to show what he knew was there, not simply what he could see from one perspective.

Further conventions, well established by the 4th dynasty, included the showing of both hands and feet, right and left, without distinction. Scenes were set on baselines, and the events were placed in sequence, usually from right to left. Unity in a scene was provided by the focal figure of the most important person, the king or tomb owner. Relative size established importance: the ruler dwarfed the generally high official, while the tomb owner dwarfed his wife and, still more so, his children.

Conservatism in artistic matters was nurtured by a relative coherence of culture, strengthened by a vigorous tradition of scribal training and tempered by a canon of proportion for the representation of the human figure. In the Old Kingdom, walls prepared for decoration were marked out with red horizontal guidelines; in later times vertical lines were added. During much of the Dynastic period a grid of 18 rows of squares was used to contain the standing figure of a man; from the 26th dynasty, 21 rows of squares were used for the same purpose. At different periods, variations in the placing of specific bodily features produced interesting and subtle nuances. During the so-called Amarna period a distinctive reappraisal of the canon took place. The full range of changes and the many variants still remain to be studied, but it is clear that the basic canon lay deeply rooted in the training of the Egyptian artist.

ARCHITECTURE

The two principal building materials used in ancient Egypt were unbaked mud brick and stone. From the Old Kingdom onward stone was generally used for tombs—the eternal dwellings of the dead—and for temples—the eternal houses of the gods. Mud brick remained the domestic material, used even for royal palaces; it was also used for fortresses, the great walls of temple precincts and towns, and for subsidiary buildings in temple complexes.

Most ancient Egyptian towns have been lost because they were situated in the cultivated and flooded area of the Nile Valley; many temples and tombs have survived because they were built on ground unaffected by the Nile flood. Any survey of Egyptian architecture will in consequence be weighted in favour of funerary and religious buildings. Yet the dry, hot climate of Egypt has allowed some mud brick structures to survive where they have escaped the destructive effects of water or humans.

TOMB ARCHITECTURE

Mortuary architecture in Egypt was highly developed and often grandiose. The tomb was a place in which a corpse might be protected from desecration and be provided with material objects to ensure continued existence after death. Part of the tomb might be decorated with scenes that would enable the individual to pursue magically an afterlife suitable and similar to his worldly existence. For a king the expectations were quite different; for him the tomb became the vehicle whereby he might achieve his exclusive destiny with the gods in a celestial afterlife.

Most tombs comprised two principal parts, the burial chamber (the tomb proper) and the chapel, in which offerings for the deceased could be made. In royal burials the chapel rapidly developed into a mortuary temple, which beginning in the New Kingdom was usually built separately and at some distance from the tomb. In the following discussion, funerary temples built separately will be discussed with temples in general and not as part of the funerary complex.

ROYAL TOMBS

In the earliest dynasties the tombs of kings and high officials were made of mud brick and of such similar size that it is difficult to distinguish between them. The tombs at Abydos are royal, whereas those at Ṣaqqārah are noble. The latter, better preserved than the former, reveal rectangular superstructures, called mastabas, with sides constructed in the form of paneled niches painted white and decorated with elaborate "matting" designs.

These great superstructures were constructed over many storage chambers stocked with food and equipment for the deceased, who lay in a rectangular burial chamber below ground. Also within the superstructure, but not always clearly evident, was a low mound of earth, possibly representing the primitive grave of earlier times.

The Step Pyramid of Djoser, second king of the 3rd dynasty, was built within a vast enclosure on a commanding site at Ṣaqqārah, overlooking the city of Memphis. A high royal official, Imhotep, has traditionally been credited with the design and with the decision to use quarried stone. This first essay in stone is remarkable for its design of six superposed stages of diminishing size, and also for its huge enclosure (1,784 by 909 feet [544 by 277 metres]) surrounded by a paneled wall faced with fine limestone and containing a series of "mock" buildings that probably represent structures associated with the heraldic shrines of Upper and Lower Egypt. There the Egyptian stonemasons made their earliest architectural innovations, using stone to reproduce the forms of primitive wood and brick buildings. Fine reliefs of the king and elaborate wall panels in glazed tiles in parts of the subterranean complexes are among the innovations found in this remarkable monument.

PYRAMID OF KHUFU

For the Old Kingdom the most characteristic form of tomb building was the true pyramid, the finest example of which is the Great Pyramid of King Khufu (Cheops) of the 4th dynasty, at Al-Jīzah (Giza). The form itself reached its maturity in the reign of Snefru, father of Khufu. Subsequently only the pyramid of Khafre (Chephren), Khufu's successor, approached the size and perfection of the Great Pyramid. The simple measurements of the Great Pyramid indicate very adequately its scale, monumentality, and precision: its sides are 755.43 feet (230.26 metres; north), 756.08 feet (230.45 metres; south), 755.88 feet (230.39 metres; east), 755.77 feet (230.36 metres; west); its orientation on the cardinal points is almost exact; its height upon completion was 481.4 feet (146.7

metres); and its area at the base is just over 13 acres (5.3 hectares). Other features in its construction contribute substantially to its remarkable character: the lofty, corbeled Grand Gallery and the granite-built King's Chamber with five relieving compartments (empty rooms for reducing pressure) above.

Khufu's pyramid is perhaps the most colossal single building ever erected on the planet. Its sides rise at an angle of 51°52' and are accurately oriented to the four cardinal points of the compass. The Great Pyramid's core is made of yellowish limestone blocks, the outer casing (now almost completely gone) and the inner passages are of finer light-coloured limestone, and the interior burial chamber is built of huge blocks of granite. Approximately 2.3 million blocks of stone were cut, transported, and assembled to create the 5.75-million-ton structure. The Great Pyramid is a masterpiece of technical skill and engineering ability. The internal walls, as well as those few outer-casing stones that still remain in place, show finer joints than any other masonry constructed in ancient Egypt.

The question of how the pyramid was built has not received a wholly satisfactory answer. The most plausible one is that the Egyptians employed a sloping and encircling embankment of brick, earth, and sand, which was increased in height and in length as the pyramid rose; stone blocks were hauled up the ramp by means of sledges, rollers, and levers. According to the ancient Greek historian Herodotus, the Great Pyramid took 20 years to construct and demanded the labour of 100,000 men. This figure is believable given the assumption that these men, who were agricultural labourers, worked on the pyramids only (or primarily) while there was little work to be done in the fields—i.e., when the Nile River was in flood. By the late 20th century, however, archaeologists found evidence that a more limited workforce may have occupied the site on a permanent rather than a seasonal basis. It was suggested that as few as 20,000 workers, with accompanying support personnel (bakers, physicians, priests, etc.), would have been adequate for the task.

The pyramid formed the focal point of a group of buildings that constituted the funerary complex of a king. Two temples linked by a causeway were essential components. The valley temple, built on the edge of the desert escarpment, was the place of reception for the royal body. The most striking valley temple is that of Khafre, a structure of massive granite blocks with huge alabaster flooring slabs, starkly simple but immensely impressive. The best-preserved causeway serves the pyramid of King Unas of the 5th dynasty; it contains low-relief wall decorations and a ceiling adorned with stars. The pyramid temple of Unas is distinguished by the extensive use of granite for architectural elements, including doorways and splendid monolithic columns with palm capitals.

The temple complexes attached to the pyramid show great mastery of architectural forms. Khufu's temple or approach causeway was decorated with impressive reliefs, fragments of which were incorporated in the 12th-dynasty pyramid of Amenemhet I at Al-Lisht.

The pyramids built for the later kings of the Old Kingdom and most kings of the Middle Kingdom were comparatively poor in size, construction, and materials. The tomb of King Mentuhotep II of the 11th dynasty is, however, of exceptional interest. Its essential components were a rectangular structure, terraced porticos, a series of pillared ambulatories, an open court, and a hypostyle hall tucked into the cliffs.

The monumentality of the pyramid made it not only a potent symbol of royal power but also an obvious target for tomb robbers. During the New Kingdom the wish to halt the robbing and desecration of royal tombs led to their being sited together in a remote valley at Thebes, dominated by a peak that itself resembled a pyramid. There, in the Valley of the Kings, tombs were carved deep into the limestone with no outward structure. The earliest tombs were entirely hidden from view; those of the Ramessid period (19th and 20th dynasties) are marked only by a doorway carved in the rock face. They had no identical plan, but most consisted of a series of corridors opening out at intervals to form rooms and ending in a large burial chamber deep in the mountain. The finest of the tombs is that of Seti I, second king of the 19th dynasty; it extends 328 feet (100 metres) into the mountain and contains a spectacular burial chamber, the barrel-shaped roof of which represents the vault of heaven.

After the abandonment of the valley at the end of the 20th dynasty, kings of the subsequent two dynasties were buried in very simple tombs within the temple enclosure of the delta city of Tanis. No later royal tombs have ever been identified in Egypt proper.

PRIVATE TOMBS

A major distinction between royal and nonroyal tombs lies in the provision of arrangements for the funerary cult of the deceased. The evidence available from the 1st dynasty onward makes it clear that king and commoner had quite different expectations. In nonroyal tombs a chapel was provided that included a formal tablet or stela on which the deceased was shown seated at a table of offerings. The earliest examples are simple and architecturally undemanding; later a suitable room, the tomb-chapel, was provided for the stela (now incorporated in a false door) in the tomb superstructure, or mastaba.

The term *mastaba* (Arabic: "bench") was first used archaeologically in the 19th century by workmen on Auguste Mariette's excavation at Ṣaqqārah to describe the rectangular, flat-topped stone superstructures of tombs. Subsequently, *mastaba* was also used to mean mud brick superstructures.

In the great cemeteries of the Old Kingdom, changes in size, internal arrangements, and groupings of the burials of nobles indicate the vicissitudes of nonroyal posthumous expectations. In the 3rd dynasty at Ṣaqqārah the most important private burials were at some distance from the step pyramids of Djoser and Sekhemkhet. Their large superstructures incorporated offering niches that were to develop into chapels (as in the tomb of Khabausokar) and corridors that could accommodate paintings of equipment for the afterlife and niches to hold carved representations of the deceased owner (as in the tomb of Hesire). During the 4th dynasty the stone mastabas of the Giza pyramid field were regularly laid out near the pyramids, and, although smaller than those at Ṣaqqārah, they show the true start of the exploitation of space within the superstructure. The niche chapel became a room for the false door and offering table, and there might also be rooms containing scenes of offering and of daily activities.

Nothing indicates more clearly the relaxation of royal authority in the later Old Kingdom than the size and decoration of the mastabas at Ṣaqqārah and Abusīr. Externally they were still rectangular structures, occasionally with a low wall establishing a precinct (as in the tomb of Mereruka). The full exploitation of internal space in the great mastabas at Abusīr (that of Ptahshepses) and Ṣaqqārah (that of Ti and the double mastaba of Akhtihotep and Ptahhotep) made ample room available for the receipt of offerings and for the representation of the milieu in which the dead owner might expect to spend his afterlife. In the mastaba of Mereruka, a vizier of Teti, first king of the 6th dynasty, there were 21 rooms for his own funerary purposes, with six for his wife and five for his son.

Contemporaneously, the provincial colleagues of the Memphite nobles developed quite different tombs in Middle and Upper Egypt. Tomb chapels were excavated into the rock of the cliffs overlooking the Nile. Rock-cut tombs subsequently were to become a more common kind of private tomb, although mastabas were built in the royal cemeteries of the 12th dynasty.

Most rock-cut tombs were fairly simple single chambers serving all the functions of the multiplicity of rooms in a mastaba. Some, however, were excavated with considerable architectural pretensions. At Aswān huge halls, often connecting to form labyrinthine complexes, were partly formal, with columns carefully cut from the rock, and partly rough-hewn. Chapels with false doors were carved out within the halls. In some cases the facades were monumental, with porticoes and inscriptions.

At Beni Hasan the local nobles during the Middle Kingdom cut large and precise tomb chambers in the limestone cliffs. Architectural features—columns, barrel roofs, and porticoes, all carved from the rock—provided fine settings for painted mural decorations. The tombs of Khnumhotep and Amenemhet are outstanding examples of fine design impeccably executed.

The most famous rock-cut private tombs are those of the New Kingdom at Thebes, their fame resting, above all, on their mural decoration. As elsewhere the excavated chambers are the tomb-chapels, mostly taking a simple T-form, in which the crossbar of the T represents the entrance hall, and the upright stroke of the T is the chapel proper. Some of the more important tombs (Rekhmire, Ramose) have open courts before their unelaborate facades and some striking internal features, but most are small in comparison with those of earlier times. A number of Theban tombs were adorned with mud brick pyramids placed above the main entrance.

A separate tradition of private tomb design was developed for important officials at Ṣaqqārah in the New Kingdom. Open courts, constructed offering chapels, and elaborate subterranean suites of rooms characterize these Memphite tombs. The tomb for Horemheb, a military commander who became the last king of the 18th dynasty, has remarkable relief decoration. The tomb of Tia (a sister of the 19th-dynasty king Ramses II) has a small pyramid behind the chapel.

TEMPLE ARCHITECTURE

Two principal kinds of temple can be distinguished—cult temples and funerary or mortuary temples. The former accommodated the images of deities, the recipients of the daily cult; the latter were the shrines for the funerary cults of dead kings.

Ancient Egyptian obelisk and statuary in the Temple of Luxor, Thebes, Egypt. © Goodshoot/
Jupiterimages

CULT TEMPLES

It is generally thought that the Egyptian cult temple of the Old Kingdom owed most to the cult of the sun god Re at Heliopolis, which was probably open in plan and lacking a shrine. Sun temples were unique among cult temples; worship was centred on a cult object, the *benben,* a squat obelisk placed in full sunlight. Among the few temples surviving from the Old Kingdom are sun temples of the 5th-dynasty kings at Abū Jirāb (Abu Gurab). That of Neuserre reveals the essential layout: a reception pavilion at the desert edge connected by a covered corridor on a causeway to the open court of the temple high on the desert, within which stood the *benben* of limestone and a huge alabaster altar. Fine reliefs embellished the covered corridor and also corridors on two sides of the court.

The cult temple achieved its most highly developed form in the great sanctuaries erected over many centuries at Thebes. Architecturally the most satisfying is the Luxor Temple, started by Amenhotep III of the 18th dynasty. The original design consists of an imposing open court with colonnades of graceful lotus columns, a smaller offering hall, a shrine for the ceremonial boat of the god, an inner sanctuary for the cult image, and a room in which the divine birth of the king was celebrated. The approach to the temple was made by a colonnade of huge columns with open papyrus-flower capitals, planned by Amenhotep III but decorated with fascinating processional reliefs under Tutankhamen and Horemheb. Later Ramses II built a wide court before the colonnade and two great pylons to form a new entrance.

The necessary elements of an Egyptian temple, most of which can be seen at Luxor, are the following: an approach avenue of sphinxes leading to the great double-towered pylon entrance fitted with flagpoles and pennants; before the pylon a pair of obelisks and colossal statues of the king; within the pylon a court leading to a pillared hall, the hypostyle, beyond which might come a further, smaller hall where offerings could be prepared; and, at the heart of the temple, the shrine for the cult image. In addition, there were storage chambers for temple equipment and, in later periods, sometimes a crypt. Outside the main temple building was a lake, or at least a well, for the water needed in the rituals; in later times there might also be a birth house (*mammisi*) to celebrate the king's divine birth. The whole, with service buildings, was contained by a massive mud brick wall.

The great precinct of the Temple of Karnak (the longest side 1,837 feet [560 metres]) contains whole buildings, or parts of buildings, dating from the early 18th dynasty down to the Roman period. Modern reconstruction work has even recovered a tiny way station of the 12th dynasty, a gem of temple building decorated with some of the finest surviving relief scenes and texts.

Entrance to the Nubian cliff temple of Ramses II at Abu Simbel, Egypt, c. 1250 BC, New Kingdom, 19th dynasty. H. Roger-Viollet

Of the structures on the main Karnak axis, the most remarkable are the hypo-style hall and the so-called Festival Hall of Thutmose III. The former contained 134 mighty papyrus columns, 12 of which formed the higher central aisle (76 feet [23 metres] high). Grill windows allowed some light to enter, but it must be supposed that even on the brightest day most of the hall was in deep gloom.

The Festival Hall is better described as a memorial hall. Its principal room is distinguished by a series of unusual columns with bell-shaped capitals, inspired by the wooden tent poles used in primitive buildings. Their lightness contrasts strikingly with the massive supports of the hypostyle hall.

Near Karnak Temple, King Akhenaton and his wife, Nefertiti, built a number of temples, later dismantled, to the sun god Aton. The vast number of blocks found in modern times indicates that these constructions were essentially open places for worship like the earlier sun temples. So, too, was the great Aton temple at Tell el-Amarna, built later in Akhenaton's reign.

The most interesting and unusual cult temple of the New Kingdom was built at Abydos by Seti I of the 19th dynasty. Principally dedicated to Osiris, it contained seven chapels dedicated to different deities, including the deified Seti himself. These chapels have well-preserved barrel ceilings and are decorated with low-relief scenes that retain much of their original colour.

The most remarkable monument of Ramses II, the great builder, is undoubtedly the temple of Abu Simbel. Although excavated from the living rock, it follows generally the plan of the usual Egyptian temple: colossal seated statues emerging from the facade, which is the cliff face; a pillared hall followed by a second leading to a vestibule; and a shrine with four statues of divinities, including one of Ramses himself.

Mention should also be made of the immense temple dedicated to the god Amon-Re at Tanis in the delta by the kings of the 21st and 22nd dynasties. Much of the stone for the so-called northern Karnak, along with colossal statues

and a dozen obelisks, was appropriated from other sanctuaries in Egypt, making this a remarkable assemblage of earlier work. It was not only a cult temple but the funerary temple for the kings who were buried within the precinct.

FUNERARY TEMPLES

Most of the New Kingdom funerary temples were built along the desert edge in western Thebes. An exception, and by far the most original and beautiful, was Queen Hatshepsut's temple, designed and built by her steward Senenmut near the tomb of Mentuhotep II at Dayr al-Baḥrī. Three terraces lead up to the recess in the cliffs where the shrine was cut into the rock. Each terrace is fronted by colonnades of square pillars protecting reliefs of unusual subjects, including an expedition to Punt and the divine birth of Hatshepsut. Ramps lead from terrace to terrace, and the uppermost level opens into a large court with colonnades. Chapels of Hathor (the principal deity of the temple) and Anubis occupy the south and north ends of the colonnade of the second terrace.

The largest conventionally planned funerary temple complex was probably that of Amenhotep III, now to be judged principally from the two huge quartzite statues, the Colossi of Memnon. These and other royal sculptures found in the ruins of the temple's courts and halls testify to the magnificence now lost. Its design, as well as much of its stone, was used by Ramses II for his own funerary

The Temple of Queen Hatshepsut at Dayr al-Baḥrī, Thebes, Egypt, 15th century BC. Katherine Young/EB Inc.

temple, the Ramesseum. The huge enclosure of the latter included not only the temple but also a royal palace (only traces of which can now be seen). The temple itself contained two huge open courts, entered through towering pylons, which led to a lofty hypostyle hall and a smaller hall with astronomical carvings on the ceiling. Statues of vast size stood before the second pylon, one of which, now toppled and ruined, has been estimated to weigh more than 1,000 tons. Mud brick storerooms in the enclosure preserve ample evidence of the use of the vault in the late 2nd millennium BC.

Ramses III's funerary temple at Madīnat Habu contains the best-preserved of Theban mortuary chapels and shrines, as well as the main temple components. The most private parts of the temple, to which few had access apart from the king and his priestly representatives, begin at the sides of the first hypostyle hall, with the temple treasury and a room for the processional boat of Ramses II (a much-honoured ancestor) on the south and shrines for various deities, including Ramses III, on the north. A second pillared hall is flanked by a solar chapel and a small Osiris complex, where the king took on the personae of Re, the sun god, and of Osiris, god of the underworld, a transfiguration considered necessary for his divine afterlife. Beyond the Osiris complex, along the temple axis, is a third small hall and the main shrine for the Theban god Amon; two lateral shrines were reserved for Amon's consort Mut and their divine child Khons.

As with most New Kingdom temples, the mural decorations on the outer walls of funerary temples, including that at Madīnat Habu, dealt mainly with the military campaigns of the king, while the inner scenes were mostly of ritual significance. Within the temple precinct lived and worked a whole community of priests and state officials. A small palace lay to the south of the main building, and a further suite of rooms for the king was installed in the castellated gate building on the east side of the precinct. The reliefs in this "high gate" suggest that the suite was used for recreational purposes by the king together with his women.

Domestic Architecture

Mud brick and wood were the standard materials for houses and palaces throughout the Dynastic period; stone was used occasionally for such architectural elements as doorjambs, lintels, column bases, and windows.

The best-preserved private houses are those of modest size in the workmen's village of Dayr al-Madīnah. Exceptional in that they were built of stone, they typically had three or four rooms, comprising a master bedroom, a reception room, a cellar for storage, and a kitchen open to the sky; accommodation on the roof, reached by a stair, completed the plan. Similar domestic arrangements are known from the workmen's village at Kabun.

Villas for important officials in Akhenaton's city of Tell el-Amarna were large and finely decorated with brightly painted murals. The house of the vizier Nakht had at least 30 rooms, including separate apartments for the master, his family, and his guests. Such houses had bathrooms and lavatories. The ceilings of large rooms were supported by painted wooden pillars, and there may have been further rooms above. Where space was restricted (as in Thebes), houses of several stories were built. Tomb scenes that show such houses also demonstrate that windows were placed high to reduce sunlight and that hooded vents on roofs were used to catch the breeze.

Palaces, as far as can be judged from remains at Thebes and Tell el-Amarna, were vast, rambling magnified versions of Nakht's villa, with broad halls, harem suites, kitchen areas, and wide courts. At Tell el-Amarna some monumental formality was introduced in the form of porticoes, colonnades, and statuary. Lavish use was made of mural and floor decoration in which floral and animal themes predominated.

SCULPTURE

The Egyptian artist, whose skills are best exemplified in sculpture, regarded himself essentially as a craftsman. Owing to his discipline and highly developed aesthetic sense, however, the products of his craft deserve to rank as art outstanding by any standards.

Much of the surviving sculpture is funerary—i.e., statues for tombs. Most of the remainder was made for placing in temples—votive for private persons and ritual for royal and divine representations. Royal colossi were ritual and also served to proclaim the grandeur and power of the king. By itself, however, a statue could represent no one unless it carried an identification in hieroglyphs.

EMERGENCE OF TYPES IN THE OLD KINGDOM

The standing male figure with left leg advanced and the seated figure were the most common types of Egyptian statuary. Traces of wooden figures found at Ṣaqqārah show that the first type was being made as early as the 1st dynasty. The earliest seated figures are two of King Khasekhem of the 2nd dynasty, which, although relatively small, already embody the essential monumentality of all royal sculpture.

Supreme sculptural competence was achieved remarkably quickly. The primitive, yet immensely impressive life-size statue of Djoser pointed the way to the

Khafre, detail of a statue with the god Horus in the shape of a falcon; in the Egyptian Museum, Cairo. Courtesy of the Egyptian Museum, Cairo; photograph, Hirmer Fotoarchiv, Munich

magnificent royal sculptures from the 4th-dynasty pyramid complexes at Giza. For subtlety of carving and true regal dignity scarcely anything of later date surpasses the diorite statue of Khafre. Scarcely less fine are the sculptures of Menkaure (Mycerinus). The pair statue of the king and his wife exemplifies wonderfully both dignity and marital affection; the triads showing the king with goddesses and nome (provincial)

Shaykh al-Balad, wood statue from Ṣaqqārah in Memphis, Egypt, 5th dynasty (c. 2400 BC); in the Egyptian Museum, Cairo. Hirmer Fotoarchiv, Munchen

deities exhibit a complete mastery of carving hard stone in many planes.

This union of skill and genius was achieved in nonroyal statuary as well as in the painted limestone statues of Prince Rahotep and his wife, Nofret, which also display the Egyptians' unsurpassed skill in inlaying eyes into sculptures, a skill further demonstrated in the wooden figure of Ka'aper, known as Shaykh al-Balad, the very epitome of the self-important official.

Among additions to the sculptural repertoire during the Old Kingdom was the scribal statue. Examples in the Louvre and in the Egyptian Museum in Cairo express brilliantly the alert vitality of the bureaucrat, who squats on the ground with brush poised over papyrus. The heads of such figures possess striking individuality, even if they are not true portraits.

REFINEMENTS OF THE MIDDLE KINGDOM

Royal sculptures, particularly of Sesostris III and Amenemhet III, achieved a high degree of realism, even of portraiture. The first true royal colossi were produced in the 12th dynasty (if the Great Sphinx of Giza is discounted) for the embellishment of cult temples. Colossi of Amenemhet I and Sesostris I exhibit a hard, uncompromising style said to typify the ruthless drive of the 12th-dynasty kings.

In this period, too, the sphinx—the recumbent lion with head or face of the king—became a commonly used image of the king as protector. The great red granite sphinx of Amenemhet II from Tanis expresses the idea most potently.

In private sculpture during the Middle Kingdom the subject is in most cases portrayed seated or squatting, occasionally standing, and wearing an all-enveloping cloak. The body was mostly concealed, but its contours were often subtly suggested in the carving, as in the figure of Khertyhotep. Of female subjects, none is more impressive than that of Sennu, a wonderful example of a figure in repose.

The simplification of the human figure was carried to its ultimate in the block statue, a uniquely Egyptian type that represents the subject squatting on the ground with knees drawn up close to his body. The arms and legs may be wholly contained within the cubic form, hands and feet alone discretely protruding. The 12th-dynasty block statue of Sihathor is the earliest dated example.

INNOVATION, DECLINE, AND REVIVAL FROM THE NEW KINGDOM TO THE LATE PERIOD

Excellence of craftsmanship is the hallmark of 18th-dynasty sculpture, in a revival of the best traditions of the Middle Kingdom. Wonderfully sensitive statues of Hatshepsut and Thutmose III confirm the return of conditions in which great work could be achieved. A seated limestone statue of Hatshepsut shows the queen as king, but with an expression of consummate grace. A schist statue

of Thutmose III, in the perfection of its execution and subtlety of its realization, epitomizes regality.

The placing of votive statues in temples led to a proliferation of private sculptures during the New Kingdom. The sculptures of Senenmut, steward of Hatshepsut, exemplify the development. At least 23 votive statues (some fragmentary) of this royal favourite are known, exhibiting many different forms.

Colossal sculpture, which reached its apogee in the reign of Ramses II, was used to splendid, and perhaps less bombastic, effect by Amenhotep III. The great sculptures of his funerary temple, including the immense Colossi of Memnon, were part of the noble designs of his master of works, also called Amenhotep (son of Hapu). Most unusually, this distinguished commoner was allowed a funerary temple for himself and larger-than-life votive sculptures that show him in contrasting attitudes, as stern-faced authoritarian and as submissive scribe.

The stylistic trends that can be noted in certain sculptures of Amenhotep III hint of an artistic change that was developed in the subsequent reign of Akhenaton. The distinctive style of this period has come to be called Amarna, after the location of Akhenaton's new capital in Middle Egypt. Colossal sculptures of the king from the dismantled Karnak temples emphasize his bodily peculiarities—elongated facial features, almost feminine breasts, and swelling hips. Sculptures of Nefertiti, his queen, are often executed in the most remarkably sensual manner

Nefertiti, painted limestone bust, c. 1350 BC; in the Egyptian Museum, Berlin. Bildarchiv Preussischer Kulturbesitz, Ägyptisches Museum, Staatliche Museen zu Berlin/ Preussischer Kulturbesitz, Berlin; photograph, Jurgen Liepe

(e.g., the Louvre torso). Sculptures from later in the reign display innovations of style with no loss of artistry, at the same time avoiding the grotesqueries of the early years. Of this period is the famous painted bust of Nefertiti.

Much of the best of the artistic legacy of Akhenaton's reign persisted in the sculpture of subsequent reigns—Tutankhamen, Horemheb, and the early kings of the 19th dynasty—but a marked change came in the reign of Ramses II. It is a commonplace to decry the quality of his monumental statuary, although little in Egypt is more dramatic and compelling than the great seated figures of this king at Abu Simbel. Nevertheless, there is much truth in the belief that the steady decline in sculpture began during Ramses II's reign. Royal portraiture subsequently became conventional. Occasionally a sculptor might produce some unusual piece, such as the extraordinary figure of Ramses VI with his lion, dragging beside him a Libyan prisoner. Among private sculptures there is the scribal statue of Ramsesnakht; the subject bends over his papyrus while Thoth (the divine scribe), in baboon form, squats behind his head.

A change was to come with the advent of the Kushite (Nubian) kings of the 25th dynasty. The portraiture of the Kushite kings exhibits a brutal realism that may owe much to the royal sculpture of the 12th dynasty; the sphinx of Taharqa, fourth king of the 25th dynasty, is a good example.

Archaism is strikingly evident in the private sculpture of the last dynasties. Types of statue common in the Middle Kingdom and 18th dynasty were revived, and many very fine pieces were produced. The sculptures of the mayor of Thebes, Montemhat, display great variety, excellent workmanship, and, in one case, a realism that transcends the dictates of convention.

In considering the clear sculptural qualities of Late period work one should never overlook the primary purpose of most Egyptian sculpture: to represent the individual in death before Osiris, or in life and death before the deities of the great temples. To this end the statue was not only a physical representation but also a vehicle for appropriate texts, which might be inscribed obtrusively over beautifully carved surfaces. The extreme example of such textual application is a so-called healing statue of which even the wig is covered with texts.

RELIEF SCULPTURE AND PAINTING

For Egyptians the decoration of tomb walls with reliefs or painted scenes provided some certainty of the perpetuation of life; in a temple, similarly, it was believed that mural decoration magically ensured the performance of important ceremonies and reinforced the memory of royal deeds.

The earliest appearance of mural decoration is to be found in tomb 100 at Hierakonpolis, presumably the grave of a powerful local chieftain; it is dated to the early Gerzean (Naqādah II) period. Although technically they are considered small objects, the large ceremonial palettes that appear around the beginning of the dynastic period represent the earliest religious relief sculptures, which would eventually find their place on the walls of temples built in stone, after the appearance of that medium.

The beginnings of the dynastic tradition can be found in tombs of the 3rd dynasty, such as that of Hesire at Ṣaqqārah; it contained mural paintings of funerary equipment and wooden panels carrying figures of Hesire in the finest low relief. Generally speaking, mural decorations were in paint when the ground was mud brick or stone of poor quality and in relief when the walls were in good stone. Painting and drawing formed the basis of what was to be carved in relief, and the finished carving was itself commonly painted.

In tombs the mural decorations might be left unfinished, being only partly sketched or partly carved by the time of the burial. Uncompleted scenes reveal clearly the methods of laying out walls for decoration. The prepared wall was marked out with red guidelines, the grid described earlier being used for major human figures and sometimes for minor ones. Preliminary outlines were corrected in black, and paint was applied usually in tempera, with pigments being mostly mineral-based.

In the Old Kingdom pure painting of the highest quality is found as early as

Egyptian dancing, detail from a tomb painting from Shaykh 'Abd al-Qurnah, Egypt, c. 1400 BC; in the British Museum, London. Courtesy of the trustees of the British Museum

the 4th dynasty, in the scene of geese from the tomb of Nefermaat and Atet at Maydum. But the glory of Old Kingdom mural decoration is the low-relief work in the royal funerary monuments of the 5th dynasty and in the private tombs of the 5th and 6th dynasties in the Memphite necropolis. Outstanding are the reliefs from the sun temple of King Neuserre at Abu Jīrab and the scenes of daily life in the tombs of Ptahhotep and Ti at Ṣaqqārah.

The tradition of fine painting was continued in the Middle Kingdom. At Beni Hasan the funerary chambers are crowded with paintings exhibiting fine draftsmanship and use of colour. The best relief work of the period, reviving the Memphite tradition, is found at Thebes in the tomb of Mentuhotep II at Dayr al-Baḥrī and in the little shrine of Sesostris I at Karnak, where the fine carving is greatly enhanced by a masterly use of space in the disposition of figures and text.

Relief sculpture from Luxor or Karnak area, Egypt. © Goodshoot/Jupiterimages

In the early 18th dynasty the relief tradition was revived at Thebes and can best be observed in the carvings in Hatshepsut's temple at Dayr al-Baḥrī. Later royal reliefs of Amenhotep III and of the post-Amarna kings show a stylistic refinement that was carried to its best in the reign of Seti I at Karnak, at Abydos, and in his tomb at Thebes.

The 18th dynasty also saw Egyptian painting reach its highest achievement in the tombs of the nobles at Thebes. The medium of decoration and an increased range of motifs felt appropriate for tomb decoration led to the introduction of small, often entertaining details into standard scenes. The tiny tombs of Menna and Nakht are full of such playful vignettes. The paintings in great tombs, such as that of Rekhmire, are more formal but still crammed with unusual detail. Fragments of mural and floor paintings from palaces and houses at Thebes and Tell el-Amarna provide tantalizing glimpses of the marsh and garden settings of everyday upper-class life.

The fine royal reliefs of the late 18th dynasty were matched by those in private tombs at Thebes (Ramose and Kheruef) and Ṣaqqārah (Horemheb); these are breathtaking in execution and, in the case of Horemheb, both moving and original. Mastery of large-scale relief compositions subsequently passed to the work in the temples of the 19th and 20th dynasties. The most dramatic subject was war, whether the so-called triumph of Ramses II at Kadesh (Thebes and Abu Simbel), or the more genuine successes of Ramses III against the Libyans and the Sea Peoples (Madīnat Habu). The size and vitality of these ostentatious scenes are stupendous, even if their execution tends to be slapdash.

The artistic renaissance of the 25th and 26th dynasties is evident in painting and relief as well as in sculpture. Although the fine work in the tomb of Montemhat at Thebes is distinctly archaizing, it is, nevertheless, exceptional in quality. The skills of the Egyptian draftsman, nurtured by centuries of exercise at large and small scale, remained highly professional. This skill is seen at its most consistent level in the illumination of papyruses. The practice of including drawings, often painted, in religious papyruses flourished from the time of the 18th dynasty and reached a high point about 1300 BC. The peak of achievement is probably represented by the Book of the Dead of the scribe Ani, in the vignettes of which both technique and the use of colour are outstanding. Subsequently, and especially in the Late period, pure line drawing was increasingly employed.

PLASTIC ARTS

In Egypt pottery provided the basic material for vessels of all kinds. Fine wares and many other small objects were made from faience. Glass arrived late on the scene and was used somewhat irregularly from the New Kingdom onward.

POTTERY

Generally speaking, Egyptian pottery had few artistic pretensions. In the tomb of Tutankhamen most of the pottery vessels were simple wine jars in the form of amphorae. It is surprising that no finer pottery vessels were found, because high-quality ware was made during the late 18th and 19th dynasties, often brightly painted with floral designs.

Pottery was rarely modeled, although human and animal figures occur in small numbers throughout the Dynastic period. Small vessels in animal form were also made, especially during the Middle and New kingdoms, and a fine category of highly burnished red pottery vases in female form was produced during the 18th dynasty.

FAIENCE

The use of pottery was filled with modeled faience objects (a glazed composition of ground quartz), most commonly blue or green in colour. In the Early Dynastic period it was much used for the making of small animal and human figures, and throughout the Dynastic period it continued to be used in this way, among the most striking results being the blue-glazed hippopotamus figures of Middle Kingdom date.

In the Late period, in particular, the making of amulets and divine figurines in faience was highly developed, and many pieces display a high standard of molding and perfection of glazing. The vast quantities of ushabti (shabti, or shawabty), small statuettes that stood in for the deceased, are mostly routine work, but the finest examples from the New Kingdom, and some of Saite date, show complete mastery of a difficult technique.

Faience tiles were also first made in the early dynasties and were used chiefly for wall decoration, as in the subterranean chambers of the Step Pyramid. In the New Kingdom, tiles with floral designs were used in houses and palaces in the reigns of Amenhotep III and his successors. During the 19th and 20th dynasties royal palaces at Per Ramessu (modern Qantīr), Tell al-Yahudīyah, and Madīnat Habu were embellished with remarkable polychrome tiles, many of which bear figures of captive foreigners.

Throughout the Dynastic period faience was regularly used for simple beads, amulets, and other components of jewelry. Quite exceptional is the extraordinary was-sceptre (a symbol of divine power) found at Tūkh, near Naqādah. It is dated to the reign of Amenhotep II and originally measured about six and a half feet (two metres) in length.

GLASS

In the form of glaze, glass was known to the ancient Egyptians from early predynastic times, but the material was not used independently until the 18th dynasty. From the mid-18th dynasty and during the 19th dynasty glass was used

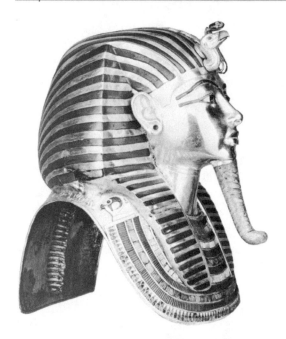

Gold funerary mask of the pharaoh Tutankhamen inlaid with lapis lazuli and coloured glass, New Kingdom, 18th dynasty (c. 1323 BC); in the Egyptian Museum, Cairo. Height 53.3 cm. Courtesy of the Egyptian Museum, Cairo. Photograph, Eliot Elisofon, Life, c. 1948, Time, Inc.

for small amulets, beads, inlays, and especially for small vessels. The material was opaque, blue being the predominant colour, although other bright colours were also achieved. The vessels, made around sand cores, were mostly drinking cups or flasks for precious liquids and were often decorated with trailed patterns applied as glass threads. Glass was certainly a material of luxury, a fact confirmed by the presence of two glass goblets with gold rims among a treasure of precious vessels from the reign of Thutmose III.

The use of glass for inlay is notably demonstrated in Tutankhamen's golden throne, in his solid gold mask, and in much of his jewelry. After the 19th dynasty, glass manufacture seems largely to have been discontinued until the Late period, when the use of glass for inlays was revived.

DECORATIVE ARTS

Among the decorative arts practiced in ancient Egypt were the making of jewelry and the creation of a variety of objects in metals, wood, ivory, and bone.

JEWELRY

Gold provided Egyptian jewelry with its richness; it was used for settings, cloisonné work, chains, and beads, both solid and hollow. Soldering, granulation, and wire making were practiced. Precious stones were not used, but a wide range of semiprecious stones was exploited: carnelian, amethyst, garnet, red and yellow jasper, lapis lazuli, feldspar, turquoise, and agate. Additional colours and textures were provided by faience and glass.

Ancient Egyptian jewelers had a fine eye for colour and an excellent sense of design. From the earliest dynasties come bracelets from the tomb of King Djer at Abydos; from the 4th dynasty, the armlets of Queen Hetepheres, of silver inlaid with carnelian, turquoise, and lapis lazuli. There are examples of splendid and delicate jewelry dating from the Middle Kingdom; in particular, pieces were found

Gold pectoral with semiprecious stones belonging to Sesostris III, Middle Kingdom, 12th dynasty (1991–1786 BC). Hirmer Fotoarchiv, Munchen

at Dahshūr and Al-Lāhūn—circlets of Princess Khnumet, pectorals of Princess Sithathor and Queen Meret, and girdles of Princess Sithathor-iunet.

The large and spectacular collection of jewelry buried with Queen Ahhotep of the early 18th dynasty includes many unusual designs; her gold chain is a masterpiece. Much fine 18th-dynasty jewelry has survived, but all is dominated by that of Tutankhamen. This huge collection demonstrates all the techniques of the goldsmith's and the lapidary's arts.

COPPER AND BRONZE

The techniques of metalworking were probably introduced into Egypt from the Middle East at a very early date. At first copper was most commonly used; but

Pectoral of gold, silver, and semiprecious stones, from the tomb of Tutankhamen, c. 1340 BC; in the Egyptian Museum, Cairo. Robert Harding Picture Library

from at least the late 3rd millennium it was often alloyed with tin, as bronze.

The skill and artistry of the metalworker is shown in the fine bowls, jugs, and other vessels from all periods and in statues and statuettes of gods, kings, and ordinary mortals. Most vessels were made by raising from metal ingots beaten on wooden anvils. In the Late period many vessels were produced by casting. Huge *situlae*, vessels used for carrying sacred liquids, are often decorated with scenes and inscriptions.

The earliest and largest metal figure from Egypt is the life-size statue of Pepi I made of copper plates fitted to a wooden core; the plates were probably beaten, not cast. Casting in open molds was developed early for tools and weapons, but the lost-wax process (*cire-perdue*), using closed molds, was not employed until the Middle Kingdom. Even in the 18th dynasty the casting of bronze figures occurred only on a relatively small scale.

The casting of large-scale bronze figures achieved its highest point in the late New Kingdom down to the 25th dynasty. The outstanding example from this period is the figure of Karomama. The exceptionally elegant modeling of the female form is greatly enriched by inlays of gold and silver reproducing the feathered pattern of the gown and an elaborate collar of floral motifs.

In the Late period huge numbers of excellent castings of conventional sacred figures and animals were produced. The so-called Gayer-Anderson cat is technically and artistically without peer.

GOLD AND SILVER

Gold was more easily obtainable in ancient Egypt than silver and was therefore less valuable (until the late New Kingdom). Gold was also easier to work and unaffected by environmental conditions. In consequence, many more gold than silver objects have survived.

Apart from jewelry, gold was lavishly used for many decorative purposes as thin sheet, leaf, and inlay, in funerary equipment, and for vessels and furniture. The range of uses is best exemplified in the objects from the tomb of Tutankhamen.

The gold-plated, gold-inlaid furniture of Queen Hetepheres of 4th-dynasty date reveals how early Egyptian craftsmen mastered the working of gold. Gold vessels have rarely survived, but those from the royal burials of Tanis preserve styles and techniques that go back to the traditions of the New Kingdom and earlier. Gold statuettes also are rare, but again, surviving examples, such as the magnificent falcon head of a cult statue of 6th-dynasty date from Hierakonpolis and the divine triad of Osiris, Isis, and Horus of the 22nd dynasty, show the achievements of early and late times.

In a hoard of precious vessels found at Bubastis and dated to the 19th dynasty, there were three silver pieces of exceptional interest, in particular a jug whose handle is of gold and in the shape of a goat. Greater availability of silver in later times is demonstrated by two massive silver coffins and a number of vessels in the royal burials at Tanis.

WOOD

The wooden sculpture of the Old Kingdom shows the carver of wood at his most skillful and sensitive. But it is in the field of cabinetmaking that the ancient woodworker excelled. Best known are the many chairs, tables, stools, beds, and chests found in Tutankhamen's tomb. Many of the designs are exceptionally practical and elegant. Techniques of inlay, veneering, and marquetry are completely mastered. One chest is veneered with strips of ivory and inlaid with 33,000

small pieces of ivory and ebony. Fine furniture was being produced in very early times, as is confirmed by the skillfully restored furniture from the secondary burial of Hetepheres.

Among the most charming and delicate products of the Egyptian woodworker are the many toilet spoons and containers in the form of graceful swimming girls, lute players in the marshes, and fishes and animals. At the other extreme, nothing is more remarkable than the great boat, more than 140 feet (43 metres) long, found in a trench by the side of the Great Pyramid.

IVORY AND BONE

Of the few small ivory figurines to have survived from pharaonic times, two royal representations found in the Early Dynastic temple at Abydos are outstanding. There can be little doubt, in spite of the paucity of survivals, that fine decorative objects of ivory were made at all periods. A gazelle and a grasshopper of the 18th dynasty may truly be described as *objets de vertu*. Many fine examples of the use of ivory were found in Tutankhamen's tomb, from simple geometric marquetry patterns to box panels carved with exquisitely informal scenes of the king with his queen.

GRECO-ROMAN EGYPT

After the conquest of Egypt by Alexander the Great, the independent rule of pharaohs in the strict sense came to an end.

Under the Ptolemies, whose rule followed Alexander's, profound changes took place in art and architecture.

The most lasting impression of the new period is made by its architectural legacy. Although very little survives of important funerary architecture, there is a group of tombs at Tunah al-Jabal of unusual form and great importance. Most interesting is the tomb of Petosiris, high priest of Thoth in nearby Hermopolis Magna in the late 4th century BC. It is in the form of a small temple with a pillared portico, elaborate column capitals, and a large forecourt. In its mural decorations a strong Greek influence merges with the traditional Egyptian modes of expression.

A boom in temple building of a more conventional kind followed the establishment of the Ptolemaic regime. At Dandarah, Esna, Idfū, Kawm Umbū (Kôm Ombo), and Philae the Egyptian cult temple can be studied better than at almost any earlier temple. Though erected by the Macedonian rulers of Egypt, these late temples employ purely Egyptian architectural conventions but include flourishes that appear only in the Ptolemaic period, such as pillars in the shape of colossal sistra, Composite capitals with elaborate floral forms, monumental screen walls, and subterranean crypts. The temple of Horus at Idfū is the most complete, displaying all the essential elements of the classical Egyptian temple, but for exploitation of setting and richness of detail it is difficult to fault the temples of Philae and Kawm Umbū, in particular.

Black diorite head of a high official, possibly a high priest of Ptah of Memphis, Ptolemaic period (c. 75 BC); in the Brooklyn Museum, New York. Height 41.4 cm. Courtesy of the Brooklyn Museum, gift of the Charles Edwin Wilbour Fund

In relief carving a noticeable change had taken place in the conventional proportions of human figures during the Saite period, and subsequently, with added influences from Greek art, a more voluptuous style of human representation developed. Yet there is much to admire in the best reliefs of the Hathor Temple at Dandarah and in the double cult temple of Sebek and Horus at Kawm Umbū.

Mummy portrait of a young girl, encaustic painting from Al-Fayyūm, Egypt, 2nd century; in the Louvre, Paris. Giraudon/Art Resource, New York

Generous representation of the human form, especially the female form, also characterizes the sculpture of the Ptolemaic period, and there is little to match the figure of Queen Arsinoe II. It is in the treatment of the head, however, that the greatest changes took place. It is a matter of debate whether the new emphasis on portraiture was attributable to influences from the Classical world or was a development of earlier Egyptian sculptural tendencies. Fine pieces such as the schist "green" head of a man could not have failed to impress the observer from the Ptolemaic court or the later Roman administration. One of the finest surviving heads, in diorite and slightly larger than life-size and of dominating appearance, is the "black" head now in the Brooklyn Museum.

Throughout the Ptolemaic period votive sculpture of private persons was made in great quantity. After the Roman conquest it became rare and of indifferent quality. Such Egyptian art as can be isolated in the Roman period is found in funerary equipment—in coffins, shrouds, and panel portraits. A mixture of Egyptian and Classical styles and of diverse symbolisms can be observed. The great shroud showing the deceased and his mummy protected by the mortuary deity, Anubis, while harking back to the traditions of pharaonic Egypt, also displays in the figure of the deceased a style that points to Byzantium.

The mummy, or Fayum, portraits are Egyptian only in that they are associated with essentially Egyptian burial customs. Painted in an encaustic technique, they represent mostly Greek inhabitants of Egypt. Seen properly in context, as in the complete mummy of Artemidorus, they provide a strange epilogue to the funerary art of 3,000 years of pharaonic Egypt. In this field and in a few others the vigour of the native tradition persisted artistically up to the Roman conquest. Thereafter the decline was rapid and complete. By the 3rd century AD Egypt was on the way to becoming a Christian country. The old tradition was not only destroyed, it was no longer valued. Coptic art was to find its inspiration elsewhere.

CHAPTER 10

EGYPTOMANIA

Fascination with Egypt has existed for millennia, Isis temples in Greece being known by the 4th century BC. Romans imported a multitude of genuine Egyptian objects and created their own "Egyptian" works: Hadrian's villa at Tivoli, built c. AD 125–134, featured an Egyptian garden with Egyptianizing statues of Antinoüs, who had been deified by Hadrian after drowning in the Nile. Romans also built pyramid tombs and worshipped Egyptian deities. Isis, one of the most important goddesses of ancient Egypt, was revered throughout the Roman Empire. Often depicted with Horus, the falcon god, on her lap, Isis became a prototype for Christian images of the Virgin and Child.

From the arrival of Islamic forces (AD 641) until the late 1600s, few Europeans visited Egypt, although they began to import mummies as early as the 13th century, usually to be ground up and used medicinally or as a pigment in paintings. Study of Egypt was thus based largely on Egyptian and Egyptianizing monuments uncovered in Roman ruins, primarily in Rome and elsewhere in Italy. The deities depicted on the Mensa Isiaca, a 1st-century-AD inlaid bronze table perhaps from an Isis sanctuary, and the statue of Antinoüs with a Classical body and pseudo-Egyptian costume became the standards for depicting Egyptian figures, while the proportions of Rome's surviving pyramid, built for Caius Cestius (c. 12 BC), was long a prototype for European representations of pyramids. Scholars began to distinguish between Roman, Egyptian, and Roman Egyptianizing works only in the late 1500s and early 1600s.

The rediscovery of Classical authors, including the Greek historian Herodotus, fueled Renaissance interest in Egypt. Of particular importance were the Hermetic texts, all allegedly composed by Hermes Trismegistus ("thrice great Thoth"), a mythical Egyptian sometimes identified with the god and credited with inventing writing and science. They have coloured Western ideas about Egypt ever since, being particularly important to esoteric movements such as Rosicrucianism—a movement begun in the late 16th and early 17th century whose central feature is the belief that its members possess secret wisdom that was handed down to them from ancient times—and Freemasonry, the largest worldwide secret society. Popes reerected obelisks in Rome, and Egyptian elements reappeared in room decorations. By the mid-1600s, the great Italian sculptor Gian Lorenzo Bernini was designing pyramid tombs for popes, and sphinxes and obelisks littered Europe's royal gardens.

The 18th century's interest in Egypt was widespread, from Enlightenment philosophers to Romantic poets. Bernard de Montfaucon (1675–1741) wrote the first nonmystical analysis of Europe's Egyptian/Egyptianizing antiquities, although depicting them in Hellenistic style. English pottery designer and manufacturer Josiah Wedgwood's first Egyptian wares appeared in 1768, and in 1769 Giovanni Battista Piranesi published

an early attempt at a coherent Egyptian style. Abbé Terrasson's novel *Séthos*, published in 1731, was a source of inspiration for Mozart's Masonic-influenced *The Magic Flute*, which debuted in 1791. Exploration of Egypt, however, began relatively late, the books by Danish traveler Frederick Norden (1737), who ventured as far as Nubia, and the Englishman Richard Pococke (1743) being among the earliest to present firsthand information about Egypt.

Interest was thus already high in 1798 when Napoleon invaded Egypt with scientists as well as soldiers. The expedition and its monumental *Description de l'Égypte*, which began publication in 1809, led to a burst of Egyptomania. Added impetus was provided by Champollion's deciphering of the hieroglyphs on the Rosetta Stone (1822), proving them to be language, not mystic symbols, and by the installation of an obelisk in Paris (1836). Scientific expeditions and enterprising individuals such as Giovanni Battista Belzoni brought back objects for new museum collections, while artists such as David Roberts and early photographers revealed Egypt to the world. International exhibitions, beginning with London's Crystal Palace Exposition (1854), also fostered Egyptomania by presenting reproductions of Egyptian buildings and exhibiting Egyptian artifacts. The Suez Canal's opening (1869) and the erection of obelisks in London (1878) and New York (1881) contributed to another spike of Egyptomania in the 1870s–80s.

Egyptian Hall, owned by British antiquities collector and promoter William Bullock. The hall, completed in 1812, was designed to capture the fancy of a public fascinated by all things Egyptian. Hulton Archive/Getty Images

Egyptianisms pervade 19th-century interior design and decorative arts. Neoclassical furniture displayed Antinoüs-type supports and lotus friezes, decorative objects (e.g., mantel clocks with a pair of vases or obelisks) and jewelry sported scarabs, cartouches, and sphinxes, and china services bore Egyptian motifs. In the 19th century, however, Egyptomania in the decorative arts remained largely the preserve of those who could afford expensive objets d'art.

Nineteenth-century architectural Egyptomania varied from Tsarskoe Selo's gateway (St. Petersburg, 1827–30), based on pylons in the *Description*, to William Bullock's fanciful Egyptian Hall (London, 1812). Designed to attract customers, it even housed an early exhibition of Egyptian antiquities (1821–22). Architects also used Egypt's associations with durability to allay fears of new technologies. Reservoirs had massive, battered walls, while pylons and obelisks supported suspension bridges. Egyptian-style university and museum buildings recalled Egypt's reputation for wisdom. In America, Egyptianizing prisons evoked the law's sublime nature to inspire reform. New garden cemeteries such as Highgate (London, 1839) invoked Egypt's time-defying traits with pylon gateways and temple-shaped mausolea.

Writers, artists, and composers also used Egyptian themes. Théophile Gauthier's novels remained popular into the 20th century, and Giuseppe Verdi's *Aida*, created for the opening of the Cairo Opera House (1871), was neither the first nor the only Egyptian-based opera. Yet, even as Egypt became better understood, allowing stage designers, for instance, to aspire to archaeological accuracy and painters to render Egyptian monuments faithfully (if often at reduced or enlarged scale), older sources and ideas of mysterious Egypt remained popular. Sarah Bernhardt played Cleopatra (1890) as the traditional seductress, while Arthur Conan Doyle's story *Lot No. 249* (1892) helped popularize the evil reanimated mummy.

In the early 20th century, mass production made Egyptianizing items more widely available. The fledgling movie industry eagerly exploited Egypt with movies like *La Roman de la momie* (1910–11, based on Gauthier's 1857 novel), Theda Bara's *Cleopatra* (1917), and biblical epics (*The Ten Commandments*, 1922–23). Bullock's Egyptian Hall showed movies from 1896 until it was demolished in 1904, and the first Egyptianizing movie palaces appeared in the early 1920s. Throughout the century, greater education, new discoveries, and, above all, the growth of mass media fostered a broader appreciation of ancient Egypt and a democratization of Egyptomania.

The 1922 discovery of Tutankhamen's tomb unleashed a wave of Egyptomania that endured until World War II, influencing the whole Art Deco movement and inspiring writers from Thomas Mann to Agatha Christie. *The Mummy* (1932) and its successors preserved the idea of mysterious Egypt, while Claudette Colbert's *Cleopatra* (1932) saw history as an excuse for spectacle, a tradition continued by Elizabeth Taylor's *Cleopatra* (1963). Architects used Egypt's pure lines and forms (now seen as modern), sometimes combining them with elaborate Egyptianizing decoration as in New York's Chrysler Building (1930). Domestic Egyptianizing architecture, however, was rare except in California, where it was perhaps inspired by the sunny climate and Hollywood's fantasy-based film industry.

After World War II, Egyptomania virtually disappeared, although the 1954 discovery of the Giza solar boat inspired Howard Hawks's *The Land of the Pharaohs* (1955), and mummies remained popular in movies and pulp fiction. The 1978 world tour of Tutankhamen artifacts sparked new interest that continues into the 21st century, as the proliferation of documentaries and books about Egypt demonstrates. Yet earlier traditions persist. Egypt's reputation for wisdom and durability promotes today's new technologies. In Tennessee, the Memphis Zoo's pylon entrance (1990–91) recalls 19th-century educational buildings, while Las Vegas's Luxor Casino (1993) is a successor to Bullock's Egyptian Hall. Evil mummies continued into the 21st century to make appearances in movies, and old ideas about "mystic Egypt" thrive. Eternal Egypt remains eternally fascinating.

APPENDIX: SELECTED SITES

ABŪ JIRĀB

Lying about 1 mile (1.6 km) north of Abū Ṣīr, between Ṣaqqārah and Al-Jīzah, Abū Jirāb (Abu Gurab, Abu Gurob) is known as the location of two 5th-dynasty (c. 2465–c. 2325 BC) sun temples. The first part of the 5th dynasty is recognized as a period of unusually strong emphasis on the worship of the sun god Re. Contemporary inscriptions record that six sun temples were built in that period. Only those of King Userkaf and King Neuserre, however, have been found and excavated, the latter one being better preserved because it was constructed entirely of stone. The temple of King Neuserre consisted of a large courtyard built on the edge of the desert and surrounded by storerooms, cult chambers, and an altar. On the western side a squat obelisk rested on a rectangular podium. A long covered passage approached the platform from the Nile River valley and was decorated with some of the most beautifully sculpted and painted scenes remaining from the Old Kingdom (c. 2575–c. 2130 BC).

ABŪ RUWAYSH

Abū Ruwaysh (Abu Roash) is the site of a 4th-dynasty (c. 2575–c. 2465 BC) pyramid built by Redjedef, usually considered the third of the seven kings of that dynasty. The site is about 5 miles (8 km) northwest of the Pyramids of Giza (Al-Jīzah) on the west bank of the Nile River. It is part of a UNESCO World Heritage site—along with Dahshūr, Ṣaqqārah, Abū Ṣīr, Memphis, and the Pyramids of Giza—that was designated in 1979. Of the pyramid superstructure very little remains, and it was probably never finished—a theory reinforced by evidence that the walls of the mortuary temple next to the pyramid were hastily made of mud brick instead of the usual cut stone. The mortuary cult of the king was certainly celebrated at Abū Ruwaysh, as indicated by the presence of large-scale statue fragments of Redjedef. Nothing remains of the pyramid's valley temple, but the causeway from it to the mortuary temple can still be traced.

An Early Dynastic (c. 2925–c. 2575 BC) private cemetery has also been found at Abu Ruwaysh.

ABŪ ṢĪR

Abū Ṣīr (also spelled Abusir) is situated between Al-Jīzah (Giza) and Ṣaqqārah, northern Egypt, where three 5th-dynasty (c. 2465–c. 2325 BC) kings (Sahure, Neferirkare, and Neuserre) built their pyramids. The pyramids were poorly constructed (in comparison with Egyptian monuments of similar types) and are now in a state of disrepair. The adjoining mortuary temples are notable for their elaborate sculptured wall reliefs and columns in the forms of palm, lotus, and papyrus plants. Near their pyramids a number of the kings, including Userkaf and Neuserre, built sanctuaries with obelisks dedicated to Re, the sun god. In 1979 Abū Ṣīr and other sites in the area—Dahshūr, Ṣaqqārah, Abū Ruwaysh, Memphis, and the Pyramids of Giza—were collectively designated a UNESCO World Heritage site.

Two significant groups of papyri have been discovered at Abū Ṣīr, one having been recovered in 1893 and another having come to light during excavations in 1982. The Abū Ṣīr papyri are the archives of the temple priesthood of the mortuary cult of Neferirkare and provide important information on the economic function of an Old Kingdom (c. 2575–c. 2130 BC) funerary endowment.

Although numerous excavations in the area have usually yielded disturbed remains, in 1998 a team of archaeologists from Charles University in Prague uncovered the intact sarcophagus of Iufaa, a priest and palace administrator who lived about 525 BC.

AL-LĀHŪN

The site of Al-Lāhūn (El Lahun, or Illahun) is located southwest of Al-Fayyūm near the southward turn of the Baḥr Yūsuf canal in Al-Fayyūm *muḥāfaẓah* (governorate). Al-Lāhūn was the location of a Middle Kingdom (1938–c. 1630 BC) pyramid and of a workmen's village of approximately the same date, and findings in the early 21st century revealed that it was a significant site in the Early Dynastic period (c. 2925–c. 2575 BC) as well.

The pyramid, built by King Sesostris II (reigned 1844–37 BC), fourth of the eight kings of the 12th dynasty (1938–c. 1756), was unusual in that the entrance to the burial chamber was not in the north side of the pyramid but was found instead to the south of the structure. Although the pyramid itself was robbed in antiquity, a treasure of jewelry was discovered in the tombs of the princesses, located within the pyramid enclosure. In technical perfection and artistic mastery this collection easily rivals all other Middle Kingdom objects of its type.

Excavation of the village, which was also inhabited during the Second Intermediate period (c. 1630–1540 BC), revealed a remarkable degree of town planning. Innumerable pieces of furniture and other household items were found, as well as a mass of papyri dealing with various topics, including letters, private wills, royal hymns, medical texts, and the temple archives of the pyramid cult. In 2009 excavations at Al-Lāhūn yielded a number of significant finds, including the body of a man identified by archaeologists as a senior government official. On the basis of engravings inscribed on its wooden coffin, the body was dated to the 2nd dynasty (c. 2775–c. 2650 BC), indicating that the site had been significant far earlier than previously thought.

AL-MAʿĀDĪ

Al-Maʿādī is a predynastic Egyptian site located just south of present-day Cairo in

Lower Egypt. The settlement at Al-Maʿādī was approximately contemporary with the Amratian and Gerzean cultures of Upper Egypt. Al-Maʿādī was apparently a village with a separate cemetery; the settlement was characterized by oval huts, ring-base vases, globular, rimmed-neck vessels, and large storage jars similar to those found at Gerzean sites. Copper was occasionally used, and Upper Egyptian stone vase types have been found. In addition to Al-Maʿādī's connections with the culture of Upper Egypt, its position on the southern leg of the Syro-Egyptian trade route also brought it under the cultural influence of Palestine.

BENI HASAN

Beni Hasan (or Banī Ḥasan) is a Middle Kingdom archaeological site (1938–c. 1630 BC), lying on the eastern bank of the Nile roughly 155 miles (245 km) south of Cairo. The site is noted for its rock-cut tombs of 11th- and 12th-dynasty officials of the 16th Upper Egyptian (Oryx) nome, or province. Some of the 39 tombs are painted with scenes of daily life and important biographical texts. The governors of the nome, whose capital was Menat Khufu, administered the eastern desert. The tomb of one, Khnumhotep II, contains a scene showing Semitic Bedouin merchants in richly coloured garments entering Egypt. Speos Artemidos, a rock-cut shrine originally dedicated to the local lion-headed goddess Pakhet, built by Queen Hatshepsut and Thutmose III of the 18th dynasty, lies

one mile (1.6 km) south in an ancient quarry, with a smaller shrine of Alexander II nearby.

DAHSHŪR

The ancient pyramid site of Dahshūr lies just south of Ṣaqqārah, northern Egypt, on the west bank of the Nile River. Dahshūr and other ruins in the area of ancient Memphis—Abū Ṣīr, Ṣaqqārah, Abū Ruwaysh, and the Pyramids of Giza—were collectively designated a UNESCO World Heritage site in 1979.

Two of its five extant pyramids date from the 4th dynasty (c. 2575–c. 2465 BC) and were built by King Snefru (reigned 2575–51). The earlier one, because of its peculiar double slope, is variously called the Blunted, Bent, False, or Rhomboidal Pyramid. It represents an early attempt to build a true pyramid, but the initial angle of slope (52°) was found to be too steep; the top portion of the pyramid was thereupon reduced to 43.5°. The best-preserved of the five, it is the only Old Kingdom (c. 2575–c. 2130 BC) pyramid with two entrances. The second of Snefru's pyramids at Dahshūr, the North Pyramid (Red Pyramid), was built at the lower slope angle of 43° and is therefore shorter. It is the first true pyramid successfully completed.

The three remaining extant pyramids belong to the 12th dynasty (1938–c. 1756 BC) and are not well preserved, their inner cores having been built largely of mud brick. The tombs of the royal families built near the 12th-dynasty pyramids contained a remarkable collection of jewelry and personal accoutrements—considered by some scholars to represent the highest stage of development in Egyptian metalworking and lapidary art. One important jewelry cache discovered at Dahshūr is that of Queen Weret, found in 1994 during excavations by the Metropolitan Museum of Art.

DAYR AL-BAḤRĪ

Dayr al-Baḥrī (Deir el-Bahri) is an archaeological site in the necropolis of Thebes. It is made up of a bay in the cliffs on the west bank of the Nile River east of the Valley of the Kings. Its name (Arabic for "northern monastery") refers to a monastery built there in the 7th century AD.

Of the three ancient Egyptian structures on the site, one, the funerary temple of King Mentuhotep II (built c. 1970 BC), has lost much of its superstructure. The second, the terraced temple of Queen Hatshepsut (built c. 1470 BC), was uncovered (1894–96) beneath the monastery ruins and subsequently underwent partial restoration. A fuller restoration of the third terrace, sanctuary, and retaining wall was started in 1968 by a Polish archaeological mission, which also found a third temple, built by Thutmose III about 1435 BC, above and between the two earlier temples. All three temples were linked by long causeways to valley temples with docking facilities. Situated under one of the cliffs, Hatshepsut's temple in particular is a famous example of creative architectural exploitation

of a site. All three temples were largely destroyed by progressive rock falls from the cliffs above.

During the Third Intermediate period (1075–656 BC) the area of Dayr al-Baḥrī was used as a private cemetery, and in the Ptolemaic period the sanctuary of Amon in Hatshepsut's temple was refurbished and rededicated to the deified individuals Imhotep and Amenhotep, son of Hapu. The temple of Hatshepsut was the site of a terrorist attack in 1997 in which more than 60 people, many of them tourists, were killed.

DAYR AL-MADĪNAH

The ancient site of Dayr al-Madīnah (Deir el-Medina) is situated on the west bank of the Nile River at Thebes in Upper Egypt. It is known primarily as the location of a settlement for craftsmen who laboured on the royal tombs, especially those in the nearby Valley of the Kings. The village, the best-preserved of its type, has provided scholars with helpful insights into the living conditions of those state labourers. The settlement has also yielded thousands of inscribed papyri fragments and ostraca; these documents have been an invaluable source of information not only about the literary and religious aspects of the workers' daily lives but also (especially regarding the 20th dynasty [1190–1075 BC]) about the economic and, less directly, the political fortunes of the time. Dayr al-Madīnah is also the location of numerous tombs of the artisans who lived in the New

Kingdom (c. 1539–1075 BC) village, private tombs from the 19th and 20th dynasties, and three temples erected for the workers' use.

KARNAK

The village of Karnak (Al-Karnak) is located in Qinā *muḥāfaẓah* (governorate), Upper Egypt, which has given its name to the northern half of the ruins of Thebes on the east bank of the Nile River, including the ruins of the Great Temple of Amon. Karnak and other areas of ancient Thebes—including Luxor, the Valley of the Kings, and the Valley of the Queens—were collectively designated a UNESCO World Heritage site in 1979.

Excavations in the 20th century pushed the history of the site back to the Gerzean period (c. 3400–c. 3100 BC), when a small settlement was founded on the wide eastern bank of the Nile floodplain. Karnak contains the northern group of the Theban city temples, called in ancient times Ipet-Isut, "Chosen of Places." The ruins cover a considerable area and are still impressive, though nothing remains of the houses, palaces, and gardens that must have surrounded the temple precinct in ancient times. The most northerly temple is the Temple of Mont, the war god, of which little now remains but the foundations. The southern temple, which has a horseshoe-shaped sacred lake, was devoted to the goddess Mut, wife of Amon; this also is much ruined. Both temples were built during the reign of Amenhotep III (1390–53 BC), whose

architect was commemorated by statues in the Temple of Mut.

Between these two precincts lay the largest temple complex in Egypt, and one of the largest in the world, the great metropolitan temple of the state god, Amon-Re. The complex was added to and altered at many periods and, in consequence, lacks a systematic plan. It has been called a great historical document in stone: in it are reflected the fluctuating fortunes of the Egyptian empire. There are no fewer than 10 pylons, separated by courts and halls and nowadays numbered for convenience, number one being the latest addition. Pylons one through six form the main east-west axis leading toward the Nile. The seventh and eighth pylons were erected in the 15th century BC by Thutmose III and Queen Hatshepsut, respectively, and the ninth and tenth during Horemheb's reign (1319–1292). These pylons formed a series of processional gateways at right angles to the main axis, linking the temple with that of Mut to the south and, farther, by way of the avenue of sphinxes, with the temple at Luxor 2 miles (3 km) away.

There are few extant traces of the original Middle Kingdom (1938–c. 1630 BC) temple save a small jubilee shrine of Sesostris I (reigned 1908–1875), now reconstructed from fragments found inside the third pylon. At the beginning of the New Kingdom (c. 1539–1075 BC), Thutmose I (reigned 1493–c. 1482) enclosed this 12th-dynasty (1938–c. 1756 BC) temple with a stone wall and fronted it with two pylons (the fourth and fifth), erecting two obelisks in front of the new temple facade. His son, Thutmose II (reigned 1482–79), added a broad festival court in front of the enlarged temple as well as another pair of obelisks. Hatshepsut then inserted a quartzite bark shrine dedicated to Amon in the centre of the temple, as well as two additional pairs of obelisks, one of which still stands. In the reign of Thutmose III (1479–26) the temple was greatly enlarged; not only did he add to the existing structures and add a pylon (the sixth) and pillared courts containing halls in which he inscribed the annals of his campaigns, but he also built to the east of the Middle Kingdom area a transverse temple in the form of a jubilee pavilion. On the walls of one of the rear rooms of this temple is carved a kind of pictorial catalog of the exotic animals and plants he had brought home from Asia in the 25th year of his reign. Other additions were made by his successors. Amenhotep III decided to demolish the festival court, building in its stead the colossal third pylon, filled largely with blocks from the dismantled structures. His son, Akhenaton (reigned 1353–36), built several large open-air temples around the periphery of Karnak in honour of his favoured deity, the Aton, all of which were later torn down following the restoration of the cult of Amon; *talatat* (small sandstone blocks that had been used in the construction of the Aton temples) were used as construction fill for the second, ninth, and tenth pylons, erected by Horemheb.

The most striking feature of the temple at Karnak is the hypostyle hall, which occupies the space between the third and second pylons. The area of this vast hall, one of the wonders of antiquity, is about 54,000 square feet (5,000 square metres). It was decorated by Seti I (reigned 1290–79) and Ramses II (reigned 1279–13), to whom much of the construction must be due. Twelve enormous columns, nearly 80 feet (24 metres) high, supported the roofing slabs of the central nave above the level of the rest so that light and air could enter through a clerestory. Seven lateral aisles on either side brought the number of pillars to 134. Historical reliefs on the outer walls show the victories of Seti in Palestine and Ramses II defeating the Hittites at the Battle of Kadesh.

Ramses III (reigned 1187–56) built a small temple to Amon outside the Ramesside pylon across from a triple shrine erected by Seti II (reigned 1204–1198). The Bubastite Gate at the southeast corner of this court commemorates the victories won by Sheshonk I (reigned 945–924), the biblical Shishak, in Palestine. The Kushite (Nubian) pharaoh Taharqa (reigned 690–664) erected a tall colonnade, of which one pillar still stands. The smaller monuments were subsequently enclosed by the addition of a vast court, probably begun during the Late Period (664–332 BC), fronted by the massive first pylon, an ambitious project that was never completed. Beyond it an avenue of sphinxes—set in place largely by Amenhotep III and usurped by Ramses II—leads to the quayside.

Within the enclosure of the Great Temple of Amon are included a number of other notable small shrines and temples. A temple to Ptah, in the north side of the enclosure, was built by Hatshepsut and Thutmose III and added to by the Ptolemies, who also embellished the Great Temple of Amon by the addition of granite shrines and gateways. To the south, Ramses III dedicated a temple to Khons, the moon god, which merits attention. A small late temple to Opet, the hippopotamus goddess, adjoins it.

The site of Karnak and other areas of ancient Thebes present a constant problem to the architects who seek to preserve them, for the foundations are inadequate, and moisture from the Nile's annual flood has disintegrated the sandstone at the base of walls and columns. The work of repairing and strengthening goes on continuously, and, as this work is carried out, new discoveries are constantly being made.

LUXOR

Luxor, the city and principal component of Al-Uqṣur urban *muḥāfaẓah* (governorate), has given its name to the southern half of the ruins of the ancient Egyptian city of Thebes.

The southern part of Thebes grew up around a beautiful temple dedicated to Amon, king of the gods, his consort Mut, and their son Khons. Commissioned by King Amenhotep III (Amenophis III; reigned 1390–53 BC) of the late 18th dynasty, the temple was built close to the Nile River and parallel with the bank and is known today as the Temple of Luxor. An avenue of sphinxes connected it to the Great Temple of Amon at Karnak. The modern name Luxor (Arabic: Al-Uqṣur) means "The Palaces" or perhaps "The Forts," from the Roman *castra*.

A small pavilion is all that is left of previous building on the site, though there probably was a temple there earlier in the 18th dynasty if not before. Amenhotep III's temple was completed by Tutankhamen (reigned 1333–23) and Horemheb (1319–1292). Ramses II (1279–13) added another court, a pylon, and obelisks; smaller additions were made to the temple in Ptolemaic times. Its hypostyle hall was at one time converted into a Christian church, and the remains of another Coptic church can be seen to the west of it.

The original part of the Temple of Luxor consisted of a large peristyle court and a complex of halls and chambers beyond. In one hall is a granite shrine of Alexander the Great. The great peristyle forecourt is surrounded on three sides by a double row of graceful papyrus-cluster columns, their capitals imitating the umbels of the papyrus plant in bud. An entrance flanked by the towers of a pylon was planned for the north end, but this design was altered, and, instead, the most striking feature of the temple, a majestic colonnade of 14 pillars, 52 feet (16 metres) high, was added. This colonnade, which also has papyrus-umbel capitals, may have been intended for the central nave of a hypostyle hall similar to that at Karnak, but the side aisles were not built; instead, enclosing walls were built down either side. Ramses II added an outer court, decorated with colossal statues of himself between the pillars of a double colonnade, and a lofty pylon on which he depicted festival scenes and episodes from his wars in Syria. In front of the pylon were colossal statues of the pharaoh (some of which remain) and a pair of obelisks, one of which still stands; the other was removed in 1831 and reerected in the Place de la Concorde in Paris.

When Thebes declined politically, Luxor remained the populated part of the town, which huddled around the Ramesside pylon. A Roman legion had its headquarters inside the 18th-dynasty temple, and Coptic churches were built around the temple and in the Ramesside court. In the Fāṭimid period (909–1171), a mosque was built over the foundations of the church in the court; the mosque was dedicated to Sheikh Yūsuf al-Ḥaggāg, a local saint who is reputed to have introduced Islam to Luxor. His feast is celebrated with a boat procession resembling an ancient rite, the festival of Opet, during which, on the 19th day of the second month, Amon was said to come from Karnak on his state barge to visit his other temple at Luxor, escorted by the people of Thebes in holiday attire. Reliefs on the walls of the great colonnade depict preparations for the procession of sacred barks during the festival.

Luxor, together with other Theban sites—Karnak, the Valley of the Queens, and the Valley of the Kings—was designated a UNESCO World Heritage site in 1979. Excavations and preservation efforts have been ongoing. In 1988 the Egyptian Antiquities Organization uncovered numerous 18th-dynasty statues at the court of Amenhotep III, and in 1995 work was initiated to preserve the columns and foundations of the court.

MAYDŪM

The ancient site of Maydūm (Medum) is located near Memphis on the west bank of the Nile River in Banī Suwayf *muḥāfaẓah* (governorate). It contains the earliest-known pyramid complex with all the parts of a normal Old Kingdom (*c.* 2575–c. 2130 BC) funerary monument. These parts included the pyramid itself, a mortuary temple, and a sloping causeway leading to a valley temple built near the Nile. The Maydūm pyramid was originally a seven-stepped pyramid to which another step was added. Finally, the steps were filled in, and the entire structure was overlaid with fine Tura limestone, giving it the appearance of a true pyramid. Most scholars agree that the pyramid was probably begun by Huni, the last king of the 3rd dynasty (*c.* 2650–c. 2575), but was apparently completed by his successor, Snefru, the first king of the 4th dynasty (*c.* 2575–c. 2465). Late in its reconstruction under Snefru, the outer casing and fill of the pyramid began to collapse. The work was abandoned, and the mortuary chapel remained uninscribed. The collapse produced the present appearance of the pyramid.

MEMPHIS

Memphis was the capital of ancient Egypt and an important centre during much of Egyptian history. It is located south of the Nile River delta, on the west bank of the river, and about 15 miles (24 km) south of modern Cairo. Closely associated with the ancient city's site are the cemeteries, or necropolises, of Memphis, where the famous pyramids of Egypt are located. From north to south the main pyramid fields are: Abū Ruwaysh, Giza, Zāwiyat al-ʿAryān, Abū Ṣīr, Ṣaqqārah, and Dahshūr. The Memphis archaeological zone was designated a UNESCO World Heritage site in 1979.

According to a commonly accepted tradition, Memphis was founded about 2925 BC by Menes, who supposedly united the two prehistoric kingdoms of Upper and Lower Egypt. The original name of the city was the White Walls, and the term may have referred originally to the king's palace, which would have been built of whitewashed brick. The modern name of Memphis is a Greek version of the Egyptian Men-nefer, the name of the nearby pyramid of the 6th-dynasty (c. 2325–c. 2150 BC) king Pepi I. Another geographic term for Memphis, Hut-ka-Ptah ("mansion of the *ka* of Ptah"), rendered

Aigyptos in Greek, was later applied to the country as a whole.

Ptah, the local god of Memphis, was a patron of craftsmen and artisans and, in some contexts, a creator god as well. The great temple of Ptah was one of the city's most prominent structures. According to an Egyptian document known as the "Memphite Theology," Ptah created humans through the power of his heart and speech; the concept, having been shaped in the heart of the creator, was brought into existence through the divine utterance itself. In its freedom from the conventional physical analogies of the creative act and in its degree of abstraction, this text is virtually unique in Egypt, and it testifies to the philosophical sophistication of the priests of Memphis.

The prominence of Memphis during the earliest periods is indicated by the extensive cemeteries of the Early Dynastic period (c. 2925–c. 2575 BC) and Old Kingdom (c. 2575–c. 2130 BC) that cluster along the desert bluffs to the west. Large elaborately niched tombs of the 1st and 2nd dynasties (c. 2925–c. 2650 BC) found at Ṣaqqārah, once argued to be royal monuments, were later accepted as private tombs of powerful courtiers.

Memphis reached preeminence by the 3rd dynasty. The 3rd-century-BC historian Manetho calls the 3rd and 4th dynasties (c. 2650–c. 2465 BC) Memphite, and the huge royal pyramid tombs of this period, in the necropolises of Memphis, confirm this. Djoser, the second king of the 3rd dynasty, was the builder of the Step Pyramid of Ṣaqqārah, the earliest royal foundation at Memphis and the first important stone building in Egypt. Imhotep, the king's architect and adviser, is credited with this architectural feat; his reputation as a wise man and physician led in later times to his deification and his identification with the Greek god Asclepius.

The remains of several unfinished or badly ruined pyramids near Memphis have been attributed to other 3rd-dynasty kings. The first king of the 4th dynasty, Snefru, built two pyramid tombs at Dahshūr. The three great pyramids of Giza belong to Khufu, Khafre, and Menkaure, later 4th-dynasty monarchs. The Great Sphinx at Giza dates from the time of Khafre. The last known king of this dynasty, Shepseskaf, built his tomb at South Ṣaqqārah. It was not a pyramid but a distinctive oblong structure with sloping sides, now called the Maṣṭabat Firʿawn.

The royal pyramids are surrounded by large cemeteries where the courtiers and officials who had served the king during his lifetime were buried. The beautiful reliefs in certain of these tombs include scenes of daily life and thus give some idea of the crafts, costumes, and occupations of the royal court of Memphis. Since little has survived of domestic architecture and household furnishings, these reliefs are a valuable source of information on such subjects. A notable exception to the general rule of loss and destruction is the hidden tomb of Queen Hetepheres, the mother of Khufu, which was discovered near the Great Pyramid of Giza.

Though the queen's body was unaccountably missing from her sarcophagus, her funerary equipment and furniture survived. The exquisite craftsmanship of these objects testify, as do the splendid low reliefs of the tombs, to the high development of the arts and crafts of the period. Indeed, it is believed by some scholars that the Old Kingdom, influenced by the craftsmen of the Memphite court and the philosopher-theologians of Ptah, reached a peak of "classic" culture that was never surpassed in Egypt.

The kings of the 5th dynasty (c. 2465–c. 2325 BC) moved south of Giza to build their funerary monuments; their pyramids, at Abū Ṣīr, are much smaller than those of the 4th dynasty, but the pyramid temples and causeways were decorated with fine reliefs. This dynasty was probably marked by a decline of Memphite influence paralleling the rise of a sun cult centred at Heliopolis. The major monuments of the period are not the pyramids but the sun temples, which were, however, also part of the so-called Memphite pyramid area, not far from Abū Ṣīr.

During the 6th dynasty, which Manetho also designates as Memphite, the funerary monuments in the pyramid field of Ṣaqqārah continued to decline in size and workmanship. At that time the influence of the centralized government at Memphis began to wane, as is indicated by the increased prominence of provincial cities and the number of fine tombs located away from the Memphis area. This process of decentralization ended in the First Intermediate Period, a time of internal breakdown. Manetho's 7th and 8th dynasties (*c.* 2150–*c.* 2130 BC) are both called Memphite, but it is believed that both dynasties together comprised a very short period and that the old Memphite house lost its control over the provincial princes soon after the end of the 6th dynasty.

Memphite influence continued during the Middle Kingdom (1938–*c.* 1630 BC), when Egypt was once more reunited, with the official residence of the 12th dynasty (1938–*c.* 1756) at nearby Itj-tawy (near modern Al-Lisht), near the entrance to Al-Fayyūm. Several 12th-dynasty monarchs erected pyramids at Dahshūr, the southernmost of the Memphite pyramid fields, but the majority of Middle Kingdom monuments were located nearer to Al-Lisht. Yet the predominant artistic and administrative influences during this period seem to be Memphite, and virtually every 12th-dynasty ruler added to the great temple of Ptah.

Another period of political and social chaos followed the 13th dynasty. This Second Intermediate Period (*c.* 1630–1540 BC) is characterized by the presence in Egypt of the Asian Hyksos peoples. According to the 1st-century-AD historian Josephus, the Hyksos king, whom he calls Salitis, made his capital at Memphis and from there ruled both Upper and Lower Egypt. Inscriptional and archaeological evidence, though it is scanty, tends to confirm the assumption that the Hyksos controlled northern Egypt, but their capital is generally supposed to have been located at Avaris, near Tanis,

in the Nile delta. Records left by Kamose, the 17th-dynasty (*c.* 1630–1540 BC) king who initiated the reconquest of Egypt from the Hyksos, describe his holdings as extending from Elephantine to Hermopolis Magna but note that he "could not pass by (the invader) as far as Memphis."

With the final expulsion of the Hyksos and the restoration of a united kingdom under the 18th dynasty (*c.* 1539–1292 BC), based at Thebes in Upper Egypt, Memphis entered a new period of prosperity. Some scholars claim that Memphis never lost its political preeminence and that during the New Kingdom (*c.* 1539–1075 BC), as in earlier times, the city was the actual political capital of Egypt, with Thebes merely the religious centre. Such a hypothesis is impossible to prove, and it may well be that such distinctions, with their rigidity and exclusiveness, are meaningless in terms of Egyptian culture.

The importance of Memphis was based to a considerable extent on its venerable religious role. Certain of the coronation ceremonies were traditionally enacted in Memphis, as was the Heb-Sed festival, a jubilee celebrated by the king after 30 years of rule and repeated every three years thereafter, perhaps a ritual reenactment of the unification of Egypt.

During the New Kingdom, Memphis probably functioned as the second, or northern, capital of Egypt. At one time it seems to have been the principal residence of the crown prince. Several 18th-dynasty inscriptions mention royal hunting parties in the desert near the Sphinx. Amenhotep II (reigned c. 1426–00 BC) was born at Memphis and held the office of high priest there. Both he and his son, Thutmose IV (reigned 1400–1390 BC), left inscriptions at Giza.

Despite the rise of the god Amon of Thebes, Ptah remained one of the principal gods of the pantheon. The great temple of Ptah was added to or rebuilt by virtually every king of the 18th dynasty. Chapels were constructed by Thutmose I, Thutmose IV, and Amenhotep III. Amenhotep III's son, the religious reformer Akhenaton, built a temple to his god, Aton, in Memphis. A number of handsome private tombs dating from this period in the Memphite necropolis testify to the existence of a sizable court.

During the New Kingdom the city shared the increasingly cosmopolitan character of the nation, as trade, foreign conquest, and travel developed. Though Memphis was not on the Nile, it was connected with it by a canal, and it was probably important as a commercial centre. Specific quarters of the city were named for the foreign colonies—slaves, prisoners of war, or merchants—who resided there. A section called the "Field of the Hittites" is known, as are, in later periods, sections inhabited by Carians and Phoenicians.

Under the 19th dynasty (1292–1190 BC) a new royal residence was built farther north at Per Ramessu in the delta, but Memphis continued to be important. The great temple of Ptah was rebuilt. The kings of that period pillaged the monuments of their predecessors for building materials, and some of the reused blocks come not only from structures in the city but also from temples and pyramid complexes in the Memphite necropolises. Ramses II (reigned 1279–13 BC) erected several colossi in the temple. The Serapeum, dedicated to the cult of Apis, the bull-god, and built in the form of a labyrinth, was begun under the son of Ramses II, Khaemwese, high priest of Ptah.

By the end of the 20th dynasty (1190–1075 BC) the united kingdom had begun to break down once again. The official capitals were Tanis and Thebes, but the royal palace at Memphis also continued to be mentioned. The growing popularity of the Apis cult led to further enlargement of the Serapeum. In the 8th century BC the Nubian king Piye conquered Egypt and restored its unity. Nubia (Kush), to the south of Egypt, had been under Egyptian political and cultural influence for centuries. An inscription describing Piye's campaign has survived, and it mentions a siege of Memphis. The city had fortified walls and was surrounded by water, presumably from its encircling canals. Piye took the city, but it was left to his brother and successor, Shabaka, to claim the royal title. There are some indications that this king made Memphis his capital. But the Kushite dynasty was overthrown shortly thereafter, when the Assyrians invaded Egypt. Records left by the Assyrian king Esarhaddon (680–669 BC) refer to the siege and destruction of Memphis, the royal residence of one Tarku (Taharqa), king of Egypt, who became pharaoh in 690 BC. After the death of Esarhaddon, Taharqa regained Memphis, but he was driven out of the city again by Ashurbanipal of Assyria, in 667/668 BC.

The collapse of Assyria (612 BC) led to brief Egyptian independence under the 26th dynasty (664–525 BC), but it was not long before new invaders appeared. The Persian Cambyses II took Memphis by siege in 525 BC. After years of Persian rule, Egypt was ready to welcome Alexander the Great in 332 BC. The conqueror used Memphis as his headquarters while making plans for his new city of Alexandria. After his death at Babylon, his body was brought to Egypt and was laid to rest temporarily in Memphis before being buried at Alexandria.

Under the Hellenistic Ptolemaic dynasty (332–30 BC), Memphis retained its cosmopolitan character and had a sizable Greek population. Some of the diversified racial types to be found in the city during Greco-Roman times are depicted in a series of striking terra-cotta heads dating from this period.

At the beginning of the Roman period (1st century BC), Memphis was still considered an important provincial capital. The serious decay of the ancient city began after the rise of Christianity, when zealots of that faith defaced and destroyed the remaining pagan temples. In the 5th century AD the Christian monastery of Apa Jeremias rose among the venerable tombs of Ṣaqqārah. The capital continued to deteriorate, receiving its death blow during the Muslim conquest

of Egypt in AD 640. A garrison and fort called Babylon occupied the eastern end of the bridge that crossed the Nile from Memphis, and after a long siege the fortress was taken by the Arab general ‘Amr ibn al-‘Āṣ. Memphis was abandoned, and later the few remaining structures were dismantled so that the stone might be reused in the neighbouring villages and in Cairo, after that city's founding in the 10th century.

The ancient city of Memphis lies near the modern village of Mīt Ruhaynah. At the beginning of the 20th century some ruined walls were still to be seen, but these have since disappeared, and the only monument above ground is a colossal statue of Ramses II, which once adorned the great temple of Ptah.

The first archaeologist to work at the city site for any prolonged period was Flinders (later Sir Flinders) Petrie, who excavated between 1908 and 1913, uncovering sections of the great temple of Ptah. These remains, left exposed, soon disappeared under the depredations of the nearby villagers. A University of Pennsylvania expedition worked at the site in 1917, finding foundations of a palace of Merneptah (1213–04 BC), east of the temple of that king. The university sponsored further digging in 1955 and 1956, excavating parts of the great temple and a small temple of Ramses II.

Since about the mid-19th century there has been hardly a season when archaeological activity was not proceeding at one or another of the pyramid sites. Almost all of the pyramids and a majority of the large private tombs were entered by treasure hunters before the beginning of scholarly excavation. One of the earliest scholars to work in the Memphite area was Auguste Mariette, who discovered the Serapeum in 1850. Among the most important of Mariette's successors were George Andrew Reisner and Hermann Junker, who excavated at Giza; Ludwig Borchardt, who excavated the sun temples and the 5th-dynasty pyramids at Abū Ṣīr; Ahmed Fakhry, who worked in the pyramids of Snefru at Dahshūr; and Zakaria Goneim, who discovered a previously unknown pyramid, probably of the 3rd dynasty, to the southwest of the Step Pyramid at Ṣaqqārah. Also noteworthy are the excavations of J.P. Lauer in the Step Pyramid complex. In the 1930s Walter Bryan Emery began the excavations that uncovered the great 1st-dynasty tombs. His work in the archaic cemetery disclosed another huge labyrinth, resembling that of the Serapeum, the precise function of which is as yet undetermined. Beginning in the 1980s, the Egypt Exploration Society sponsored a long-range survey of the Memphite area to determine its extent and development from different historical periods. Large sculptural and architectural elements recovered from various excavations are displayed at an outdoor museum at Mīt Ruhaynah.

ṢAQQĀRAH

Ṣaqqārah (Sakkara) is part of the necropolis of the ancient Egyptian city of Memphis, 15 miles (24 km) southwest of Cairo and west of the modern Arab village of Ṣaqqārah. The site extends along the edge of the desert plateau for about 5 miles (8 km), bordering Abū Ṣīr to the north and Dahshūr to the south. In 1979 the ancient ruins of the Memphis area, including Ṣaqqārah, Abū Ṣīr, Dahshūr, Abū Ruwaysh, and the Pyramids of Giza, were collectively designated a UNESCO World Heritage site.

The earliest remains at Ṣaqqārah are those in the early dynastic cemetery at the northernmost end of the site, where large mud-brick tombs, or mastabas, have been found that date to the very beginning of Egyptian history. Although storage jars found in the mastabas bore the names of the kings of the 1st dynasty (c. 2925–c. 2775 BC), it seems that these tombs were those of high officials of the period.

South of the Early Dynastic cemetery lies the Step Pyramid complex of Djoser, second king of the 3rd dynasty (c. 2650–c. 2575 BC). Djoser's architect Imhotep designed a new form of burial structure for the king in the shape of a pyramid in six stages. Around the pyramid lies a huge complex of halls and courts in which the prototype structures of mud brick, wood, and reed were for the first time translated into fine limestone. Shepseskaf of the 4th dynasty (c. 2575–c. 2465 BC) built Maṣṭabat Firʿawn, a coffin-shaped tomb, and several kings of the 5th dynasty (c. 2465–c. 2325 BC) also constructed their pyramids at Ṣaqqārah. Unas, the last king of the 5th dynasty, was the first to inscribe on the walls of his pyramid chambers the Pyramid Texts, which were designed to protect the dead king and to ensure him life and sustenance in the hereafter. Succeeding kings of the 6th dynasty (c. 2325–c. 2150 BC) continued the practice of inscribing Pyramid Texts in the underground chambers. With the exception of Teti, the 6th-dynasty kings built their pyramids to the south of Unas's pyramid, and the most southerly is that of a 13th-dynasty (c. 1756–c. 1630 BC) king.

Around the pyramids of their sovereigns, the Old Kingdom (c. 2575–c. 2130 BC) nobles were buried in mastabas. The wall carvings within their tombs depict scenes of daily life.

During the Middle Kingdom (1938–c. 1630 BC) relatively few tombs were added

to in the Ṣaqqārah necropolis. In the New Kingdom (c. 1539–1075 BC), however, Memphis became a principal administrative and military centre, and a number of tombs from that period have been found, including the finely decorated tomb of the general, later king, Horemheb, rediscovered in 1975. Also, in that era and later the sacred Apis bulls were buried at Ṣaqqārah in large subterranean galleries, the most famous of which is the Serapeum. The last imposing tombs to be built in Ṣaqqārah were those of several great officials of the Saite and Persian periods. In the northeastern part of the necropolis, beneath a field of mastabas of the 3rd and 4th dynasties, another complex of underground passages contains thousands of ibis mummies of the Ptolemaic period.

GLOSSARY

bitumen Any of various solid or semi-solid mixtures of hydrocarbons that occur in nature or that are obtained as residues from the distillation of petroleum or coal.

caliph A religious and civil leader of a Muslim state; literally "successor."

cataract A spot in a river where large volumes of water fall over a cliff; a waterfall.

cartouche An oval or oblong frame enclosing a sovereign's name. It is one of the most characteristic Egyptian symbols.

consanguineous marriage A union between two blood relatives who, because of the nature of their relationships, traditionally are prohibited from intermarrying.

Coptic language The Afro-Asian language—written using the Greek alphabet—that succeeded hieroglyphics and hieratic and demotic script in ancient Egypt.

cryptography Practice of the enciphering and deciphering of messages in secret code in order to render them unintelligible to all but the intended receiver.

cuneiform System of writing with wedge-shaped characters that was used in the ancient Middle East.

ennead The oldest of all numeric god groupings in ancient Egypt, consisting of nine deities.

faience A glazed composition of ground quartz.

funerary temple A highly decorated building or complex created as a shrine to honour a dead king or queen.

gnostic Any of a number of philosophical and religious movements prominent in the Greco-Roman world in the early Christian era.

hieroglyphics A system of writing that utilizes drawn characters or symbols to represent a word or its phonetic sound.

Hittites An ancient Indo-European people who by 1340 BC had become one of the dominant powers of the Middle East.

Hyksos Mixed Semitic-Asiatics who settled Egypt's delta region during the 18th century BC.

isthmus A narrow strip of land that connects two larger land masses that otherwise would be separated by the sea.

logogram Written letter, pictorial symbol, or sign intended to represent a whole word.

mastaba An oblong tomb with a burial chamber dug beneath it, common at earlier nonroyal sites.

necropolis The section of an ancient city dedicated to burial; literally "city of the dead."

nomarch Governor of the ancient Egyptian administrative division called the nome.

papyrus Writing material of ancient times; also the plant from which the material was derived.

Philistines Aegean people who settled on the southern coast of Palestine in the 12th century BC, arriving there about the same time as the Israelites.

Pyramid Texts A collection of Egyptian mortuary prayers, hymns, and spells intended to protect royalty in the afterlife.

satrap A provincial governor in ancient Egypt, appointed by the king.

scarab An important ancient Egyptian symbol in the form of the dung beetle, which was associated with the qualities of development, growth, and effectiveness.

Sea Peoples Seafaring invaders of Egypt toward the end of the Bronze Age, especially in the 13th century BC.

sinecure An office or position of power that requires little work of its occupant in return for income.

stela A vertical stone slab used primarily to mark grave sites or as a commemoration.

suzerainty Having power over a territory or vassal state, yet allowing it control of its own internal affairs.

syncretism The fusion of religious beliefs and practices. In ancient Egypt, syncretism often took the form of creating a composite identity when combining two or more gods.

triad A triumvirate of three gods worshipped in ancient Egypt; a common grouping from the New Kingdom onward.

vassal One who received protection or land in exchange for loyalty to a feudal lord.

viceroy One who rules a country or province as the empowered representative of the king.

vizier A chief administrative officer in various Muslim countries; a supreme caliph.

BIBLIOGRAPHY

Kathryn A. Bard, *An Introduction to the Archaeology of Ancient Egypt*. Malden, MA: Blackwell Pub., 2008.

Nina Burleigh, *Mirage: Napoleon's Scientists and the Unveiling of Egypt*. New York: Harper, 2007.

Jean-François Champollion, *The Code Breaker's Secret Diaries: The Perilous Expedition Through Plague-ridden Egypt to Uncover the Ancient Mysteries of the Hieroglyphs*; translated by Martin Rynja. London: Gibson Square, 2009.

Elliott Colla, *Conflicted Antiquities: Egyptology, Egyptomania, Egyptian Modernity*. Durham, N.C.: Duke University Press, 2007.

A. Rosalie David, *The Experience of Ancient Egypt*. London; New York: Routledge, 2000.

Aidan Dodson, *Ancient Egypt: Pyramids and Hieroglyphs: Enduring Symbols of a Great Civilization*. London: New Holland, 2006.

Brian M. Fagan, *The Rape of the Nile: Tomb Robbers, Tourists, and Archaeologists in Egypt*, rev. ed. Boulder, Colo.: Westview Press, 2004.

Nicolas-Christoph Grimal, *A History of Ancient Egypt*. Cambridge, USA: Blackwell, 1992.

Bruno Halioua and Bernard Ziskind, *Medicine in the Days of the Pharoahs*. Cambridge, MA: Belknap Press of Harvard University Press, 2005.

Michael A. Hoffman, *Egypt Before the Pharaohs: The Prehistoric Foundations of Egyptian Civilization*. Austin: University of Texas Press, 1991.

Jean-Marcel Humbert, and Clifford Price (eds.), *Imhotep Today: Egyptianizing Architecture*. London: UCL Press, Institute of Archaeology, 2003.

Norma Jean Katan, *Hieroglyphs: The Writing of Ancient Egypt*, rev. ed. London: Published for the Trustees of the British Museum by British Museum Publications, 1985.

Valeria Manferto, Rosanna Pirelli, Angela Arnone, and Dorothea Arnold, *The Queens of Ancient Egypt*. Vercelli, Italy: White Star Pub.; New York: Distributed in the US and Canada by Rizzoli International Pub., 2008.

Béatrix Midant-Reynes, *The Prehistory of Egypt from the First Egyptians to the First Pharaohs*. Oxford, UK; Malden, MA: Blackwell Publishers, 2000.

Lorna Oakes and Lucia Gahlin, *Ancient Egypt: An Illustrated Reference to the Myths, Religions, Pyramids, and Temples of the Land of the Pharoahs*. London: Hermes House, 2003.

David O'Connor and Eric H. Cline (eds.), *Amenhotep III: Perspectives on His Reign*. Ann Arbor: University of Michigan Press, 1998.

Delia Pemberton, *Treasures of the Pharoahs*. San Francisco: Chronicle Books, 2004.

Geraldine Pinch, *Magic in Ancient Egypt*. London: British Museum Press, 2006.

J.D. Ray, *The Rosetta Stone and the Rebirth of Ancient Egypt*. Cambridge, Mass.: Harvard University Press, 2007.

Corinna Rossi, *Architecture and Mathematics in Ancient Egypt*. Cambridge; New York: Cambridge University Press, 2004.

Ian Shaw, *Ancient Egypt: A Very Short Introduction*. Oxford; New York: Oxford University Press, 2004.

Ian Shaw (ed.), *The Oxford History of Ancient Egypt*. Oxford; New York: Oxford University Press, 2003.

Alberto Siliotti, *Luxor, Karnak, and the Theban Temples*. Cairo; New York: American University in Cairo Press, 2002.

Francesco Tiradritti, *Ancient Egypt: Art, Architecture, and History*. London : British Museum, 2002.

Amanda Doering Tourville, *King Tut's Tomb*. Mankato, Minn.: Capstone Press, 2009.

Joyce Tyldesley, *Hatchepsut: The Female Pharaoh*. New York, N.Y.: Viking, 1996.

Richard H. Wilkinson (ed.), *Egyptology Today*. New York: Cambridge University Press, 2008.

Richard H. Willkinson, *Reading Egyptian Art: A Hieroglyphic Guide to Ancient Egyptian Painting and Sculpture*. London: Thames and Hudson, 1992.